RAND McNALLY

Atlas
of WORLD GEOGRAPHY

Editor

Brett R. Gover

Design

Rand McNally Design

Cartographic Direction

Howard Veregin

Cartography

Robert K. Argersinger

Gregory P. Babiak

Marzee L. Eckhoff

Robert L. Merrill

Thomas F. Vitacco

Research

Susan Hudson

Felix Lopez

Raymond Tobiaski

Photograph Credits:

l = left, r = right, c = center, t = top, b = bottom.

Cover photo ©Torleif Svensson/Corbis, art ©istockphoto; p. 4 tl Courtesy Image Science and Analysis Laboratory, NASA-Johnson Space Center, tr ©World History Archive/Alamy, bl ©Zev Radovan/BibleLandPictures/Alamy, br ©The Art Gallery Collection/Alamy; p. 7 earth Courtesy Image Science and Analysis Laboratory, NASA-Johnson Space Center, bkgd ©Felix Stensson/Alamy; p. 11 Courtesy Image Science and Analysis Laboratory, NASA-Johnson Space Center; p. 16 ©Stacey Putman/istockphoto; p. 17 ©Steve Terrill/Corbis; p. 19 ©Natalia Tsarkova/ imagebroker/Alamy; p. 20-21 ©Jose Fuste Raga/Corbis; p. 21 ©Herve Collart/ Corbis Sygma; p. 24 ©Shutterstock; p. 28 t ©Corbis, b ©Nikola Bilic/Alamy; p. 29 t _____, b ©Douglas Peebels Photography/Alamy; p. 30 ©DanieleC/ Alamy; p. 31 t ©Jo Stephens/Alamy, b ©Felix Stensson/Alamy; p. 32 t ©Danita Delimont/Alamy, b ©Aivar Mikko/Alamy; p. 33 t ©Photos 12/Alamy, b ©Visions of America, LLC/Alamy; p. 34 t ©uwesSERENGETI/Alamy, b ©Joerg Boethling/ Alamy; p. 35 t ©Suzanne Porter/Alamy, b ©Joshua Baker/Alamy; p. 36 ©Image Source/Superstock; p. 37 t ©Amana Images Inc./Alamy, b ©Photodisc/Getty Images; p. 38 t ©Craig Ruaux/Alamy, b ©Photodisc/Getty Images; p. 62 (l to r) ©Amana Images Inc./Alamy, ©Corbis/Alamy, ©Inaquim/Alamy, ©Amana Images Inc./Alamy, ©Panorama Media (Beijing) Ltd./Alamy; p. 63 (l to r) ©Radius Images/Alamy, ©Ron Chapple Stock/Alamy, ©Oleksandr Buzko/Alamy, ©Aristidis Vafeiadakis/Alamy, ©Vibe Images/Alamy; p. 66 ©Bill Warchol/Alamy; p. 68 ©Outer Focus Photos/Alamy; p. 69 ©Benedicte Desrus/Alamy; p. 98 ©Jacques Jangoux/Alamy, b ©Steve Allen Travel Photography/Alamy; p. 100 ©Rosewood/ Alamy; p. 101 ©Michael Doolittle/Alamy; p. 108 ©allOver photography/Alamy; p. 110 ©Owen Franken/Alamy; . 111 ©Armin Puschmann/Alamy; p. 122 t ©Bart Pro/Alamy , b ©Photowood Inc./Alamy; p. 124 t ©Andrew McConnell/Alamy, b ©Wildlife GmbH/Alamy; p. 125 ©Michele Burgess/Alamy; p. 132 ©Robert Harding Picture Library Ltd/Alamy; p. 134 ©Robert Fried/Alamy; p. 150 t ©Image Source/Alamy, b ©National Geographic Image Collection/Alamy; p. 152 t ©Radius Images/Alamy, b ©Bill Bachman/Alamy; p. 153 ©Paul Dymond/Alamy.

Information Credits:

Volcano data, pages 29, 32, and 36: Tom Simkin, Smithsonian Institution Global Volcanism Program

Earthquake data, page 37: Paula Dunbar, National Geophysical Data Center, National Oceanic and Atmospheric Administration

Australia information, page 38: Australian Tourist Commission

Much of the information on the destruction of the Amazonian rain forest, page 101, was provided by Fred Engel of the Center for Earth and Planetary Science, National Air and Space Museum, Smithsonian Institution, Washington, D.C.

Atlas of World Geography

Manufactured by Rand McNally
Skokie, Illinois 60077

Printed in Madison, WI, U.S.A.
Revised 2009 Edition
11 Printing

PO# 5305
ISBN 0-528-00482-4
ISBN-13: 978-0-528-00482-7

For information about ordering the *Atlas of World Geography* or the *Atlas of World Geography Teacher's Guide*, call **1-800-333-0136** or visit our website at **www.randmcnally.com/education**

Table of Contents

Using the Atlas

Maps and Atlases

Today, satellite images (Figure 1) and aerial photography show us the face of the Earth in precise detail. It is hard to imagine how difficult it once was to ascertain what our planet looked like—even small parts of it. Yet from earliest history we have evidence of humans trying to depict the world through maps and charts.

Figure 1

Twenty-five hundred years ago, on a tiny clay tablet the size of a hand, the Babylonians inscribed the earth as a flat disk (Figure 2) with Babylon at the center.

The section of the Cantino map of 1502 (Figure 3) is an example of a portolan chart used by mariners to chart the newly discovered Americas. Handsome and useful maps have been produced by many cultures. The Mexican map (Figure 4) drawn in 1583 marks hills with wavy lines and roads with footprints between parallel lines. The methods and materials used to create these maps were dependent upon the technology available, and their accuracy suffered considerably. The maps in this atlas show the detail and accuracy that cartographers are now able to achieve. They benefit from our ever-increasing technology, including satellite imagery and computer-assisted cartography.

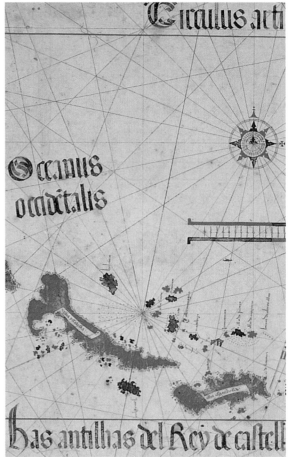

Figure 3

Figure 4

Figure 2

In 1589, Gerardus Mercator used the word "atlas" to describe a collection of maps. Atlases have become a unique and indispensable reference for graphically defining the world and answering the question "Where?" Only on a map can the countries, cities, roads, rivers, and lakes covering a vast area be simultaneously viewed in their relative locations. Routes between places can be traced, trips planned, boundaries of neighboring states and countries examined, distances between places measured, the meandering of rivers and streams and the sizes of lakes visualized, and remote places imagined.

Getting the Information

An atlas can be used for many purposes, from planning a trip to finding hot spots in the news and supplementing world knowledge. To realize the potential of an atlas, the user must be able to:

1) Find places on the maps

2) Measure distances

3) Determine directions

4) Understand map symbols

Finding Places

One of the most common and important tasks facilitated by an atlas is finding the location of a place in the world. A river's name in a book, a city mentioned in the news, or a potential vacation spot may prompt your need to know where the place is located. The illustrations and text below explain how to find Lagos, Nigeria.

1) Look up the place-name in the index at the back of the atlas. Lagos, Nigeria can be found in the map on page 128, and it can be located on the map by its latitude and longitude, expressed in degrees: 7 North Latitude, 3 East Longitude (Figure 5).

La Fayette, In., U.S. 40N	87W	**90**
Lafayette, La., U.S. 30N	92W	**95**
Laghouat, Alg. 34N	3 E	**128**
Lagos, Nig. 7N	3 E	**128**
La Grande, Or., U.S. 45N	118W	**82**
LaGrange, Ga., U.S. 33N	85W	**92**
Lahore, Pak. 32N	74 E	**143**
Lahti, Fin......................61N	26 E	**116**

Figure 5

2) Turn to the map of Northern Africa on page 128. Note that the latitude appears in the right and left margins of the map, and the longitude in the upper and lower margins.

3) To find Lagos on the map, place your left index finger on the left margin at 7 degrees (between 5 and 10); and your right index finger in the top margin at 3 degrees East (between 0 and 5). Move your left finger across the map and your right finger down the map. Your fingers will meet in the area in which Lagos is located (Figure 6).

Figure 6

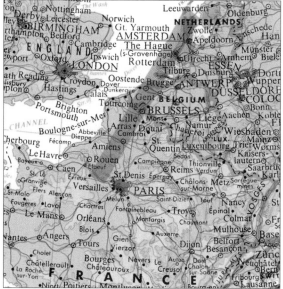

Figure 7

Measuring Distances

In planning trips, determining the distances between two places is essential, and an atlas can help in travel preparation. For instance, to determine the approximate distance between Paris, France and Amsterdam, Netherlands, follow these three steps:

1) Lay a slip of paper on the map on page 117 so that its edge touches the two cities. Adjust the paper so only one corner touches Paris. Mark the paper directly at the spot where Amsterdam is located (Figure 7).

2) Place the paper along the scale of miles beneath the map. Position the corner at 0 and line up the edge of the paper along the scale. The pencil mark on the paper indicates Amsterdam is between 250 and 300 miles from Paris (Figure 8).

3) To find the exact distance, make a second pencil mark at the 250-mile point of the scale. Then slide the paper to the left so that this second mark is lined up with 0 on the scale (Figure 9). The Amsterdam mark now falls at the third 10-mile point on the scale. This means that Paris and Amsterdam are approximately 250 plus 30—or 280—miles apart.

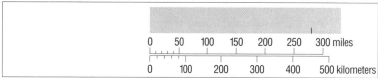

Figure 8

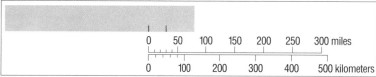

Figure 9

Determining Directions

Most of the maps in the atlas are drawn so that when oriented for normal reading, north is at the top of the map, south is at the bottom, west is at the left, and east is at the right. Most maps have a series of lines drawn across them—the lines of latitude and longitude. Lines of latitude, or parallels of latitude, are drawn east and west. Lines of longitude, or meridians of longitude, are drawn north and south (Figure 10, at bottom of page).

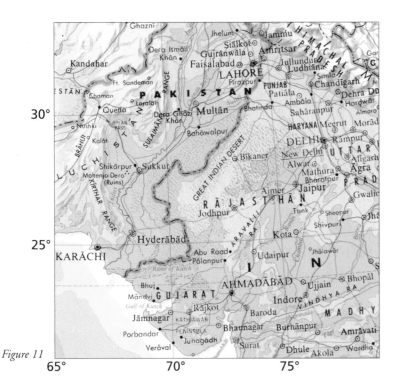

Figure 11

Parallels and meridians appear as either curved or straight lines. For example, in the section of the map of Southwestern Asia (Figure 11), from page 143, the parallels of latitude appear as curved lines. The meridians of longitude are curved vertical lines.

Latitude and longitude lines help locate places on maps. Parallels of latitude are numbered in degrees north and south of the Equator. Meridians of longitude are numbered in degrees east and west of a line called the Prime Meridian, which runs through Greenwich, England, near London. Any place on Earth can be located by the latitude and longitude lines running through it.

To determine directions or locations on the map, you must use the parallels and meridians. For example, suppose you want to know which is farther north, Karachi, Pakistan or Delhi, India. The map in Figure 11 shows that Karachi is south of the 25° parallel of latitude and that Delhi is north of it. Therefore Delhi is farther north than Karachi. By looking at the meridians of longitude, you can determine which city is farther east. Karachi is approximately 2° east of the 65° meridian, and Delhi is about 2° east of the 75° meridian. Delhi is farther east than Karachi.

Understanding Map Symbols

In a very real sense, every map is a symbol representing the world or part of it. It is a reduced representation of the Earth: each of the world's features —cities, rivers, etc.—is represented by a symbol. Map symbols may take the form of points, such as dots or squares (often used for cities, capital cities, or points of interest) or lines (roads, railroads, rivers). Symbols may also occupy an area, showing extent of coverage (terrain, forests, deserts). They seldom look like the feature they represent and therefore must be identified and interpreted. For instance, some of the maps in this atlas define political units by a colored line depicting their boundaries. Neither the colors nor the boundary lines are actually found on the surface of the Earth, but because countries and states are such important political components of the world, strong symbols are used to represent them. The Legend on page 51 of this atlas identifies the symbols used on the maps.

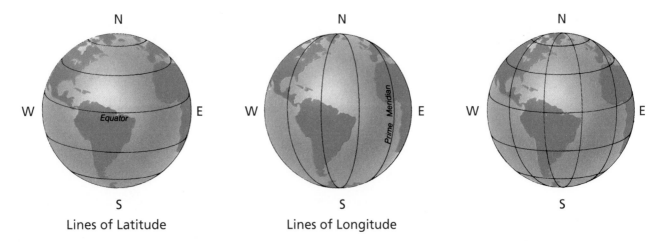

Lines of Latitude   Lines of Longitude

Figure 10

Geographic Tables, Charts, and Graphs

This section provides an interesting way to learn key geographic information about your country and the world. Locate places referred to in the questions on Atlas of World Geography maps.

The Universe and Solar System

The Milky Way Galaxy

The Milky Way Galaxy is large spiral galaxy that contains hundreds of billions of stars. One of these stars is the Sun. This galaxy is but one of billions of galaxies in the universe.

The Milky Way measures 100,000 light-years in diameter. This means that light—which travels at 186,000 miles per second—takes 100,000 years to go from one edge of the galaxy to the other.

Statistical Data for the Milky Way Galaxy
Diameter: 100,000 light-years
Estimated thickness of galactic disk: 2,300 to 2,600 light-years
Estimated thickness of galaxy's central bulge: 16,000 light-years
Mass: At least 200 billion stars
Distance from the Sun to the center of the galaxy: About 28,000 light years

Sun

The Sun is our solar system's star. It is almost unimaginably large. Its diameter is 109 times that of Earth, and its mass is 332,900 times that of Earth. It contains 99.86% of the mass of the entire solar system.

Diameter: 864,300 miles (1,391,000 km)
Mass: 332,900 times Earth's mass
Surface temperature: 10,000° F (5,500° C)
Core temperature: 27 million° F (15 million° C)
Composition: 72% hydrogen, 26% helium
Surface gravity: 2,800% of the gravity on Earth. A 100-pound person would weigh 2,800 pounds on the Sun.
Rotational period: 26 days, 19 hours

Mercury

Average distance from the Sun: 35,980,000 miles (57,910,000 km), or 39% that of Earth
Diameter: 3,032 miles (4,879 km), or 39% that of Earth
Mass: 6% of Earth's mass
Surface temperature range: −279 to 801° F (−173 to 427° C)
Atmosphere: 42% oxygen, 29% sodium, 22% hydrogen, 6% helium, 0.5% potassium
Surface gravity: 38% of the gravity on Earth. A 100-pound person would weigh 38 pounds on Mercury.
Length of day (rotational period): 1,407.5 hours (58 Earth days)
Length of year (orbital period): 88.0 Earth days
Moons: None

Venus

Average distance from the Sun: 67,240,000 miles (108,200,000 km), or 72% that of Earth
Diameter: 7,521 miles (12,104 km), or 95% that of Earth
Mass: 82% of Earth's mass
Surface temperature: 864° F (462° C) (The temperature remains constant.)
Atmosphere: 96.5% carbon dioxide, 3.5% nitrogen
Surface gravity: 91% of the gravity on Earth. A 100-pound person would weigh 91 pounds on Venus.
Length of day (rotational period): 5,832.5 hours (243 Earth days). The planet rotates opposite to the rotation of Earth.
Length of year (orbital period): 224.7 Earth days
Moons: None

Earth

Average distance from the Sun: 92,960,000 miles (149,600,000 km)
Diameter: 7,926 miles (12,760 km)
Surface temperature range: −126 to 136° F (−88 to 58° C)
Atmosphere: 78% nitrogen, 21% oxygen
Length of day (rotational period): 23.9 hours
Length of year (orbital period): 365.24 days
Moons: 1

The Moon

The Moon is Earth's only natural satellite. It is an airless, waterless world just one–fourth the size of Earth. It makes a complete orbit around Earth every 27 days.

Average distance from Earth: 238,900 miles (384,400 km)
Diameter: 2,159 miles (3,475 km)
Mass: 1% of Earth's mass
Surface temperature range: −387 to 253° F (−233 to 123° C)
Surface gravity: 16% that of Earth. A 100-pound person would weigh 16 pounds on the Moon.
Orbital period (around Earth): 27.3 Earth days

Mars

Average distance from the Sun: 141,600,000 miles (227,900,000 km), or about 1.5 times that of Earth
Diameter: 4,222 miles (6,794 km), or 53% that of Earth
Mass: 11% of Earth's mass
Surface temperature range: −125 to 23° F (−87 to −5° C)
Atmosphere: 95.3% carbon dioxide, 2.7% nitrogen, 1.6% argon
Surface gravity: 38% of the gravity on Earth. A 100-pound person would weigh 38 pounds on Mars.
Length of day (rotational period): 24.62 hours
Length of year (orbital period): 686.93 Earth days (1 Earth year, 322 Earth days)
Moons: 2

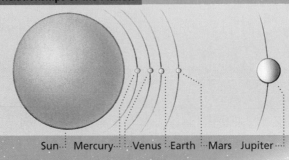

Spatial Relationships of the Planets

Sun · Mercury · Venus · Earth · Mars · Jupiter · Saturn

Jupiter

By any measure, Jupiter is the solar system's giant. To equal Jupiter's bulk would take 318 Earths. Over 1,300 Earth-sized balls could fit within this enormous planet.

Average distance from the Sun: 483,700,000 miles (778,400,000 km), or 5.2 times that of Earth
Diameter: 88,846 miles (142,984 km), or 11.2 times that of Earth
Mass: 318 times Earth's mass
Surface temperature: −234° F (−148° C)
Atmosphere: 89.8% hydrogen, 10.2% helium
Surface gravity: 214% of the gravity on Earth. A 100-pound person would weigh 214 pounds on Jupiter.
Length of day (rotational period): 9.9 hours
Length of year (orbital period): 4,330.6 Earth days (11 Earth years, 313 Earth days)
Moons: 63

Uranus

Average distance from the Sun: 1,784,000,000 miles (2,871,000,000 km), or 19.2 times that of Earth
Diameter: 31,760 miles (51,120 km), or four times that of Earth
Mass: 15 times Earth's mass
Surface temperature: −357° F (−216° C)
Atmosphere: 82.5% hydrogen, 15.2% helium, 2.3% methane
Surface gravity: 86% of the gravity on Earth. A 100-pound person would weigh 86 pounds on Uranus.
Length of day (rotational period): 17.24 hours. The planet rotates opposite to the rotation of Earth.
Length of year (orbital period): 30,687.2 Earth days (84 Earth years, 7 Earth days)
Moons: 27

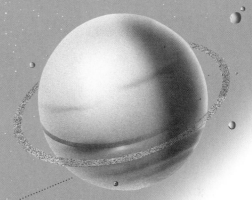

Neptune

Average distance from the Sun: 2,795,000,000 miles (4,498,000,000 km) or 30 times that of Earth
Diameter: 30,776 miles (49,528 km), or 3.9 times that of Earth
Mass: 17 times Earth's mass
Surface temperature: −353° F (−214° C)
Atmosphere: 80% hydrogen, 18.5% helium, 1.5% methane
Surface gravity: 110% of the gravity on Earth. A 100-pound person would weigh 110 pounds on Neptune.
Length of day (rotational period): 16.11 hours
Length of year (orbital period): 60,190 Earth days (164 Earth years, 288 Earth days)
Moons: 13

Saturn

Average distance from the Sun: 886,500,000 miles (1,426,000,000 km), or 9.4 times that of Earth
Diameter: 74,900 miles (120,500 km), or 9.4 times that of Earth
Mass: 95 times Earth's mass
Surface temperature: −288° F (−178° C)
Atmosphere: 96.3% hydrogen, 3.25% helium
Surface gravity: 91% of the gravity on Earth. A 100-pound person would weigh 91 pounds on Saturn.
Length of day (rotational period): 10.7 hours
Length of year (orbital period): 10,755.7 Earth days (29 Earth years, 163 Earth days)
Moons: 61

Uranus

Neptune

Isn't Pluto a Planet?

Discovered in 1930, Pluto was considered to be our solar system's ninth planet. However, in 2006 it was downgraded from planet to "dwarf planet" by the International Astronomical Union (IAU). In addition to Pluto, the IAU has so far classified four other celestial bodies as dwarf planets. Their names are Ceres, Eris, Haumea, and Makemake.

The Earth

History of the Earth

Estimated age of the Earth:
At least 4.6 billion (4,600,000,000) years.

Formation of the Earth: It is generally thought that the Earth was formed from a cloud of gas and dust (A) revolving around the early Sun. Gravitational forces pulled the cloud's particles together into an ever denser mass (B), with heavier particles sinking to the center. Heat from radioactive elements caused the materials of the embryonic Earth to melt and gradually settle into core and mantle layers. As the surface cooled, a crust formed. Volcanic activity released vast amounts of steam, carbon dioxide, and other gases from the Earth's interior. The steam condensed into water to form the oceans, and the gases, prevented by gravity from escaping, formed the beginnings of the atmosphere (C).

The calm appearance of our planet today (D) belies the intense heat of its interior and the violent tectonic forces which are constantly reshaping its surface.

Periods in Earth's history

Earth's history is divided into different **eras**, which are subdivided into **periods**.

The most recent periods are themselves subdivided into **epochs**. The main divisions and subdivisions are shown below.

	Began	Ended	
	(million years ago)		
Precambrian Era			
Archean Period	3,800	2,500	Start of life
Proterozoic Period	2,500	590	Life in the seas
Paleozoic Era			
Cambrian Period	590	500	Sea life
Ordovician Period	505	438	First fishes
Silurian Period	438	408	First land plants
Devonian Period	408	360	Amphibians
Carboniferous Period	360	286	First reptiles
Permian Period	286	248	Spread of reptiles
Mesozoic Era			
Triassic Period	248	213	Reptiles and early mammals
Jurassic Period	213	144	Dinosaurs
Cretaceous Period	144	65	Dinosaurs, dying out at the end
Cenozoic Era			
Tertiary Period			
Paleocene	65	55	Large mammals
Eocene	55	38	Primates begin
Oligocene	38	25	Development of primates
Miocene	25	5	Modern-type animals
Pliocene	5	2	Australopithecus ape, ancestor to the human race
Quaternary Period			
Pleistocene	2	0.01	Ice ages; true humans
Holocene	0.01	Present	Modern humans

Source: *Atlas of the Universe* by Patrick Moore, Reed International Books Limited, 1994.

Internal Structure of the Earth

In its simplest form, the Earth is composed of a crust, a mantle with an upper and lower layer, and a core, which has an inner region.

Temperatures in the Earth increase with depth, as is observed in a deep mine shaft or bore-hole, but the prediction of temperatures within the Earth is made difficult by the fact that different rocks conduct heat at different rates: rock salt, for example, has 10 times the heat conductivity of coal. Also, estimates have to take into account the abundance of heat-generating atoms in a rock. Radioactive atoms are concentrated toward the Earth's surface, so the planet has, in effect, a thermal blanket to keep it warm. The temperature at the center of the Earth is believed to be approximately 5,400° F (3,000° C).

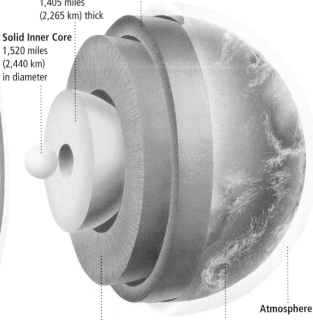

Upper Mantle
415 miles
(667 km) thick

Molten Outer Core
1,405 miles
(2,265 km) thick

Solid Inner Core
1,520 miles
(2,440 km)
in diameter

Atmosphere

Lower Mantle
1,365 miles
(2,200 km) thick

Solid Crust
0–19 miles
(0–33 km) thick

Chemical composition of the Earth:

The chemical composition of the Earth varies from crust to core. The upper crust of continents, called sial, is mainly granite, rich in aluminum and silicon. Oceanic crust, or sima, is largely basalt, made of magnesium and silicon. The mantle is composed of rocks that are rich in magnesium and iron silicates, whereas the core, it is believed, is made of iron and nickel oxides.

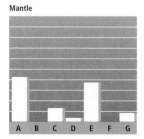

- Sial
- Sima
- Upper Mantle
- Lower Mantle
- Outer Core
- Inner Core

A. Silicon
B. Aluminum
C. Iron
D. Calcium
E. Magnesium
F. Nickel
G. Other

Sial (upper crust of continents) · **Sima (oceanic crust)** · **Mantle** · **Core**

Measurements of the Earth

Equatorial circumference of the Earth: 24,901.45 miles (40,066.43 km)

Polar circumference of the Earth: 24,855.33 miles (39,992.22 km)

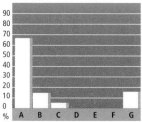

Equatorial diameter of the Earth: 7,926.38 miles (12,753.54 km)

Polar diameter of the Earth: 7,899.80 miles (12,710.77 km)

Equatorial radius of the Earth: 3,963.19 miles (6,376.77 km)

Polar radius of the Earth: 3,949.90 miles (6,355.38 km)

Estimated weight of the Earth: 6,600,000,000,000,000,000,000 tons, or 6,600 billion billion tons (5,940 billion billion metric tons)

Total surface area of the Earth: 197,000,000 square miles (510,230,000 sq km)

Total land area of the Earth (including inland water and Antarctica): 57,900,000 square miles (150,100,000 sq km)

Total ocean area of the Earth: 139,200,000 square miles (360,528,000 sq km), or 70% of the Earth's surface area

Total area of the Earth's surface covered with water (oceans and all inland water): 147,750,000 square miles (382,672,500 sq km), or 75% of the Earth's surface area

Types of water: 97% of the Earth's water is salt water; 3% is fresh water

Life on Earth
Number of plant species on Earth: About 350,000

Number of animal species on Earth: More than one million

Estimated total human population of the Earth: 6,195,885,000

Movements of the Earth
Mean distance of the Earth from the Sun: About 93 million miles (149.6 million km)

Period in which the Earth makes one complete orbit around the Sun: 365 days, 5 hours, 48 minutes, and 46 seconds

Speed of the Earth as it orbits the Sun: 66,700 miles (107,320 km) per hour

Period in which the Earth makes one complete rotation on its axis: 23 hours, 56 minutes and 4 seconds

Equatorial speed at which the Earth rotates on its axis: More than 1,000 miles (1,600 km) per hour

The Shape of the Earth

Comparing the Earth's equatorial and polar dimensions reveals that our planet is actually not a perfect sphere but rather an oblate spheroid, flattened at the poles and bulging at the Equator. This is the result of a combination of gravitational and centrifugal forces.

An even more precise term for the Earth's shape is "geoid" — the actual shape of sea level, which is lumpy, with variations away from spheroid of up to 260 feet (80 m). This lumpiness reflects major variations in density in the Earth's outer layers.

The Seasons
(Northern Hemisphere)

Summer Solstice Noon sun is directly overhead at 23½° N. Longest day of year.

Autumnal Equinox Noon sun is directly overhead at the Equator, on its apparent migration south. Day and night are equal.

Vernal Equinox Noon sun is directly overhead at the Equator, on its apparent migration North. Day and night are equal.

Winter Solstice Noon sun is directly overhead at 23½° S. Shortest day of year.

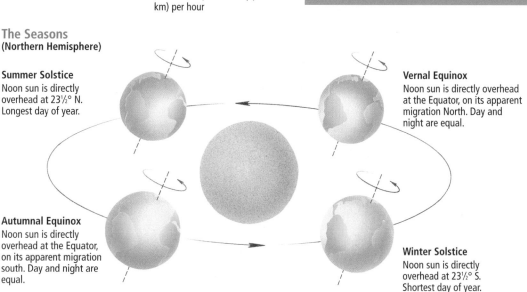

Plate Tectonics

Continental Drift

225 million years ago: The supercontinent of Pangaea exists and Panthalassa forms the ancestral ocean. Tethys Sea separates Eurasia and Africa.

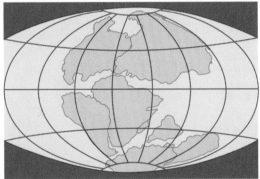

180 million years ago: Pangaea splits, Laurasia drifts north. Gondwanaland breaks into South America/Africa, India, and Australia/Antarctica.

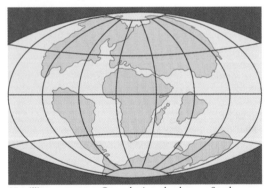

65 million years ago: Ocean basins take shape as South America and India move from Africa and the Tethys Sea closes to form the Mediterranean Sea.

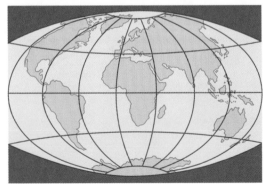

The present day: India has merged with Asia, Australia is free of Antarctica, and North America is free of Eurasia.

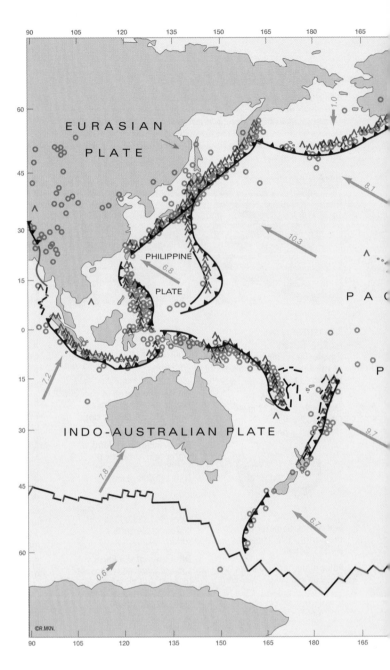

PLATE TECTONICS

Types of plate boundaries

— **Divergent:** Magma emerges from the earth's mantle at the mid-ocean ridges, forming new crust and forcing the plates to spread apart at the ridges.

▲▲▲ **Convergent:** Plates collide at subduction zones where the denser plate is forced back into the earth's mantle, forming deep ocean trenches.

— **Transform:** Plates slide past one another, producing faults and fracture zones.

Other map symbols

→ Direction of plate movement

6.7 → Length of arrow is proportional to the amount of plate movement (number indicates centimeters of movement per year)

○ Earthquake of magnitude 7.5 and above (from 10 A.D. to the present)

∧ Volcano (eruption since 1900)

✳ Selected hot spots

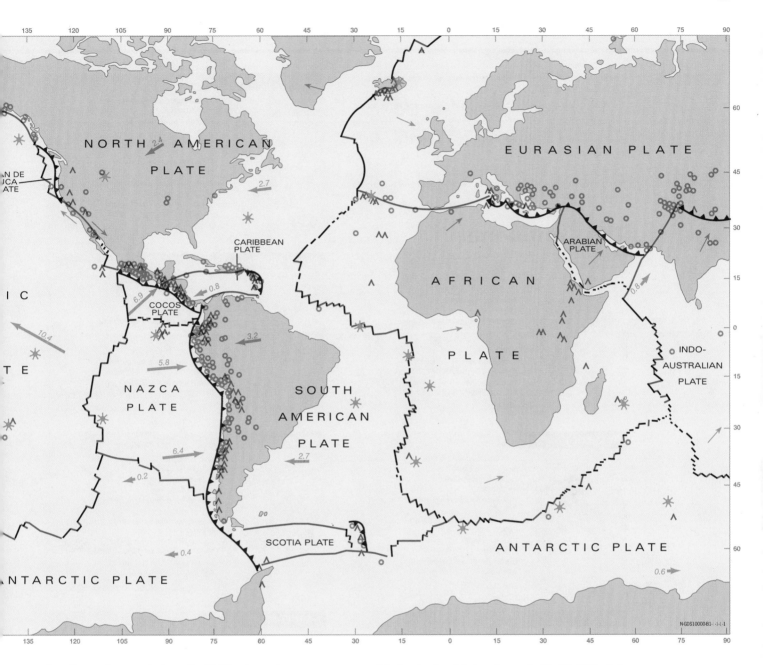

According to plate tectonic theory, Earth's lithosphere—the crust and uppermost rigid part of the mantle—is divided into plates that move relative to one another. The map above shows the locations and names of the major plates.

These rigid plates move on a molten layer of Earth's mantle called the asthenosphere. The moving plates meet at three different types of boundaries—divergent, convergent, and transform. (See map legend at the left.)

Divergent Boundaries

At divergent boundaries, plates are pushed apart by currents in the asthenosphere in a process called rifting. Most rifting occurs on the ocean floors. In ocean floor rifting, molten material from the asthenosphere wells up between the separated plates, hardens, and forms ridges. (See World Physical Map and Ocean Depths Profile, pages 54 and 55.) This process of adding to the Earth's crust is called seafloor spreading.

Convergent Boundaries

At convergent boundaries, the moving plates collide with one another. The edge of the heavier plate sinks under the crust of the lighter plate, and is consumed back into Earth's mantle in a process called subduction. Subduction can create deep ocean trenches as the

crust of the heavier plate sinks into the mantle. (See World Physical Map, pages 54 and 55.) The colliding plates also create mountain chains as the lighter plate is pushed up over the heavier plate.

Transform Boundaries

When plates meet at transform boundaries or faults, they grind past each other. This movement neither increases nor destroys Earth's crust. The San Andreas Fault, north of San Francisco, is a famous example of a transform boundary.

Earthquakes and Volcanoes

Most of Earth's volcanoes and earthquakes occur along plate boundaries. The ring of volcanic and seismic activity along the west coasts of North and South America and the east coast of Asia, known as the Ring of Fire, follows plate boundaries. Volcanoes and earthquakes also occur at locations known as hot spots, where hot rock from deep in the mantle rises to the surface, creating some of Earth's tallest mountains.

Continental Drift

Plate tectonic theory assumes that the rigid plates have moved slowly through the millennia, carrying the continents with them. The history of this continental drifting is illustrated by the four maps to the left.

Continents and Islands

The word "continents" designates the largest continuous masses of land in the world.

For reasons that are mainly historical, seven continents are generally recognized: Africa, Antarctica, Asia, Australia, Europe, North America, and South America. Since Asia and Europe actually share the same landmass, they are sometimes identified as a single continent, Eurasia.

The lands of the central and south Pacific, including Australia, New Zealand, Micronesia, Melanesia, and Polynesia, are sometimes grouped together as Oceania.

The Continents

Africa

Area in square miles (sq km):
11,700,000 (30,300,000)

Estimated population:
985,490,000

Population per square mile (sq km):
84 (33)

Mean elevation in feet (meters):
1,900 (580)

Highest elevation in feet (meters):
Kilimanjaro, Tanzania, 19,340 (5,895)

Lowest elevation in feet (meters):
Lac 'Assal, Djibouti, 515 (157) below sea level

Antarctica

Area in square miles (sq km):
5,400,000 (14,000,000)

Estimated population:
Uninhabited

Population per square mile (sq km):
0 (0)

Mean elevation in feet (meters):
6,000 (1,830)

Highest elevation in feet (meters):
Vinson Massif, 16,066 (4,897)

Lowest elevation in feet (meters):
Deep Lake, 184 (56) below sea level

Asia

Area in square miles (sq km):
17,300,000 (44,900,000)

Estimated population:
4,078,790,000

Population per square mile (sq km):
236 (91)

Mean elevation in feet (meters):
3,000 (910)

Highest elevation in feet (meters):
Mt. Everest, China (Tibet)–Nepal, 29,028 (8,848)

Lowest elevation in feet (meters):
Dead Sea, Israel–Jordan, 1,339 (408) below sea level

Australia

Area in square miles (sq km):
2,969,910 (7,692,030)

Estimated population:
21,135,000

Population per square mile (sq km):
7.1 (2.7)

Mean elevation in feet (meters):
1,000 (305)

Highest elevation in feet (meters):
Mt. Kosciuszko, New South Wales, 7,313 (2,229)

Lowest elevation in feet (meters):
Lake Eyre, South Australia, 52 (16) below sea level

Europe

Area in square miles (sq km):
3,800,000 (9,900,000)

Estimated population:
728,420,000

Population per square mile (sq km):
192 (74)

Mean elevation in feet (meters):
980 (300)

Highest elevation in feet (meters):
Gora El'brus, Russia, 18,510 (5,642)

Lowest elevation in feet (meters):
Caspian Sea, Asia-Europe, 92 (28) below sea level

North America

Area in square miles (sq km):
9,500,000 (24,700,000)

Estimated population:
531,180,000

Population per square mile (sq km):
56 (22)

Mean elevation in feet (meters):
2,000 (610)

Highest elevation in feet (meters):
Mt. McKinley, Alaska, U.S., 20,320 (6,194)

Lowest elevation in feet (meters):
Death Valley, California, U.S., 282 (86) below sea level

Oceania (incl. Australia)

Area in square miles (sq km):
3,300,000 (8,500,000)

Estimated population:
34,605,000

Population per square mile (sq km):
10 (4.1)

Mean elevation in feet (meters):
1,000 (305)

Highest elevation in feet (meters):
Mt. Wilhelm, Papua New Guinea, 14,793 (4,509)

Lowest elevation in feet (meters):
Lake Eyre, South Australia, 52 (16) below sea level

South America

Area in square miles (sq km):
6,900,000 (17,800,000)

Estimated population:
391,890,000

Population per square mile (sq km):
57 (22)

Mean elevation in feet (meters):
1,800 (550)

Highest elevation in feet (meters):
Cerro Aconcagua, Argentina, 22,831 (6,959)

Lowest elevation in feet (meters):
Laguna del Carbón, Argentina, 344 (105) below sea level

World

Area in square miles (sq km):
57,900,000 (150,100,000)

Estimated population:
6,750,375,000

Population per square mile (sq km):
117 (45)

Mean elevation in feet (meters):
0 (0)

Highest elevation in feet (meters):
Mt. Everest, China (Tibet)–Nepal, 29,028 (8,848)

Lowest elevation in feet (meters):
Dead Sea, Israel–Jordan, 1,339 (408) below sea level

Largest Islands

Rank	Name	Area square miles	square km
1	Greenland, North America	840,000	2,175,600
2	New Guinea, Asia-Oceania	309,000	800,000
3	Borneo (Kalimantan), Asia	287,300	744,100
4	Madagascar, Africa	226,500	587,000
5	Baffin Island, Canada	195,928	507,451
6	Sumatra (Sumatera), Indonesia	182,860	473,606
7	Honshū, Japan	89,176	230,966
8	Great Britain, United Kingdom	88,795	229,978
9	Victoria Island, Canada	83,897	217,291
10	Ellesmere Island, Canada	75,767	196,236
11	Celebes (Sulawesi), Indonesia	73,057	189,216
12	South Island, New Zealand	57,708	149,463
13	Java (Jawa), Indonesia	51,038	132,187
14	North Island, New Zealand	44,332	114,821
15	Cuba, North America	42,800	110,800
16	Newfoundland, Canada	42,031	108,860
17	Luzon, Philippines	40,420	104,688
18	Iceland, Europe	39,800	103,000
19	Mindanao, Philippines	36,537	94,630
20	Ireland, Europe	32,600	84,400
21	Hokkaidō, Japan	32,245	83,515
22	Sakhalin, Russia	29,500	76,400
23	Hispaniola, North America	29,400	76,200
24	Banks Island, Canada	27,038	70,028
25	Tasmania, Australia	26,200	67,800
26	Sri Lanka, Asia	24,900	64,600
27	Devon Island, Canada	21,331	55,247
28	Berkner Island, Antarctica	20,005	51,829
29	Alexander Island, Antarctica	19,165	49,652
30	Tierra del Fuego, South America	18,600	48,200
31	Novaya Zemlya, north island, Russia	18,436	47,764
32	Kyūshū, Japan	17,129	44,363
33	Melville Island, Canada	16,274	42,149
34	Southampton Island, Canada	15,913	41,214
35	Axel Heiberg, Canada	15,498	40,151
36	Spitsbergen, Norway	15,260	39,523
37	New Britain, Papua New Guinea	14,093	36,500
38	Taiwan, Asia	13,900	36,000
39	Hainan Dao, China	13,100	34,000
40	Prince of Wales Island, Canada	12,872	33,339
41	Novaya Zemlya, south island, Russia	12,633	32,730
42	Vancouver Island, Canada	12,079	31,285
43	Sicily, Italy	9,926	25,709
44	Somerset Island, Canada	9,570	24,786
45	Sardinia, Italy	9,301	24,090
46	Bathurst Island, Canada	7,600	19,684
47	Shikoku, Japan	7,258	18,799
48	Ceram (Seram), Indonesia	7,191	18,625
49	North East Land, Norway	6,350	16,446
50	New Caledonia, Oceania	6,252	16,192
51	Prince Patrick Island, Canada	5,986	15,509
52	Timor, Asia	5,743	14,874
53	Sumbawa, Indonesia	5,549	14,377
54	Ostrov Oktyabr'skoy Revolyutsii, Russia	5,511	14,279
55	Flores, Indonesia	5,502	14,250
56	Samar, Philippines	5,100	13,080
57	King William Island, Canada	4,961	12,853
58	Negros, Philippines	4,907	12,710
59	Thurston Island, Antarctica	4,854	12,576
60	Palawan, Philippines	4,550	11,785

Islands, Islands, Everywhere

Four islands—Hokkaidō, Honshū, Kyūshū, and Shikoku—constitute 98% of Japan's total land area, but the country is actually comprised of more than 3,000 islands. Similarly, two islands—Great Britain and Ireland—make up 93% of the total land area of the British Isles, but the island group also includes more than 5,000 smaller islands.

Greenland

New Guinea

Borneo

Madagascar

Baffin Island

Sumatra

Honshū

Great Britain

Victoria Island

Ellesmere Island

Major World Island Groups

Aleutian Islands (Pacific Ocean)

Alexander Archipelago (Pacific Ocean)

Azores (Atlantic Ocean)

Bahamas (Atlantic Ocean)

Balearic Islands (Mediterranean Sea)

Bismarck Archipelago (Pacific Ocean)

British Isles (Atlantic Ocean)

Cape Verde Islands (Atlantic Ocean)

Dodecanese (Mediterranean Sea)

Faroe Islands (Atlantic Ocean)

Falkland Islands (Atlantic Ocean)

Fiji Islands (Pacific Ocean)

Galapagos Islands (Pacific Ocean)

Greater Sunda Islands (Indian/Pacific Oceans)

Hawai'ian Islands (Pacific Ocean)

Ionian Islands (Mediterranean Sea)

Islas Canarias (Atlantic Ocean)

Japan (Pacific Ocean)

Kikládhes (Mediterranean Sea)

Kuril Islands (Pacific Ocean)

Lesser Sunda Islands (Indian Ocean)

Moluccas (Pacific Ocean)

Nansei Shotō (Pacific Ocean)

New Hebrides (Atlantic Ocean)

New Siberian Islands (Arctic Ocean)

Novaya Zemlya (Arctic Ocean)

Philippine Islands (Pacific Ocean)

Severnaya Zemlya (Arctic Ocean)

Solomon Islands (Pacific Ocean)

Spitsbergen (Arctic Ocean)

West Indies (Atlantic Ocean)

Contrasting Population Densities

Some islands are among the most densely populated places on Earth, while others are among the least densely populated. This fact is dramatically illustrated by the following comparison of five islands:

Manhattan, N.Y., U.S., (pop. 1,537,000) 69,864/sq mile (26,965/sq km)

Singapore Island, Singapore (pop. 4,375,000) 17,785/sq mile (6,879/sq km)

Long Island, N.Y., U.S. (pop. 7,449,000) 5,410/sq mile (2,089/sq km)

Population per square mile (sq km)

Baffin Island, Canada (pop. 11,700) 0.06/sq mile (0.02/sq km)

Greenland (pop. 56,000) 0.07/sq mile (0.03/sq km)

Mountains, Volcanoes, and Earthquakes

The Tallest Mountain in the World

With its peak reaching 29,028 feet (8,848 m) above sea level, Mt. Everest ranks as the highest mountain in the world, but not the tallest. That title goes to Mauna Kea, one of the five volcanic mountains that make up the island of Hawai'i. From its base on the floor of the Pacific Ocean, Mauna Kea rises 33,476 feet (10,210 m)—more than six miles—although only the top 13,796 feet (4,205 m) are above sea level.

Seafloor Atop Mt. Everest

When Sir Edmund Percival Hillary and Tenzing Norgay reached the summit of Mt. Everest in 1953, they probably did not realize they were standing on the seafloor.

The Himalayan mountain system was formed through the process of plate tectonics. Ocean once separated India and Asia, but 180 million years ago the Indo-Australian crustal plate, on which India sits, began a northward migration and eventually collided with the Eurasian plate. The seafloor between the two landmasses crumpled and was slowly thrust upward. Rock layers that once lay at the bottom of the ocean now crown the peaks of the highest mountains in the world.

Principal Mountain Systems and Ranges of the World

Alaska Range (North America)
Alps (Europe)
Altai (Asia)
Andes (South America)
Appennino (Europe)
Atlas Mountains (Africa)
Appalachian Mountains (North America)
Brooks Range (North America)
Carpathian Mountains (Europe)
Cascade Range (North America)
Caucasus (Europe/Asia)
Coast Mountains (North America)
Coast Ranges (North America)
Great Dividing Range (Australia)
Greater Khingan Range (Asia)
Himalayas (Asia)
Hindu Kush (Asia)
Karakoram Range (Asia)
Kunlun Shan (Asia)
Madre Occidental, Sierra (North America)
Madre Oriental, Sierra (North America)
Nevada, Sierra (North America)
Pamirs (Asia)
Pyrenees (Europe)
Rocky Mountains (North America)
Sayan Khrebet (Asia)
Southern Alps (New Zealand)
Tien Shan (Asia)
Urals (Europe)
Zagros Mountains (Asia)

Principal Mountains of the World

Δ = Highest mountain in range, region, country, or state named

Location	Height Feet	Height Meters	Location	Height Feet	Height Meters
Africa			Dufourspitze, Italy-Δ Switzerland	15,203	4,634
Kilimanjaro, Δ Tanzania (Δ Africa)	19,340	5,895	Weisshorn, Switzerland	14,783	4,506
Kirinyaga (Mount Kenya), Δ Kenya	17,058	5,199	Matterhorn, Italy-Switzerland	14,692	4,478
Margherita Peak, Δ Uganda-Δ Dem. Rep. of the Congo	16,763	5,109	Finsteraarhorn, Switzerland	14,022	4,274
Ras Dashen Terara, Δ Ethiopia	15,158	4,620	Jungfrau, Switzerland	13,642	4,158
Meru, Mount, Tanzania	14,978	4,565	Écrins, Barre des, France	13,458	4,102
Karisimbi, Volcan, Δ Rwanda-Dem. Rep. of the Congo	14,787	4,507	Viso, Monte, Italy (Δ Cottian Alps)	12,602	3,841
Elgon, Mount, Kenya-Uganda	14,178	4,321	Grossglockner, Δ Austria	12,461	3,798
Toubkal, Jebel, Δ Morocco (Δ Atlas Mts.)	13,665	4,165	Teide, Pico de, Δ Spain (Δ Canary Is.)	12,188	3,715
Cameroon Mountain, Δ Cameroon	13,451	4,100	**North America**		
Antarctica			McKinley, Mt., Δ Alaska (Δ United States; Δ North America)	20,320	6,194
Vinson Massif, Δ Antarctica	16,066	4,897	Logan, Mt., Δ Canada (Δ Yukon; Δ St. Elias Mts.)	19,551	5,959
Kirkpatrick, Mount	14,856	4,528	Orizaba, Pico de, Δ Mexico	18,406	5,610
Markham, Mount	14,049	4,282	St. Elias, Mt., Alaska-Canada	18,008	5,489
Jackson, Mount	13,747	4,190	Popocatépetl, Volcán, Mexico	17,930	5,465
Sidley, Mount	13,717	4,181	Foraker, Mt., Alaska	17,400	5,304
Wade, Mount	13,396	4,083	Iztaccíhuatl, Mexico	17,159	5,230
Asia			Lucania, Mt., Canada	17,147	5,226
Everest, Mount, Δ China-Δ Nepal (Δ Tibet; Δ Himalayas; Δ Asia; Δ World)	29,028	8,848	Fairweather, Mt., Alaska-Canada (Δ British Columbia)	15,300	4,663
K2 (Qogir Feng), China-Δ Pakistan (Δ Kashmir; Δ Karakoram Range)	28,250	8,611	Whitney, Mt., Δ California	14,494	4,418
Kanchenjunga, Δ India-Nepal	28,208	8,598	Elbert, Mt., Δ Colorado (Δ Rocky Mts.)	14,433	4,399
Makalu, China-Nepal	27,825	8,481	Massive, Mt., Colorado	14,421	4,396
Dhawalāgiri, Nepal	26,810	8,172	Harvard, Mt., Colorado	14,420	4,395
Nanga Parbat, Pakistan	26,660	8,126	Rainier, Mt., Δ Washington (Δ Cascade Range)	14,410	4,392
Annapurna, Nepal	26,504	8,078	Williamson, Mt., California	14,370	4,380
Gasherbrum, China-Pakistan	26,470	8,068	La Plata Pk., Colorado	14,361	4,377
Xixabangma Feng, China	26,286	8,012	Blanca Pk., Colorado (Δ Sangre de Cristo Mts.)	14,345	4,372
Nanda Devi, India	25,645	7,817	Uncompahgre Pk., Colorado (Δ San Juan Mts.)	14,309	4,361
Kamet, China-India	25,447	7,756	Grays Pk., Colorado (Δ Front Range)	14,270	4,349
Namjagbarwa Feng, China	25,446	7,756	Evans, Mt., Colorado	14,264	4,348
Muztag, China (Δ Kunlun Shan)	25,338	7,723	Longs Pk., Colorado	14,255	4,345
Tirich Mir, Pakistan (Δ Hindu Kush)	25,230	7,690	Wrangell, Mt., Alaska	14,163	4,317
Gongga Shan, China	24,790	7,556	Shasta, Mt., California	14,162	4,317
Kula Kangri, Δ Bhutan	24,784	7,554	Pikes Pk., Colorado	14,110	4,301
Ismail Samani, pik, Δ Tajikistan (Δ Pamir)	24,590	7,495	Colima, Nevado de, Mexico	13,991	4,240
Nowshak, Δ Afghanistan-Pakistan	24,557	7,485	Tajumulco, Volcán, Δ Guatemala (Δ Central America)	13,845	4,220
Pobedy, Pik, China-Russia	24,406	7,439	Gannett Pk., Δ Wyoming	13,804	4,207
Chomo Lhari, Bhutan-China	23,997	7,314	Mauna Kea, Δ Hawaii	13,796	4,205
Muztag, China	23,891	7,282	Grand Teton, Wyoming	13,770	4,197
Lenina, Pik, Δ Kyrgyzstan-Tajikistan	23,406	7,134	Mauna Loa, Hawaii	13,679	4,169
Api, Nepal	23,399	7,132	Kings Pk., Δ Utah	13,528	4,123
Kangrinboqê Feng, China	22,028	6,714	Cloud Pk., Wyoming (Δ Bighorn Mts.)	13,167	4,013
Hkakabo Razi, Δ Myanmar	19,296	5,881	Waddington, Mt., Canada (Δ Coast Mts.)	13,163	4,012
Damavand, Qolleh-ye, Δ Iran	18,386	5,604	Wheeler Pk., Δ New Mexico	13,161	4,011
Agri Dagi (Mount Ararat), Δ Turkey	16,854	5,137	Boundary Pk., Δ Nevada	13,140	4,005
Fuladi, Kuh-e, Afghanistan	16,847	5,135	Robson, Mt., Canada (Δ Canadian Rockies)	12,972	3,954
Jaya, Puncak, Δ Indonesia (Δ New Guinea)	16,503	5,030	Granite Pk., Δ Montana	12,799	3,901
Klyuchevskaya, Vulkan, Russia (Δ Poluostrov Kamchatka)	15,584	4,750	Borah Pk., Δ Idaho	12,662	3,859
Trikora, Puncak, Indonesia	15,584	4,750	Humphreys Pk., Δ Arizona	12,633	3,851
Belukha, Gora, Kazakhstan-Russia	14,783	4,506	Chirripó, Volcán, Δ Costa Rica	12,530	3,819
Turgen, Mount, Mongolia	14,311	4,362	Columbia, Mt., Canada (Δ Alberta)	12,294	3,747
Kinabalu, Gunong, Δ Malaysia (Δ Borneo)	13,455	4,101	Adams, Mt., Washington	12,276	3,742
Yü Shan, Δ Taiwan	13,114	3,997	Gunnbjørn Fjeld, Δ Greenland	12,139	3,700
Erciyes Dagı, Turkey	12,851	3,917	**South America**		
Kerinci, Gunung, Indonesia (Δ Sumatra)	12,467	3,800	Aconcagua, Cerro, Δ Argentina (Δ Andes; Δ South America)	22,831	6,959
Fuji San, Δ Japan (Δ Honshu)	12,388	3,776	Ojos del Salado, Nevado, Argentina-Δ Chile	22,615	6,893
Rinjani, Gunung, Indonesia (Δ Lombok)	12,224	3,726	Bonete, Cerro, Argentina	22,546	6,872
Semeru, Gunung, Indonesia (Δ Java)	12,060	3,676	Huascarán, Nevado, Δ Peru	22,133	6,746
Hadūr Shu'ayb, Jabal an-, Δ Yemen (Δ Arabian Peninsula)	12,008	3,660	Llullaillaco, Volcán, Argentina-Chile	22,110	6,739
Australia / Oceania			Yerupaja, Nevado, Peru	21,765	6,634
Wilhelm, Mt., Δ Papua New Guinea	14,793	4,509	Tupungato, Cerro, Argentina-Chile	21,555	6,570
Giluwe, Mt., Papua New Guinea	14,330	4,368	Sajama, Nevado, Bolivia	21,463	6,542
Bangeta, Mt., Papua New Guinea	13,520	4,121	Illampu, Nevado, Bolivia	21,066	6,421
Victoria, Mt., Papua New Guinea (Δ Owen Stanley Range)	13,238	4,035	Illimani, Nevado, Bolivia	20,741	6,322
Aoraki (Mt. Cook), Δ New Zealand (Δ South Island)	12,316	3,754	Chimborazo, Δ Ecuador	20,702	6,310
Europe			Antofalla, Volcán, Argentina	20,013	6,100
El'brus, Gora, Δ Russia (Δ Caucasus; Δ Europe)	18,510	5,642	Cotopaxi, Ecuador	19,347	5,897
Dykhtau, Mt., Russia	17,073	5,204	Misti, Volcán, Peru	19,101	5,822
Blanc, Mont (Monte Bianco) Δ France-Δ Italy (Δ Alps)	15,771	4,807	Huila, Nevado de, Colombia (Δ Cordillera Central)	18,865	5,750
			Bolívar, Pico, Δ Venezuela	16,427	5,007

Notable Volcanic Eruptions

Year	Volcano Name, Location	Comments
ca. 4895 B.C.	Crater Lake, Oregon, U.S.	Collapse forms caldera that now contains Crater Lake.
ca. 4350 B.C.	Kikai, Ryukyu Islands, Japan	Japan's largest known eruption.
ca. 1628 B.C.	Santorini (Thira), Greece	Eruption devastates late Minoan civilization.
79 A.D.	Vesuvius (Vesuvio), Italy	Roman towns of Pompeii and Herculaneum are buried.
ca. 180	Taupo, New Zealand	Area measuring 6,200 square miles (16,000 sq km) is devastated.
ca. 260	Ilopango, El Salvador	Thousands killed, with major impact on Mayan civilization.
915	Towada, Honshu, Japan	Japan's largest historic eruption.
ca. 1000	Baitoushan, China/Korea	Largest known eruption on Asian mainland.
1259	Unknown	Evidence from polar ice cores suggests that a huge eruption, possibly the largest of the millennium, occurred in this year.
1586	Kelut, Java	Explosions in crater lake; mudflows kill 10,000.
1631	Vesuvius (Vesuvio), Italy	Eruption kills 4,000.
ca. 1660	Long Island, Papua New Guinea	"The time of darkness" in tribal legends on Papua New Guinea.
1672	Merapi, Java	Pyroclastic flows and mudflows kill 3,000.
1711	Awu, Sangihe Islands, Indonesia	Pyroclastic flows kill 3,000.
1760	Makian, Halmahera, Indonesia	Eruption kills 2,000; island evacuated for seven years.
1772	Papandayan, Java	Debris avalanche causes 2,957 fatalities.
1783	Lakagigar, Iceland	Largest historic lava flows; 9,350 deaths.
1790	Kīlauea, Hawai'i	Hawai'i's last large explosive eruption.
1792	Unzen, Kyushu, Japan	Tsunami and debris avalanche kill 14,500.
1815	Tambora, Indonesia	History's most explosive eruption; 92,000 deaths.
1822	Galunggung, Java	Pyroclastic flows and mudflows kill 4,011.
1856	Awu, Sangihe Islands, Indonesia	Pyroclastic flows kill 2,806.
1883	Krakatau, Indonesia	Caldera collapse; 36,417 people killed, most by tsunami.
1888	Ritter Island, Papua New Guinea	3,000 killed, most by tsunami created by debris avalanche.
1902	Mont Pelee, West Indies	Town of St. Pierre destroyed; 28,000 people killed.
1902	Santa Maria, Guatemala	5,000 killed as 10 villages are buried by volcanic debris.
1912	Novarupta (Katmai), Alaska	Largest 20th-century eruption.
1914	Lassen, California, U.S.	California's last historic eruption.
1919	Kelut, Java	Mudflows devastate 104 villages and kill 5,110 people.
1930	Merapi, Java	1,369 people are killed as 42 villages are totally or partially destroyed.
1943	Parícutin, Mexico	Fissure in cornfield erupts, building cinder cone 1,500 feet (460 m) high within two years. One of the few volcano births ever witnessed.
1951	Lamington, Papua New Guinea	Pyroclastic flows kill 2,942.
1963	Surtsey, Iceland	Submarine eruption builds new island.
1977	Nyiragongo, Dem. Rep. of the Congo	One of the shortest major eruptions and fastest lava flows ever recorded.
1980	St. Helens, Washington, U.S.	Lateral blast; 230-square-mile (600 sq km) area devastated.
1982	El Chichón, Mexico	Pyroclastic surges kill 1,877.
1985	Ruiz, Colombia	Mudflows kill 23,080.
1991	Pinatubo, Luzon, Philippines	Major eruption in densely populated area prompts evacuation of 250,000 people; fatalities number fewer than 800. Enormous amount of gas released into stratosphere lowers global temperatures for more than a year.
1995	Soufriere Hills Volcano, Montserrat Island	Forced evacuation of the southern half of the island, destroyed capital city of Plymouth.

Sources: Smithsonian Institution Global Volcanism Program; Volcanoes of the World, Second Edition, by Tom Simkin and Lee Siebert, Geoscience Press and Smithsonian Institution, 1994. USGS National Earthquake Information Center.

Eruption of Mt. St. Helens in 1980

Significant Earthquakes through History

Year	Estimated Magnitude	Number of Deaths	Place
365		50,000	Knossos, Crete
844		50,000	Damascus, Syria; Antioch, Turkey
856		150,000	Dāmghān, Kashan, Qumis, Iran
893		150,000	Caucasus region
894		180,000	western India
1042		50,000	Palmyra, Baalbek, Syria
1138		230,000	Aleppo, Gansana, Syria
1139	6.8	300,000	Gäncä, Kiapas, Azerbaijan
1201		50,000	upper Egypt to Syria
1290	6.7	100,000	eastern China
1556		820,000	Shanxi Province, China
1662		300,000	China
1667	6.9	80,000	Caucusus region, northern Iran
1668		50,000	Shandong Province, China
1693		93,000	Sicily, Italy
1727		77,000	Tabrīz, Iran
1731		100,000	Beijing, China
1739		50,000	China
1755		62,000	Morocco, Portugal, Spain
1780	6.7	100,000	Tabrīz, Iran
1868	7.7	70,000	Ecuador, Colombia
1908	7.5	83,000	Calabria, Messina, Italy
1920	8.5	200,000	Gansu and Shanxi provinces, China
1923	8.2	142,807	Tokyo, Yokohama, Japan
1927	8.3	200,000	Gansu and Qinghai provinces, China
1932	7.6	70,000	Gansu Province, China
1970	7.8	66,794	northern Peru
1976	7.8	242,000	Tangshan, China
1990	7.7	50,000	northwestern Iran
2004	9.0	280,000	Sumatra, Indonesia
2008	7.9	69,000	Sichuan Province, China

Some Significant U.S. Earthquakes

Year	Estimated Magnitude	Number of Deaths	Place
1811–12	8.6, 8.4, 8.7	<10	New Madrid, Missouri (series)
1886	7.0	60	Charleston, South Carolina
1906	8.3	3,000	San Francisco, California
1933	6.3	115 ‡	Long Beach, California
1946	7.4	5	Alaska
1964	8.4	125	Anchorage, Alaska
1971	6.8	65	San Fernando, California
1989	7.1	62	San Francisco Bay Area, California
1994	6.8	58	Northridge, California

‡ A tsunami generated by this earthquake struck Hilo, Hawaii, killing 159 people.

Oceans and Lakes

Oceans, Seas, Gulfs, and Bays

	Area		Volume of water		Mean depth		Greatest known depth		
	sq. miles	sq. km.	cubic miles	cubic km.	feet	meters	feet	meters	
Pacific Ocean	63,800,000	165,200,000	169,650,000	707,100,000	12,987	3,957	35,810	10,922	Mariana Trench
Atlantic Ocean	31,800,000	82,400,000	79,199,000	330,100,000	11,821	3,602	28,232	8,611	Puerto Rico Trench
Indian Ocean	28,900,000	74,900,000	68,282,000	284,600,000	12,261	3,736	23,812	7,258	Weber Basin
Arctic Ocean	5,400,000	14,000,000	4,007,000	16,700,000	3,712	1,131	17,897	5,453	Lat. 77° 45'N, long. 175°W
Coral Sea	1,850,000	4,791,000	2,752,000	11,470,000	7,857	2,394	30,079	9,165	
Arabian Sea	1,492,000	3,864,000	2,416,000	10,070,000	8,973	2,734	19,029	5,803	
South China Sea	1,331,000	3,447,000	943,000	3,929,000	3,741	1,140	18,241	5,563	
Caribbean Sea	1,063,000	2,753,000	1,646,000	6,860,000	8,175	2,491	25,197	7,685	Off Cayman Islands
Mediterranean Sea	967,000	2,505,000	901,000	3,754,000	4,916	1,498	16,470	5,023	Off Cape Matapan, Greece
Bering Sea	876,000	2,269,000	911,000	3,796,000	5,382	1,640	25,194	7,684	Off Buldir Island
Bengal, Bay of	839,000	2,173,000	1,357,000	5,616,000	8,484	2,585	17,251	5,261	
Okhotsk, Sea of	619,000	1,603,000	316,000	1,317,000	2,694	821	1,029	3,374	Lat. 146° 10'E, long. 46° 50'N
Norwegian Sea	597,000	1,546,000	578,000	2,408,000	5,717	1,742	13,189	4,022	
Mexico, Gulf of	596,000	1,544,000	560,000	2,332,000	8,205	2,500	14,370	4,382	Sigsbee Deep
Hudson Bay	475,000	1,230,000	22,000	92,000	328	100	850	259	Near entrance
Greenland Sea	465,000	1,204,000	417,000	1,740,000	4,739	1,444	15,899	4,849	
Japan, Sea of	413,000	1,070,000	391,000	1,630,000	5,037	1,535	12,041	3,669	
Arafura Sea	400,000	1,037,000	49,000	204,000	646	197	12,077	3,680	
East Siberian Sea	357,000	926,000	14,000	61,000	216	66	508	155	
Kara Sea	349,000	903,000	24,000	101,000	371	113	2,034	620	
East China Sea	290,000	752,000	63,000	263,000	1,145	349	7,778	2,370	
Banda Sea	268,000	695,000	511,000	2,129,000	10,056	3,064	24,418	7,440	
Baffin Bay	263,000	681,000	142,000	593,000	2,825	861	7,010	2,136	
Laptev Sea	262,000	678,000	87,000	363,000	1,772	540	9,780	2,980	
Timor Sea	237,000	615,000	60,000	250,000	1,332	406	10,863	3,310	
Andaman Sea	232,000	602,000	158,000	660,000	3,597	1,096	13,777	4,198	
Chukchi Sea	228,000	590,000	11,000	45,000	252	77	525	160	
North Sea	214,000	554,000	12,000	52,000	315	96	2,655	809	
Java Sea	185,000	480,000	5,000	22,000	147	45	292	89	
Beaufort Sea	184,000	476,000	115,000	478,000	3,295	1,004	12,245	3,731	
Red Sea	174,000	450,000	60,000	251,000	1,831	558	8,648	2,635	
Baltic Sea	173,000	448,000	5,000	20,000	157	48	1,506	459	
Celebes Sea	168,000	435,000	380,000	1,586,000	11,962	3,645	19,173	5,842	
Black Sea	166,000	431,000	133,000	555,000	3,839	1,170	7,256	2,211	
Yellow Sea	161,000	417,000	4,000	17,000	131	40	344	105	
Sulu Sea	134,000	348,000	133,000	553,000	5,221	1,591	18,300	5,576	
Molucca Sea	112,000	291,000	133,000	554,000	6,242	1,902	16,311	4,970	
Ceram Sea	72,000	187,000	54,000	227,000	3,968	1,209	17,456	5,319	
Flores Sea	47,000	121,000	53,000	222,000	6,003	1,829	16,813	5,123	
Bali Sea	46,000	119,000	12,000	49,000	1,349	411	4,253	1,296	
Savu Sea	41,000	105,000	43,000	178,000	5,582	1,701	11,060	3,370	
White Sea	35,000	91,000	1,000	4,400	161	49	1,083	330	
Azov, Sea of	15,000	40,000	100	400	29	9	46	14	
Marmara, Sea of	4,000	11,000	1,000	4,000	1,171	357	4,138	1,261	

Source: Atlas of World Water Balance, USSR National Committee for the International Water Decade and UNESCO, 1977.

Note: In 2000, the International Hydrographic Organization delimited a fifth world ocean: the Southern Ocean. This ocean, which encircles Antarctica, is not included in this chart.

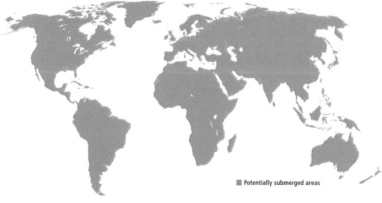

■ Potentially submerged areas

Fluctuating Sea Level

Changes in the Earth's climate have a dramatic effect on the sea level. Only 20,000 years ago, at the height of the most recent ice age, a vast amount of the Earth's water was locked up in ice sheets and glaciers, and the sea level was 330 feet (100 meters) lower than it is today. As the climate warmed slowly, the ice began to melt and the oceans began to rise.

Today there is still a tremendous amount of ice on the Earth. More than nine-tenths of it resides in the enormous ice cap which covers Antarctica. Measuring about 5.4 million square miles (14 million sq km) in surface area, the ice cap is on average one mile (1.6 km) thick but in some places is nearly three miles (4.8 km) thick. If it were to melt, the oceans would rise another 200 feet (60 m), and more than half of the world's population would have to relocate.

Ocean Depths in Profile

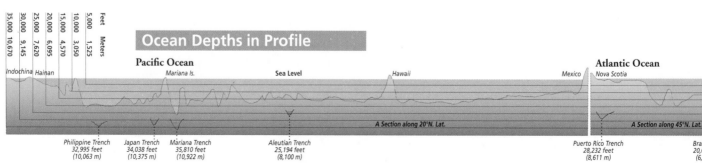

Deepest Lakes

	Lake	Greatest depth feet	meters
1	Baikal, Lake, Russia	5,315	1,621
2	Tanganyika, Lake, Africa	4,800	1,464
3	Caspian Sea, Asia-Europe	3,363	1,025
4	Nyasa, Lake (Lake Malawi), Malawi-Mozambique-Tanzania	2,317	706
5	Issyk-Kul', Lake, Kyrgyzstan	2,303	702
6	Great Slave Lake, NWT, Canada	2,015	614
7	Matana, Lake, Indonesia	1,936	590
8	Crater Lake, Oregon, U.S.	1,932	589
9	Toba, Lake (Danau Toba), Indonesia	1,736	529
10	Sarez, Lake, Tajikistan	1,657	505
11	Tahoe, Lake, California-Nevada, U.S.	1,645	502
12	Kivu, Lake, Rwanda-Dem. Rep. of the Congo	1,628	496
13	Chelan, Lake, Washington, U.S.	1,605	489
14	Quesnel Lake, BC, Canada	1,560	476
15	Adams Lake, BC, Canada	1,500	457

Lakes with the Greatest Volume of Water

	Lake	Volume of water cubic mi	cubic km
1	Caspian Sea, Asia-Europe	18,900	78,200
2	Baikal, Lake, Russia	5,500	23,000
3	Tanganyika, Lake, Africa	4,500	18,900
4	Superior, Lake, Canada-U.S.	2,900	12,200
5	Nyasa, Lake (Lake Malawi), Malawi-Mozambique-Tanzania	1,900	7,725
6	Michigan, Lake, U.S.	1,200	4,910
7	Huron, Lake, Canada-U.S.	860	3,580
8	Victoria, Lake, Kenya-Tanzania-Uganda	650	2,700
9	Issyk-Kul', Lake, Kyrgyzstan	415	1,730
10	Ontario, Lake, Canada-U.S.	410	1,710
11	Great Slave Lake, Canada	260	1,070
12	Great Bear Lake, Canada	240	1,010
13	Ladozhskoye, Ozero, Russia	220	908
14	Titicaca, Lago, Bolivia-Peru	170	710

Sources for volume and depth information: Atlas of World Water Balance, *USSR National Committee for the International Water Decade and UNESCO, 1977;* Principal Rivers and Lakes of the World, *National Oceanic and Atmospheric Administration, 1982.*

Principal Lakes

	Lake	Area sq mi	sq km
1	Caspian Sea, Asia-Europe	143,240	370,990
2	Superior, Lake, Canada-U.S.	31,700	82,100
3	Victoria, Lake, Kenya-Tanzania-Uganda	26,820	69,463
4	Huron, Lake, Canada-U.S.	23,000	60,000
5	Michigan, Lake, U.S.	22,300	57,800
6	Tanganyika, Lake, Africa	12,350	31,986
7	Baikal, Lake, Russia	12,200	31,500
8	Great Bear Lake, Canada	12,095	31,326
9	Nyasa, Lake (Lake Malawi), Malawi-Mozambique-Tanzania	11,150	28,878
10	Aral Sea, Kazakhstan-Uzbekistan	11,100	28,700
11	Great Slave Lake, Canada	11,030	28,568
12	Erie, Lake, Canada-U.S.	9,910	25,667
13	Winnipeg, Lake, Canada	9,416	24,387
14	Ontario, Lake, Canada-U.S.	7,540	19,529
15	Balqash koli (Lake Balkhash), Kazakhstan	7,100	18,300
16	Ladozhskoye, Ozero, Russia	6,833	17,700
17	Chad, Lake (Lac Tchad), Cameroon-Chad-Nigeria	6,300	16,300
18	Onezhskoye, Ozero, Russia	3,753	9,720
19	Eyre, Lake, Australia	3,700	9,500
20	Titicaca, Lago, Bolivia-Peru	3,200	8,300
21	Nicaragua, Lago de, Nicaragua	3,150	8,158
22	Mai-Ndombe, Lac, Dem. Rep. of the Congo	3,100	8,000
23	Athabasca, Lake, Canada	3,064	7,935
24	Reindeer, Lake, Canada	2,568	6,650
25	Tônlé Sap, Cambodia	2,500	6,500
26	Rudolf, Lake, Ethiopia-Kenya	2,473	6,405
27	Issyk-Kul', Ozero, Kyrgyzstan	2,425	6,280
28	Torrens, Lake, Australia	2,300	5,900
29	Albert, Lake, Uganda-Dem. Rep. of the Congo	2,160	5,594
30	Vänern, Sweden	2,156	5,584
31	Nettilling Lake, Canada	2,140	5,542
32	Winnipegosis, Lake, Canada	2,075	5,374
33	Bangweulu, Lake, Zambia	1,930	4,999
34	Nipigon, Lake, Canada	1,872	4,848
35	Orumiyeh, Daryacheh-ye, Iran	1,815	4,701
36	Manitoba, Lake, Canada	1,785	4,624
37	Woods, Lake of the, Canada-U.S.	1,727	4,472
38	Kyoga, Lake, Uganda	1,710	4,429

Lake Baikal

Russia's Great Lake

On a map of the world, Lake Baikal is easy to overlook — a thin blue crescent adrift in the vastness of Siberia. But its inconspicuousness is deceptive, for Baikal is one of the greatest bodies of fresh water on Earth.

Although lakes generally have a life span of less than one million years, Baikal has existed for perhaps as long as 25 million years, which makes it the world's oldest body of fresh water. It formed in a rift that tectonic forces had begun to tear open in the Earth's crust. As the rift grew, so did Baikal. Today the lake is 395 miles (636 km) long and an average of 30 miles (48 km) wide. Only six lakes in the world have a greater surface area.

Baikal is the world's deepest lake. Its maximum depth is 5,315 feet (1,621 m) — slightly over a mile, and roughly equal to the greatest depth of the Grand Canyon. The lake bottom lies 4,250 feet (1,295 m) below sea level and two-and-a-third miles (3.75 km) below the peaks of the surounding mountains. The crustal rift which Baikal occupies is the planet's deepest land depression, extending to a depth of more than five-and-a-half miles (9 km). The lake sits atop at least four miles (6.4 km) of sediment, the accumulation of 25 million years.

More than 300 rivers empty into Baikal, but only one, the Angara, flows out of it. Despite having only 38% of the surface area of North America's Lake Superior, Baikal contains more water than all five of the Great Lakes combined. Its volume of 5,500 cubic miles (23,000 cubic km) of water is greater than that of any other freshwater lake in the world and represents approximately one-fifth of all of the Earth's unfrozen fresh water.

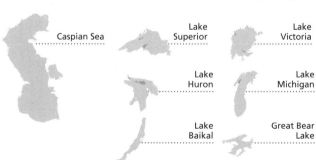

Caspian Sea

Lake Superior

Lake Victoria

Aral Sea

Lake Huron

Lake Michigan

Lake Tanganyika

Lake Baikal

Great Bear Lake

Lake Nyasa (Malawi)

Mediterranean Sea

France · Gibraltar · Malta · Israel

Indian Ocean

Sea Level

Sumba · 65°N

Arctic Ocean

North Pole · 65°N · 65°S

Pacific Ocean

South Pole

A Section along 10°N. Lat.

Rivers

World's Longest Rivers

Rank	River	Length Miles	Length Kilometers	Rank	River	Length Miles	Length Kilometers
1	Nile, Africa	4,145	6,671	36	Murray, Australia	1,566	2,520
2	Amazon (Amazonas)-Ucayali, South America	4,000	6,400	37	Ganges, Asia	1,560	2,511
3	Yangtze (Chang), Asia	3,900	6,300	38	Pilcomayo, South America	1,550	2,494
4	Mississippi-Missouri, North America	3,740	6,019	39	Euphrates, Asia	1,510	2,430
5	Huang (Yellow), Asia	3,395	5,464	40	Ural, Asia	1,509	2,428
6	Ob'-Irtysh, Asia	3,362	5,410	41	Arkansas, North America	1,459	2,348
7	Río de la Plata-Paraná, South America	3,030	4,876	42	Colorado, North America (U.S.-Mexico)	1,450	2,334
8	Congo, Africa	2,900	4,700	43	Aldan, Asia	1,412	2,273
9	Paraná, South America	2,800	4,500	44	Syr Darya, Asia	1,370	2,205
10	Amur-Argun, Asia	2,761	4,444	45	Dnieper, Europe	1,350	2,200
11	Lena, Asia	2,700	4,400	46	Araguaia, South America	1,350	2,200
12	Mackenzie, North America	2,635	4,241	47	Cassai (Kasai), Africa	1,338	2,153
13	Mekong, Asia	2,600	4,200	48	Tarim, Asia	1,328	2,137
14	Niger, Africa	2,600	4,200	49	Kolyma, Asia	1,323	2,129
15	Yenisey, Asia	2,543	4,092	50	Orange, Africa	1,300	2,100
16	Missouri-Red Rock, North America	2,533	4,076	51	Negro, South America	1,300	2,100
17	Mississippi, North America	2,348	3,779	52	Ayeyarwady (Irrawaddy), Asia	1,300	2,100
18	Murray-Darling, Australia	2,330	3,750	53	Red, North America	1,270	2,044
19	Missouri, North America	2,315	3,726	54	Juruá, South America	1,250	2,012
20	Volga, Europe	2,194	3,531	55	Columbia, North America	1,240	2,000
21	Madeira, South America	2,013	3,240	56	Xingu, South America	1,230	1,979
22	São Francisco, South America	1,988	3,199	57	Ucayali, South America	1,220	1,963
23	Grande, Rio (Río Bravo), North America	1,885	3,034	58	Saskatchewan-Bow, North America	1,205	1,939
24	Purús, South America	1,860	2,993	59	Peace, North America	1,195	1,923
25	Indus, Asia	1,800	2,900	60	Tigris, Asia	1,180	1,899
26	Danube, Europe	1,776	2,858	61	Don, Europe	1,162	1,870
27	Brahmaputra, Asia	1,770	2,849	62	Songhua, Asia	1,140	1,835
28	Yukon, North America	1,770	2,849	63	Pechora, Europe	1,124	1,809
29	Salween (Nu), Asia	1,750	2,816	64	Kama, Europe	1,122	1,805
30	Zambezi, Africa	1,700	2,700	65	Limpopo, Africa	1,120	1,800
31	Vilyuy, Asia	1,647	2,650	66	Angara, Asia	1,105	1,779
32	Tocantins, South America	1,640	2,639	67	Snake, North America	1,038	1,670
33	Orinoco, South America	1,615	2,600	68	Uruguay, South America	1,025	1,650
34	Paraguay, South America	1,610	2,591	69	Churchill, North America	1,000	1,600
35	Amu Darya, Asia	1,578	2,540	70	Marañón, South America	995	1,592

The World's Greatest River

Although the Nile is slightly longer, the Amazon surpasses all other rivers in volume, size of drainage basin, and in nearly every other important category. If any river is to be called the greatest in the world, surely it is the Amazon.

It has been estimated that one-fifth of all of the flowing water on Earth is carried by the Amazon. From its 150-mile (240-km)-wide mouth, the river discharges 6,180,000 cubic feet (174,900 cubic m) of water per second — four-and-a-half times as much as the Congo, ten times as much as the Mississippi, and fifty-six times as much as the Nile. The Amazon's tremendous outflow turns the waters of the Atlantic from salty to brackish for more than 100 miles (160 km) offshore.

Drainage basin of the Amazon River

Covering more than one-third of the entire continent of South America, the Amazon's vast drainage basin measures 2,669,000 square miles (6,915,000 sq km) and is nearly twice as large as that of the second-ranked Congo. The Amazon begins its 4,000-mile (6,400-km) journey to the Atlantic from high up in the Andes, only 100 miles (160 km) from the Pacific. Along its course it receives the waters of more than 1,000 tributaries, which rise principally from the Andes, the Guiana Highlands, and the Brazilian Highlands. Seven of the tributaries are more than 1,000 miles (1,600 km) long, and one, the Madeira, is more than 2,000 miles (3,200 km) long.

The depth of the Amazon throughout most of its Brazilian segment exceeds 150 feet (45 m). Depths of more than 300 feet (90 m) have been recorded at points near the mouth. The largest ocean-going vessels can sail as far inland as Manaus, 1,000 miles (1,600 km) from the mouth. Freighters and small passenger vessels can navigate to Iquitos, 2,300 miles (3,700 km) from the mouth, even during times of low water.

Rivers with the Greatest Volume of Water

Rank	River Name	Flow of water per second at mouth		Rank	River Name	Flow of water per second at mouth	
		cubic feet	cubic meters			cubic feet	cubic meters
1	Amazon (Amazonas), South America	6,180,000	174,900	18	Para-Tocantins, South America (joins Amazon at mouth)	360,000	10,200
2	Congo, Africa	1,377,000	39,000	19	Salween, Asia	353,000	10,000
3	Negro, South America (tributary of Amazon)	1,236,000	35,000	20	Cassai (Kasai), Africa (trib. of Congo)	351,000	9,900
4	Orinoco, South America	890,000	25,200	21	Mackenzie, North America	343,000	9,700
5	Río de la Plata-Paraná, South America	809,000	22,900	22	Volga, Europe	271,000	7,700
6	Yangtze (Chang), Asia;	770,000	21,800	23	Ohio, North America (trib. of Mississippi)	257,000	7,300
	Madeira, South America (trib. of Amazon)	770,000	21,800	24	Yukon, North America	240,000	6,800
7	Missouri, North America (trib. of Mississippi)	763,000	21,600	25	Indus, Asia	235,000	6,600
8	Mississippi, North America*	640,300	18,100	26	Danube, Europe	227,000	6,400
9	Yenisey, Asia	636,000	18,000	27	Niger, Africa	215,000	6,100
10	Brahmaputra, Asia	575,000	16,300	28	Atchafalaya, North America	181,000	5,100
11	Lena, Asia	569,000	16,100	29	Paraguay, South America	155,000	4,400
12	Zambezi, Africa	565,000	16,000	30	Ob'-Katun, Asia	147,000	4,200
13	Mekong, Asia	500,000	14,100	31	São Francisco, South America	120,000	3,400
14	Saint Lawrence, North America	460,000	13,000	32	Tunguska, Asia	118,000	3,350
15	Ayeyarwady (Irrawaddy), Asia	447,000	12,600	33	Huang (Yellow), Asia	116,000	3,300
16	Ob'-Irtysh, Asia; Ganges, Asia	441,000	12,500	34	Nile, Africa	110,000	3,100
17	Amur, Asia	390,000	11,000				

*Approximately one-third of the Mississippi's water is diverted above Baton Rouge, Louisiana, and reaches the Gulf of Mexico via the Atchafalaya River.

Principal Rivers of the Continents

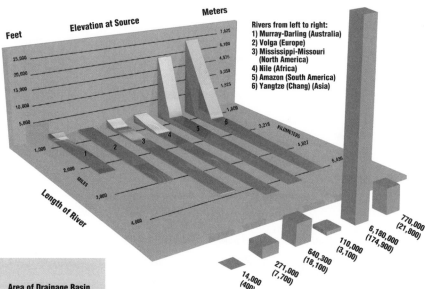

Rivers from left to right:
1) Murray-Darling (Australia)
2) Volga (Europe)
3) Mississippi-Missouri (North America)
4) Nile (Africa)
5) Amazon (South America)
6) Yangtze (Chang) (Asia)

Average volume of discharge at mouth, in cubic feet (cubic meters) per second

Rivers with the Largest Drainage Basins

Rank	River	Area of Drainage Basin	
		Square Miles	Square Kilometers
1	Amazon (Amazonas), South America	2,669,000	6,915,000
2	Congo, Africa	1,474,500	3,820,000
3	Mississippi-Missouri, North America	1,243,000	3,220,000
4	Río de la Plata-Paraná, South America	1,197,000	3,100,000
5	Ob'-Irtysh, Asia	1,154,000	2,990,000
6	Nile, Africa	1,108,000	2,870,000
7	Yenisey-Angara, Asia	1,011,000	2,618,500
8	Lena, Asia	961,000	2,490,000
9	Niger, Africa	807,000	2,090,000
10	Amur-Argun, Asia	792,000	2,051,300
11	Yangtze (Chang), Asia	705,000	1,826,000
12	Volga, Europe	525,000	1,360,000
13	Zambezi, Africa	513,500	1,330,000
14	St. Lawrence, North America	503,000	1,302,800
15	Huang (Yellow), Asia	486,000	1,258,700

Sources for volume and drainage basin information: Atlas of World Water Balance, *USSR National Committee for the International Hydrological Decade and UNESCO, 1977;* Principal Rivers and Lakes of the World, *National Oceanic and Atmospheric Administration, 1982.*

Climate and Weather

Temperature Extremes by Continent

Africa

Highest recorded temperature
Al 'Azīzīyah, Libya, September 13, 1922:
136° F (58° C),
Lowest recorded temperature
Ifrane, Morocco, February 11, 1935:
-11° F (-24° C)

Antarctica

Highest recorded temperature
Vanda Station, January 5, 1974:
59° F (15° C)
Lowest recorded temperature
Vostok, July 21, 1983:
-129° F (-89° C)

Asia

Highest recorded temperature
Tirat Zevi, Israel, June 21, 1942:
129° F (54° C)
Lowest recorded temperature
Oymyakon, Russia, February 6, 1933,
and Verkhoyansk, Russia, February 7, 1892:
-90° F (-68° C)

Australia / Oceania

Highest recorded temperature
Cloncurry, Queensland, Australia,
January 16, 1889: 128° F (53° C)
Lowest recorded temperature
Charlotte Pass, New South Wales, Australia,
June 29, 1994: -9.4° F (-22° C)

Europe

Highest recorded temperature
Sevilla, Spain, August 4, 1881:
122° F (50° C)
Lowest recorded temperature
Ust' Ščugor, Russia, (date not known):
-67° F (-55° C)

North America

Highest recorded temperature
Death Valley, California, United States,
July 10, 1913: 134° F (57° C)
Lowest recorded temperature
Northice, Greenland, January 9, 1954:
-87° F (-66° C)

South America

Highest recorded temperature
Rivadavia, Argentina, December 11, 1905:
120° F (49° C)
Lowest recorded temperature
Sarmiento, Argentina, June 1, 1907:
-27° F (-33° C)

World

Highest recorded temperature
Al 'Azīzīyah, Libya, September 13, 1922:
136° F (58° C)
Lowest recorded temperature
Vostok, Antarctica, July 21, 1983:
-129° F (-89° C)

World Temperature Extremes

Highest mean annual temperature Dalol, Ethiopia, 94° F (34° C)
Lowest mean annual temperature Plateau Station, Antarctica: -70° F (-57° C)

Greatest difference between highest and lowest recorded temperatures
Verkhoyansk, Russia. The highest temperature ever recorded there is 93.5° F (34.2° C); the lowest is -89.7° F (-67.6° C)
— a difference of 183° F (102° C).

Highest temperature ever recorded at the South Pole 7.5° F (-14° C) on December 27, 1978

Most consecutive days with temperatures of 100° F (38° C) or above Marble Bar, Australia, 162 days: October 30, 1923 to April 7, 1924

Greatest rise in temperature within a 12-hour period
Granville, North Dakota, on February 21, 1918. The temperature rose 83° F (46° C), from -33° F (-36° C)
in early morning to +50° F (10° C) in late afternoon.

Greatest drop in temperature within a 12-hour period
Fairfield, Montana, on December 24, 1924. The temperature dropped 84° F (46° C), from 63° F (17° C)
at noon to -21° F (-29° C) by midnight.

Temperature Ranges for 14 Major Cities around the World

City	Mean Temperature		City	Mean Temperature	
	Coldest Winter Month	Hottest Summer Month		Coldest Winter Month	Hottest Summer Month
Buenos Aires, Argentina	Aug: 51.3° F (10.7° C)	Jan: 75.0° F (23.9° C)	Mumbai (Bombay), India	Jan: 74.3° F (23.5° C)	May: 85.5° F (29.7° C)
Kolkata (Calcutta), India	Jan: 67.5° F (19.7° C)	May: 88.5° F (31.4° C)	New York City, U.S.	Jan: 32.9° F (0.5° C)	Jul: 77.0° F (25.0° C)
London, England	Feb: 39.4° F (4.1° C)	Jul: 63.9° F (17.7° C)	Osaka, Japan	Jan: 40.6° F (4.8° C)	Aug: 82.2° F (27.9° C)
Los Angeles, U.S.	Jan: 56.3° F (13.5° C)	Jul: 74.1° F (23.4° C)	Rio de Janeiro, Brazil	Jul: 70.2° F (21.2° C)	Jan: 79.9° F (26.6° C)
Manila, Philippines	Jan: 77.7° F (25.4° C)	May: 84.9° F (29.4° C)	São Paulo, Brazil	Jul: 58.8° F (14.9° C)	Jan: 71.1° F (21.7° C)
Mexico City, Mexico	Jan: 54.1° F (12.3° C)	May: 64.9° F (18.3° C)	Seoul, South Korea	Jan: 23.2° F (-4.9° C)	Aug: 77.7° F (25.4° C)
Moscow, Russia	Feb: 14.5° F (-9.7° C)	Jul: 65.8° F (18.8° C)	Tokyo, Japan	Jan: 39.6° F (4.2° C)	Aug: 79.3° F (26.3° C)

Precipitation

Greatest local average annual rainfall
Mt. Waialeale, Kaua'i, Hawaii,
460 inches (1,168 cm)

Lowest local average annual rainfall
Arica, Chile, .03 inches (.08 cm)

Greatest rainfall in 12 months
Cherrapunji, India, August 1860 to August 1861:
1,042 inches (2,646 cm)

Greatest rainfall in one month
Cherrapunji, India, July 1861: 366 inches (930 cm)

Greatest rainfall in 24 hours
Cilaos, Reunion, March 15 and 16, 1952:
74 inches (187 cm)

Greatest rainfall in 12 hours
Belouve, Reunion, February 28 and 29, 1964:
53 inches (135 cm)

Most thunderstorms annually
Kampala, Uganda, averages 242 days per
year with thunderstorms

Between 1916 and 1920, Bogor, Indonesia,
averaged 322 days per year with thunderstorms

Longest dry period
Arica, Chile, October, 1903
to January, 1918 — over 14 years

Largest hailstone ever recorded
Aurora, Nebraska, U.S., June 22, 1993:
circumference 18.75 inches (47.6 cm),
diameter 7 inches (17.8 cm)

Heaviest hailstone ever recorded
Kazakhstan, 1959: 4.18 pounds (1.9 kilograms)

North America's greatest snowfall in one season
Rainier Paradise Ranger Station, Washington,
U.S., 1971–1972: 1,122 inches (2,850 cm)

North America's greatest snowfall in one storm
Mt. Shasta Ski Bowl, California, U.S.,
February 13 to 19, 1959: 189 inches (480 cm)

North America's greatest snowfall in 24 hours
Silver Lake, Colorado, U.S., April 14 and 15, 1921:
76 inches (192.5 cm)

N. America's greatest depth of snowfall on the ground
Tamarack, California, U.S., March 11, 1911:
451 inches (1,145.5 cm)

Foggiest place on the U.S. West Coast
Cape Disappointment, Washington,
averages 2,552 hours of fog per year

Foggiest place on the U.S. East Coast
Mistake Island, Maine, averages
1,580 hours of fog per year

Wind

Highest 24-hour mean surface wind speed
Mt. Washington, New Hampshire, U.S.,
April 11 and 12, 1934: 128 mph (206 kph)

Highest 5-minute mean surface wind speed
Mt. Washington, New Hampshire, U.S.,
April 12, 1934: 188 mph (303 kph)

Highest surface wind peak gust:
Mt. Washington, New Hampshire, U.S.,
April 12, 1934: 231 mph (372 kph)

Windiest U.S. Cities

Chicago is sometimes called "The Windy City."
It earned this nickname because of long-winded politicians,
not because it has the strongest gales.

The windiest cities in the U.S. are as follows:

Cities	Average wind speed	
	mph	kph
Dodge City, Kansas	13.9	22.4
Amarillo, Texas	13.5	21.7
Cheyenne, Wyoming	12.9	20.8
Rochester, Minnesota	12.9	20.8
Casper, Wyoming	12.7	20.4

Chicago has an average wind speed of 10.3 mph (16.6 kph).

Deadliest Hurricanes in the U.S. since 1890

Rank	Place	Year	Number of Deaths
1	Texas (Galveston)	1900	8,000
2	Louisiana	1893	2,000
3	Florida (Lake Okeechobee)	1928	1,836
4	Louisiana (New Orleans), Mississippi— "Hurricane Katrina"	2005	>1,800
5	South Carolina, Georgia	1893	>1,000
6	Florida (Keys)	1919	>600
7	New England	1938	600
8	Florida (Keys)	1935	408
9	Southwest Louisiana, north Texas— "Hurricane Audrey"	1957	390
	Northeast U.S.	1944	390
10	Louisiana (Grand Isle)	1909	350

Tornadoes in the U.S., 1950—2003

Rank	State	Total Number of Tornadoes	Yearly Average	Total Number of Deaths
1	Texas	7,411	137	527
2	Florida	4,268	79	159
3	Oklahoma	3,183	59	263
4	Kansas	3,047	56	214
5	Nebraska	2,386	44	575
	U.S. Total	53,052	982	5,186

Deadliest Floods in the U.S. since 1900

Rank	Place	Year	Number of Deaths
1	Ohio River and tributaries	1913	467
2	Mississippi Valley	1927	246
3	Black Hills, South Dakota	1972	237
4	Willow Creek, Oregon	1903	225
5	Texas rivers	1921	215
6	Texas rivers	1913	180
7	Northeastern U.S., following Hurricane Diane	1955	180
8	New England	1936	150+
9	Big Thompson Canyon, Colorado	1976	144
10	Ohio and Lower Mississippi river basins	1937	137
11	Buffalo Creek, West Virginia	1972	125
12	James River basin, Virginia, following Hurricane Camille	1969	117

Population

World Population

During the first two million years of our species' existence, human population grew at a very slow rate, and probably never exceeded 10 million. With the development of agriculture circa 8000 B.C., the growth rate began to rise sharply: by the year A.D. 1, the world population stood at approximately 250 million.

By 1650, the population had doubled to 550 million, and within only 200 years it doubled again, reaching almost 1.2 billion by 1850. Each subsequent doubling has taken only half as long as the previous one: it took just 100 years to reach 2.5 billion, and 40 years to reach 5.2 billion.

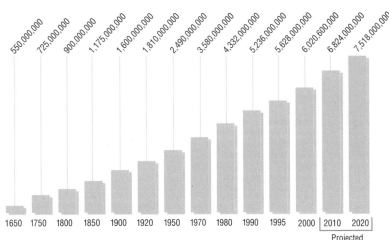

Year	1650	1750	1800	1850	1900	1920	1950	1970	1980	1990	1995	2000	2010	2020
Population	550,000,000	725,000,000	900,000,000	1,175,000,000	1,600,000,000	1,810,000,000	2,490,000,000	3,580,000,000	4,332,000,000	5,236,000,000	5,628,000,000	6,020,600,000	6,824,000,000	7,518,000,000

Projected Population

Historical Populations of the Continents and the World

Year	Africa	Asia	Australia	Europe	North America	Oceania, incl. Australia	South America	World
1650	100,000,000	335,000,000	<1,000,000	100,000,000	5,000,000	2,000,000	8,000,000	550,000,000
1750	95,000,000	476,000,000	<1,000,000	140,000,000	5,000,000	2,000,000	7,000,000	725,000,000
1800	90,000,000	593,000,000	<1,000,000	190,000,000	13,000,000	2,000,000	12,000,000	900,000,000
1850	95,000,000	754,000,000	<1,000,000	265,000,000	39,000,000	2,000,000	20,000,000	1,175,000,000
1900	118,000,000	932,000,000	4,000,000	400,000,000	106,000,000	6,000,000	38,000,000	1,600,000,000
1920	140,000,000	1,000,000,000	6,000,000	453,000,000	147,000,000	9,000,000	61,000,000	1,810,000,000
1950	199,000,000	1,418,000,000	8,000,000	530,000,000	219,000,000	13,000,000	111,000,000	2,490,000,000
1970	346,900,000	2,086,200,000	12,460,000	623,700,000	316,600,000	19,200,000	187,400,000	3,580,000,000
1980	463,800,000	2,581,000,000	14,510,000	660,000,000	365,000,000	22,700,000	239,000,000	4,332,000,000
1990	648,300,000	3,156,100,000	16,950,000	688,000,000	423,600,000	26,300,000	293,700,000	5,236,000,000
2000	781,300,000	3,676,700,000	19,050,000	709,500,000	478,200,000	30,500,000	344,400,000	6,020,600,000

Figures for years prior to 1970 are rounded to the nearest million. Figures in italics represent rough estimates.

The Most Populous City in the World, through History

With more than 25 million people, Japan's Tokyo-Yokohama agglomeration ranks as the most populous metropolitan area in the world today. New York City held this title from the mid-1920s through the mid-1960s. But what city was the most populous in the world five hundred years ago? Five thousand years ago?

The following time line represents one expert's attempt to name the cities that have reigned as the most populous in the world since 3200 B.C. The time line begins with Memphis, the capital of ancient Egypt, which was possibly the first city in the world to attain a population of 20,000.

Listed after each city name is the name of the political entity to which the city belonged during the time that it was the most populous city in the world. The name of the modern political entity in which the city, its ruins, or its site is located, where this entity differs from the historic political entity, is listed in parentheses.

For the purpose of this time line, the word "city" is used in the general sense to denote a city, metropolitan area, or urban agglomeration.

It is important to note that reliable census figures are not available for most of the 5,200 years covered by this time line. Therefore the time line is somewhat subjective and conjectural.

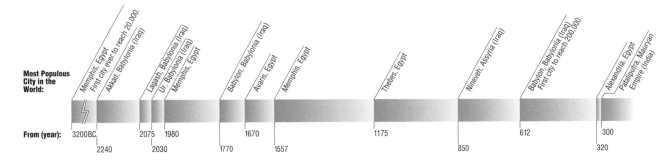

Most Populous City in the World:

Memphis, Egypt
First city ever to reach 20,000.
Akkad, Babylonia (Iraq)
Lagash, Babylonia (Iraq)
Ur, Babylonia (Iraq)
Memphis, Egypt
Babylon, Babylonia (Iraq)
Avaris, Egypt
Memphis, Egypt
Thebes, Egypt
Nineveh, Assyria (Iraq)
Babylon, Babylonia (Iraq)
First city to reach 200,000.
Alexandria, Egypt
Pataliputra, Mauryan Empire (India)

From (year): 3200 B.C. 2240 2075 2030 1980 1770 1670 1557 1175 850 612 300 320

Most Densely Populated Countries

Rank	Country (Population)	Population per Sqaure Mile	Kilometer
1	Monaco (33,000)	41,250	16,500
2	Singapore (4,635,000)	17,557	6,786
3	Vatican City (800)	4,000	2,000
4	Maldives (395,000)	3,435	1,326
5	Malta (405,000)	3,320	1,282
6	Bangladesh (155,045,000)	2,789	1,077
7	Bahrain (725,000)	2,715	1,049
8	Guernsey (66,000)	2,200	846
9	Jersey (92,000)	2,044	793
10	Nauru (14,000)	1,728	667
11	Barbados (285,000)	1,717	663
12	Taiwan (22,950,000)	1,651	637
13	Mauritius (1,280,000)	1,624	627
14	Aruba (100,000)	1,333	518
15	South Korea (48,445,000)	1,264	488

Least Densely Populated Countries

Rank	Country (Population)	Population per Sqaure Mile	Kilometer
1	Greenland (58,000)	0.07	0.03
2	Mongolia (3,020,000)	5	1.9
3	Namibia (2,100,000)	6.6	2.6
4	Australia (21,135,000)	7.1	2.7
5	Suriname (480,000)	7.6	2.9
6	Iceland (305,000)	7.7	3
7	Mauritania (3,090,000)	7.8	3
8	Canada (33,350,000)	8.7	3.3
9	Botswana (1,970,000)	8.8	3.4
10	Libya (6,240,000)	9.2	3.5
11	Guyana (770,000)	9.3	3.6
12	Gabon (1,500,000)	15	5.6
13	Kazakhstan (15,370,000)	15	5.7
14	Niue (1,500)	15	5.8
15	Central African Republic (4,480,000)	19	7.2

Most Highly Urbanized Countries

Country	Urban pop. as a % of total pop.
Singapore	100%
Monaco	100%
Anguilla	100%
Nauru	100%
Vatican City	100%
Kuwait	98.3%
Puerto Rico	98.2%
Belgium	97.3%
Qatar	95.6%
San Marino	94.2%
Malta	94.1%
Venezuela	93.1%
Netherlands Antilles	92.5%
Uruguay	92.2%
Iceland	92.2%

Least Urbanized Countries

Country	Urban pop. as a % of total pop.
Burundi	10.1%
Papua New Guinea	12.5%
Uganda	12.8%
Trinidad and Tobago	12.9%
Liechtenstein	14.3%
Sri Lanka	15.1%
Niger	16.4%
Ethiopia	16.6%
Nepal	16.7%
Solomon Islands	17.6%
Rwanda	18.2%
Malawi	18.3%
Burkina Faso	19.1%
Eritrea	20.2%
Cambodia	20.9%

World's Largest Metropolitan Areas

Rank	Name	Population
1	Tōkyō, Japan	35,700,000
2	New York-Newark, U.S.	19,000,000
3	Mexico City, Mexico	19,000,000
4	Mumbai (Bombay), India	19,000,000
5	São Paulo, Brazil	18,800,000
6	Delhi, India	15,900,000
7	Shanghai, China	15,000,000
8	Kolkata (Calcutta), India	14,800,000
9	Dhaka, Bangladesh	13,500,000
10	Buenos Aires, Argentina	12,800,000
11	Los Angeles-Long Beach-Santa Ana, U.S.	12,500,000
12	Karāchi, Pakistan	12,100,000
13	Cairo, Egypt	11,900,000
14	Rio de Janeiro, Brazil	11,700,000
15	Ōsaka-Kōbe, Japan	11,300,000

The 50 Most Populous Countries

Rank	Name	Population	Rank	Name	Population	Rank	Name	Population
1	China	1,341,820,000	18	Dem. Rep. of the Congo	67,590,000	35	Morocco	34,600,000
2	India	1,157,055,000	19	Iran	66,135,000	36	Algeria	33,975,000
3	United States	305,710,000	20	Thailand	65,705,000	37	Canada	33,350,000
4	Indonesia	238,910,000	21	France	62,260,000	38	Afghanistan	33,170,000
5	Brazil	197,550,000	22	United Kingdom	61,030,000	39	Uganda	31,935,000
6	Pakistan	174,525,000	23	Italy	58,140,000	40	Peru	29,365,000
7	Bangladesh	155,045,000	24	South Africa	48,985,000	41	Iraq	28,585,000
8	Nigeria	147,735,000	25	South Korea	48,445,000	42	Saudi Arabia	28,420,000
9	Russia	140,370,000	26	Myanmar	47,950,000	43	Nepal	28,380,000
10	Japan	127,200,000	27	Ukraine	45,845,000	44	Uzbekistan	27,475,000
11	Mexico	110,585,000	28	Colombia	45,330,000	45	Venezuela	26,615,000
12	Philippines	97,020,000	29	Argentina	40,700,000	46	Malaysia	25,495,000
13	Vietnam	86,545,000	30	Sudan	40,650,000	47	Ghana	23,610,000
14	Ethiopia	83,870,000	31	Tanzania	40,630,000	48	Yemen	23,410,000
15	Egypt	82,400,000	32	Spain	40,510,000	49	Taiwan	22,950,000
16	Germany	82,350,000	33	Poland	38,490,000	50	North Korea	22,620,000
17	Turkey	76,300,000	34	Kenya	38,475,000			

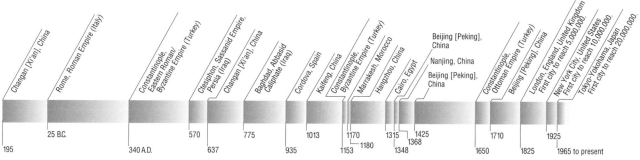

Source: Four Thousand Years of Urban Growth *by Tertius Chandler, Edwin Mellen Press, 1987.*

Economics and Energy

Annual World Production

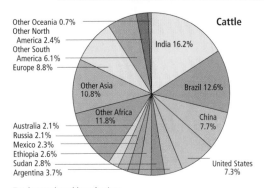

Cattle

Other Oceania 0.7%
Other North America 2.4%
Other South America 6.1%
Europe 8.8%
Other Asia 10.8%
Other Africa 11.8%
Australia 2.1%
Russia 2.1%
Mexico 2.3%
Ethiopia 2.6%
Sudan 2.8%
Argentina 3.7%
India 16.2%
Brazil 12.6%
China 7.7%
United States 7.3%

Total annual world production:
1,346,583,000 head

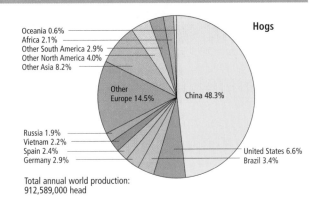

Hogs

Oceania 0.6%
Africa 2.1%
Other South America 2.9%
Other North America 4.0%
Other Asia 8.2%
Other Europe 14.5%
Russia 1.9%
Vietnam 2.2%
Spain 2.4%
Germany 2.9%
China 48.3%
United States 6.6%
Brazil 3.4%

Total annual world production:
912,589,000 head

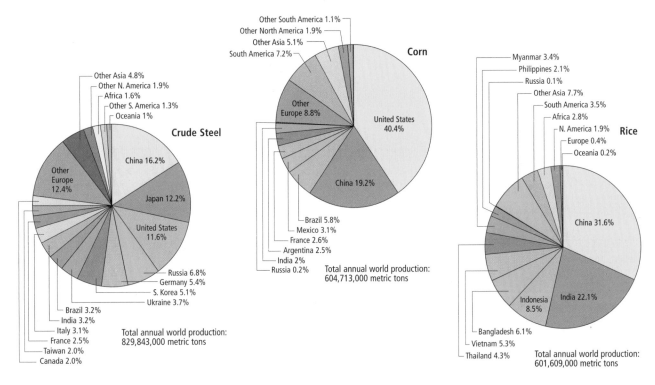

Crude Steel

Other Asia 4.8%
Other N. America 1.9%
Africa 1.6%
Other S. America 1.3%
Oceania 1%
Other Europe 12.4%
China 16.2%
Japan 12.2%
United States 11.6%
Russia 6.8%
Germany 5.4%
S. Korea 5.1%
Ukraine 3.7%
Brazil 3.2%
India 3.2%
Italy 3.1%
France 2.5%
Taiwan 2.0%
Canada 2.0%

Total annual world production:
829,843,000 metric tons

Corn

Other South America 1.1%
Other North America 1.9%
Other Asia 5.1%
South America 7.2%
Other Europe 8.8%
United States 40.4%
China 19.2%
Brazil 5.8%
Mexico 3.1%
France 2.6%
Argentina 2.5%
India 2%
Russia 0.2%

Total annual world production:
604,713,000 metric tons

Rice

Myanmar 3.4%
Philippines 2.1%
Russia 0.1%
Other Asia 7.7%
South America 3.5%
Africa 2.8%
N. America 1.9%
Europe 0.4%
Oceania 0.2%
China 31.6%
India 22.1%
Indonesia 8.5%
Bangladesh 6.1%
Vietnam 5.3%
Thailand 4.3%

Total annual world production:
601,609,000 metric tons

Gross Domestic Product

Annual Gross Domestic Product (GDP) is the total market value of all the goods and services produced by a nation in a year. GDP is not an indicator of personal income; it is a measure of economic performance at the national level. Most governments carefully analyze changes in GDP from year to year. A GDP growth rate of about 2% per year is an indicator of a healthy national economy.

The most striking thing this bar graph shows is the economic power of the United States. With just 4.6% of the world's population, the United States accounts for 21.2% of the world's GDP. The ten countries with the highest GDPs account for nearly two-thirds of the world total. At the other end of the spectrum is the continent of Africa, which holds 13.3% of the world's people but represents just 3.7% of the GDP.

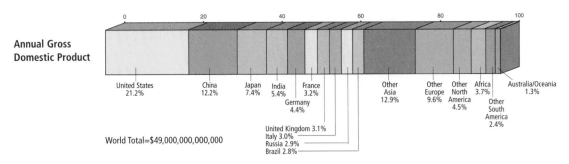

Annual Gross Domestic Product

United States 21.2%
China 12.2%
Japan 7.4%
India 5.4%
France 3.2%
Germany 4.4%
Other Asia 12.9%
Other Europe 9.6%
Other North America 4.5%
Africa 3.7%
Australia/Oceania 1.3%
Other South America 2.4%
United Kingdom 3.1%
Italy 3.0%
Russia 2.9%
Brazil 2.8%

World Total=$49,000,000,000,000

Electricity

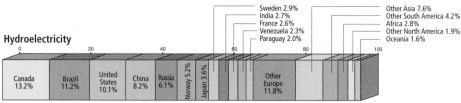

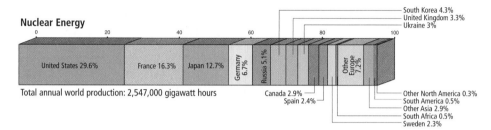

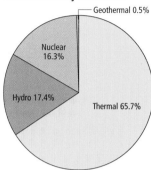

Petroleum

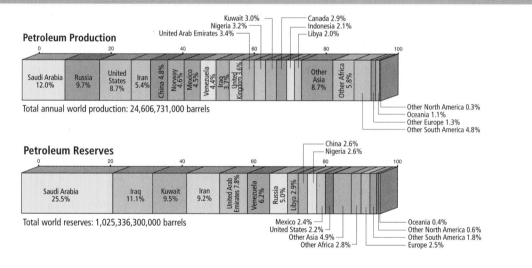

Commercial Energy

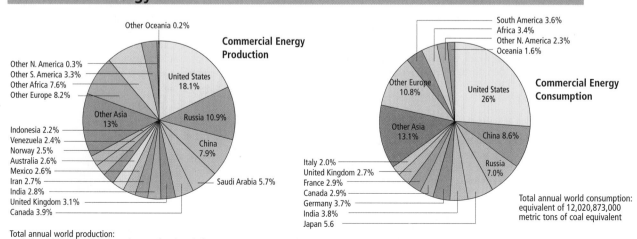

Questions and Answers

North America

Q What is the difference between "Central America" and "Middle America"?

A The term "Central America" refers to the North American countries which lie south of Mexico and north of Colombia: Belize, Guatemala, Honduras, El Salvador, Nicaragua, Costa Rica, and Panama. The Caribbean islands are not considered part of Central America. "Middle America" is comprised of Central America as well as Mexico and all of the Caribbean islands.

Q What is the largest U.S. city east of Reno, Nevada and west of Chicago?

A Surprisingly, the answer is Los Angeles. Although Los Angeles is located on the Pacific Coast, it actually lies slightly farther east than Reno. The coast, which forms the western edge of the U.S., curves dramatically eastward below Cape Mendocino in northern California. San Diego, at the southern end of California's coast, is approximately as far east as the eastern borders of Washington and Oregon. *(Refer to map on pages 74-75.)*

Los Angeles, California

Q Which is the southernmost U.S. state? The northernmost? The westernmost? The easternmost?

A Hawaii is the southernmost state; Alaska is both the westernmost and the northernmost. The question of which state is the easternmost is a bit problematic. Generally, Maine is considered to be the easternmost, since it extends farther east than any other state along the Atlantic seaboard. However, Alaska is technically the easternmost state, since the Aleutian Islands cross the 180° longitude line which divides the globe into eastern and western hemispheres. These islands sit at the eastern edge of the eastern hemisphere.

Q How many national flags have flown over Texas?

A Six. Spain (1682-1821), France (1685-1686), Mexico (1821-1836), the Republic of Texas (1836-1845), the United States (1845-1861), the Confederate States of America (from 1861 until the state was re-admitted to the Union in 1870), and the United States again (1870 through the present). Texas is the only U.S. state to have existed as an independent country.

Q What is the oldest city in the United States to be founded by Europeans?

A St. Augustine, Florida. Spanish explorer Juan Ponce de León, searching for the Fountain of Youth, landed nearby and claimed the area for Spain in 1513. The French established a colony on the site in 1564, but it was destroyed in 1565 by the Spanish, who then founded the present city. The oldest U.S. state capital is Santa Fe, New Mexico, which was founded in 1609, also by the Spanish.

Q What is Papiamento?

A Papiamento is a language which blends Dutch, Spanish, Portuguese, English, and Indian words. It is the principal language of Aruba and other islands in the Dutch Caribbean, and is spoken by an estimated 200,000 people.

Q If you were on a ship sailing from the Atlantic Ocean to the Pacific Ocean, in which direction would you be traveling as you passed through the Panama Canal?

A Southeast. The Pacific lies west of the Atlantic, and it would seem that a ship passing through the canal from the Atlantic would be sailing west. However, because of the twisting shape of the Isthmus of Panama, the canal's Pacific end lies south and east of its Atlantic end. *(Refer to inset map on page 96.)*

Q Into what body of water does the Colorado River empty?

A Currently, it doesn't empty into any body of water. Until recently, the river flowed into the Gulf of California. As the populations of water-poor Arizona and California have soared, more and more water has been drawn from the river for farms, industry, and homes. Today the Colorado is barely a trickle when it crosses the border into Mexico, and it disappears in the desert before it reaches the Gulf of California.

Q What is Canada's smallest province? Its largest?

A Prince Edward Island is Canada's smallest province, at 2,185 square miles (5,660 sq km). Canada's largest province is Quebec, which covers 594,860 square miles (1,540,680 sq km). The territory of Nunavut represents the country's largest administrative division: It spreads over an area of 733,594 square miles (1,900,000 sq km), much of which lies within the Arctic Circle. If Nuvavut were an independent country, it would be larger than all but 15 of the world's countries.

Q What is the Continental Divide?

A An imaginary line running down the backbone of North America. Except for those which empty into the Great Basin and other basins, rivers to the west of this line flow into the Pacific Ocean, including its bays and gulfs; rivers to the east flow into the Atlantic or Arctic oceans, including their bays and gulfs. From northwest Canada south to New Mexico, the Divide runs along the crest of the Rocky Mountains, and in northern Mexico it follows the ridge of the Sierra Madre Occidental. All continents except frozen Antarctica have "divides."

Q Is Niagara Falls the highest waterfall in the world?

A Not even close. Niagara Falls' maximum drop of 167 feet (51 m) is surpassed by at least 22 waterfalls in North America alone. The highest waterfall in the world is Angel Falls in Venezuela, which spills 3,212 feet (979 m) from a flat mountain plateau. North America's highest waterfall is Yosemite National Park's Yosemite Falls, which drops 2,425 feet in two separate steps.

Niagara Falls actually consists of two separate waterfalls: American Falls, above, and Canadian (Horseshoe) Falls.

Q What did ships do before the Panama Canal was built?

A Before the canal opened, ships traveling between New York and San Francisco would sail 13,000 miles (21,000 km) around the entire continent of South America. When the canal opened in 1914, this journey was shortened to 5,200 miles (8,400 km). However, the canal is now too narrow for many of today's largest ocean-going vessels, so they must once again sail around South America to reach their destination. A project to widen the canal began in 1992.

Gatun Lake, Panama Canal

Q What is the largest inland body of water in Central America?

A Lake Nicaragua, which has a surface area of 3,150 square miles (8,158 sq km). Its only outlet is the San Juan River, which flows into the Caribbean Sea. Lying in a lowland region called the Nicaragua Depression, the lake was once part of the sea but became separated when the land began to rise. The freshwater lake is home to many species of fish usually found only in salt water, including sharks, tuna, and swordfish.

Q Why does Minnesota have so many lakes?

A During the height of the most recent Ice Age, glaciers moved southward from the Arctic regions to cover Canada and much of the northern U.S., including Minnesota. As they advanced, the glaciers scoured the landscape, gouging out countless depressions. When the Earth's climate grew warmer, the glaciers began to melt and retreat, and the depressions filled with meltwater to become lakes. Although Minnesota bills itself as the "Land of 10,000 Lakes," it actually has more than 15,000 lakes. Other areas of the world which experienced extreme glaciation, including parts of Europe and Siberia, also contain many lakes.

Q What is the most popular U.S. national park?

A Great Smoky Mountains National Park. Covering over 521,500 acres (211,200 hectares) in eastern Tennessee, the park receives approximately 9.1 million visitors each year. Arizona's Grand Canyon National Park has the second-highest visitor count: it receives around 4.6 million people annually.

Q What two U.S. states share borders with the most other states?

A Missouri and Tennessee, which each border eight other states. Missouri borders Iowa, Illinois, Kentucky, Tennessee, Arkansas, Oklahoma, Kansas, and Nebraska. Tennessee borders Kentucky, Virginia, North Carolina, Georgia, Alabama, Mississippi, Arkansas, and Missouri.

Q How many U.S. states border only one other state?

A One: Maine, which borders only New Hampshire. Two states, Alaska and Hawaii, border no others.

Q What is the one place in North America where you can see both the Atlantic Ocean and the Pacific Ocean?

A Irazú, a volcano in central Costa Rica. From its summit, both the Atlantic and Pacific oceans can be seen on a clear day.

Q Where is the Yucatan Peninsula?

A This thumb of land juts off of southeastern Mexico, separating the Gulf of Mexico from the Caribbean Sea. Yucatan was the center of the Maya civilization from about the first century B.C. through the tenth century A.D. Extensive Mayan ruins can be found at Chichén Itzá, Cobá, Mayapán, Tulum, and Uxmal. Near the town of Chicxulub at the northern tip of the peninsula, there is evidence of an enormous crater which is thought to be the point of impact of a meteorite 65 million years ago. The impact would have sent so much dust into the atmosphere that the sun's rays would have been blocked for months or perhaps years, lowering temperatures globally and possibly causing the extinction of the dinosaurs.

Q What is the oldest capital city in the Americas?

A Mexico City. The city originated as Tenochtitlán, the capital of the Aztecs, founded in the mid-1300s. By the early 1500s, the city had a population of perhaps 150,000, which was not only greater than any other city in the Americas but also greater than any European city at the time. In 1521, after a three-month siege, Spanish invaders under Hernán Cortés captured Tenochtitlán, razed the entire city, and founded Mexico City upon its ruins.

Q What is the most densely populated country in North America?

A El Salvador, which has a density of 775 people per square mile (299 per sq km). The U.S. ranks eighth, with 75 people per square mile (29 per sq km). Canada, the continent's largest country, is by far the least densely populated: it averages only 8.2 people per square mile (3.2 per sq km).

Q What is the largest island in Caribbean Sea?

A Cuba, the world's 15th-largest island. It has a land area of 42,800 square miles (110,800 sq km). The second-largest Caribbean island is Hispaniola, which covers 29,400 square miles (76,200 sq km) and contains the countries of Haiti and the Dominican Republic. Jamaica, measuring 4,200 square miles (11,000 sq km), is the third-largest Caribbean island.

Q How many U.S. states have volcanoes that were active in the 20th century?

A Four. Alaska has the most: 34 of its volcanoes, most of which are located on the Alaska Peninsula and the Aleutian Islands, have erupted since 1900. The other states with documented eruptions in the 20th century are: Hawaii (3), Washington (1), and California (1).

Caldera and lava lake of Kīlauea, on the island of Hawai'i

Q What is the only Caribbean island with large oil reserves?

A Trinidad. The island's economy is based on oil, which accounts for about 80% of its exports. As a result of oil wealth, Trinidadians enjoy a higher standard of living than the people of most other Caribbean countries.

Q Which U.S. state has the highest average elevation?

A Colorado, with an average elevation of 6,800 feet (2,074 m) above sea level. However, the four highest peaks in the U.S. are found not in Colorado but in Alaska.

Questions and Answers

South America

Q What is Latin America?

A The term "Latin America" designates the parts of North and South America which were settled by Spanish and Portuguese colonists and still retain a Hispanic character. These include Mexico, Cuba, Puerto Rico, the Dominican Republic, some of the smaller islands in the West Indies, all of Central America except for Belize, and all of South America except for Guyana, Suriname, and French Guiana.

Q If you flew due south from Chicago, which South American country would you fly over first?

A You wouldn't fly over any South American countries. A straight line drawn south from Chicago passes through the Gulf of Mexico, Central America, and the Pacific Ocean. Point Parinas, Peru, the westernmost point of mainland South America, is about 500 miles (800 km) east of this line. The Galapagos Islands, which belong to Ecuador, lie about 75 miles (120 km) west of the line.

Q What percentage of the world's coffee beans come from South America?

A South America currently produces approximately 45% of the world's coffee beans. Brazil leads the continent, producing just under one-quarter of the world total. Another 16% are grown in Colombia. Coffee plants require hot, moist climates, and they yield the most flavorful beans when cultivated at elevations between 3,000 and 6,000 feet (900 and 1800 m). South America's principal coffee-growing regions are found in the Brazilian and Guiana Highlands, and in the valleys and foothills of the Andes.

Giant Galapagos turtle

Q What scientist made the Galapagos Islands famous?

A Charles Darwin, who visited the islands during his 1831-1836 expedition on the H.M.S. Beagle. Darwin's observations of how various animal species had adapted to life on the islands contributed to his ground-breaking theory of evolution, which he presented in the 1859 book *On the Origin of Species*.

Q Where are the Falkland Islands?

A In the Atlantic Ocean, about 275 miles (440 km) off the east coast of Argentina. The Falklands are a dependency of the United Kingdom, and nearly all of the residents are English-speakers of British descent. Argentina, which has asserted claims to the Falklands since 1816, invaded and occupied the islands in 1982. The U.K. sent a large task force that defeated the Argentineans in a war lasting less than a month.

Q What South American country is the longest when measured from north to south?

A Brazil. The country measures 2,725 miles (4,395 km) north to south, which is the approximate distance from New York City to Reno, Nevada. The second-longest country is Chile, with a length of 2,647 miles (4,270 km). In contrast to its great length, Chile measures only 235 miles (380 km) east to west at its widest point.

Q What was discovered in Venezuela's Lake Maracaibo in 1914?

A Oil. Maracaibo sits above one of the world's largest oil fields, and today the lake's surface is a thicket of oil derricks. Wealth from oil exportation has helped to make Venezuela one of the richest countries in Latin America.

Q What is Patagonia?

A Patagonia is a wind-swept plateau region occupying the southern third of South America, east of the Andes. The plateau receives little precipitation, and its only vegetation is scrubby grasses and thorny desert shrubs. The name "Patagonia" probably comes from the Grand Patagon, a dog-headed monster in a European romance called *Primaleon of Greece*. In 1592, the crew members of the ship Desire were attacked by a war-party of Tehuelche Indians wearing dog masks.

Q What South American city is the world's highest national capital?

A La Paz, Bolivia. The city sprawls across the floor of a deep canyon high in the Andes, at an elevation of 12,000 feet (19,350 km)—approximately the same height as the summit of Japan's Mt. Fuji. The canyon walls protect the city from the bitterly cold winds that whip across the surrounding plateau. Visitors from lower elevations often suffer from altitude sickness for several days until their bodies adjust to the thin, oxygen-poor air.

Q What is the southernmost city in the world?

A Ushuaia, Argentina, on the island of Tierra del Fuego. This city of 29,452 people lies at 54°48' south latitude, less than 700 miles (1,100 km) from Antarctica. The world's southernmost city with a population greater than 100,000 is Punta Arenas, Chile, located 150 miles (240 km) northwest of Ushuaia.

Q How many South American countries are named for famous people or cities?

A Three. Bolivia was named for Simón Bolívar, the revolutionary who helped to liberate much of northern South America from Spanish rule. Colombia takes its name from the explorer Christopher Columbus, who "discovered" South America in 1498 and sailed along the coast of present-day Colombia in 1502. The name "Venezuela" is Spanish for "Little Venice." When European explorers reached Lake Maracaibo in 1499, they found villages built on pilings over the shallow waters, which reminded them of Venice, Italy.

Q Why is South America sometimes referred to as "the hollow continent"?

A South America earned this nickname because most of its people live on or near the coasts; the interior is sparsely populated. Sixteen of the 20 largest metropolitan areas lie within 200 miles (320 km) of the coast. The continent's uneven population distribution has both a historical and a geographical explanation. Beginning in the 16th century, European colonists settled in the coastal regions from which raw materials were shipped back to Europe. The Amazon rain forest—hot, humid, and nearly impenetrable in places—has discouraged settlement of the northern half of the continent, and the Andes present a formidable barrier to eastward expansion from the Pacific coast. *(Refer to population map on page 99.)*

Q How many of South America's 20 longest rivers empty into the Pacific Ocean?

A None. South America's continental divide runs along the crest of the Andes at the continent's western edge. In most places the divide lies within 200 miles (320 km) of the Pacific coast. Rivers originating west of the divide have only a short distance to travel before reaching the Pacific. Rivers flowing east from the divide have nearly the whole expanse of the continent to cross before emptying into the Atlantic.

Q What South American city was the capital of the Inca empire?

A Cusco, Peru. The city was built by the Incas in the fourteenth century and served as their capital for 200 years until it was destroyed by Francisco Pizarro in 1533.

Cathedral and rooftops in Cusco

Today, Cusco thrives as a major tourist attraction. Many of its houses and buildings are constructed on foundations of stone first cut by the Incas. Lying about 50 miles (80 km) northwest of Cusco is Machu Picchu, a well-preserved mountaintop Inca city, which was rediscovered in 1911.

Q What stretch of ocean off the South American coast is considered one of the most treacherous to ships?

A The Drake Passage. Approximately 500 miles (1,800 km) wide, this strait separates Cape Horn—at the southern tip of South America—from the South Shetland Islands which lie just north of Antarctica. First traversed in 1615, the passage was part of a major trade route between the Atlantic and Pacific oceans until 1914, when the Panama Canal opened. Frigid temperatures, rough waters, and high winds make the passage treacherous for all vessels but especially for the sailing ships of centuries past. Because the passage is so perilous, many ships avoid it by cutting through the Strait of Magellan to the north. However, this strait has its own dangers: it is narrow and twisting, and has been the site of numerous major shipwrecks.

Q Where is the Land of Fire?

A At the southern tip of South America. Tierra del Fuego, Spanish for "Land of Fire," is a group of islands lying south of the Strait of Magellan. When Portuguese explorer Ferdinand Magellan arrived in 1520, he named the islands after observing the native inhabitants carrying torches. The largest island, also called Tierra del Fuego, accounts for two-thirds of the land area of the island group. The eastern third of the islands belong to Argentina, and the rest belong to Chile.

Q What are the Nazca Lines?

A The Nazca Lines are gigantic drawings that were etched into Peru's desert floor by the Nazca people between 500 B.C. and A.D. 500. Scattered across 200 square miles (520 sq km), they form the world's largest display of art. The drawings fall into two categories: animal motifs and geometric patterns of crisscrossing straight lines. They were made by scraping away the top layer of red gravel to reveal the yellow sand below it. Archaeologists still disagree about the purpose of the Nazca Lines, but some theories hold that the lines formed ancient highways or were used as a giant calendar.

Q What is "El Niño"?

A El Niño is a seasonal ocean current that flows south along the Pacific coast of South America. The current takes its name—which is Spanish for "the Child"—from its usual arrival during the Christmas season. In normal years, when El Niño reaches northern Peru, southeasterly trade winds push its warm surface waters westward across the Pacific, away from the coast. Every four or five years, these trade winds weaken, allowing El Niño to travel farther south along the coast, raising local water temperatures by several degrees. This warmer water kills plankton and fish, crippling the fishing industry. Increased evaporation leads to excessive rainfall over parts of South America. The change in El Niño's normal flow pattern affects other ocean currents which often leads to dramatic climatic changes around the world.

Q How many of the Earth's species are found in the Amazon rain forest?

A Most of the Amazon basin has not been fully explored, and therefore most of its plant and animal species have not yet been catalogued. However, scientists estimate that the Amazon rain forest, which covers less than 5% of the Earth's total land area, contains almost one-half of the planet's animal and plant species. One in ten of the most common medicines we use today comes from rain forest plants, and scientists believe that cures for many diseases, such as cancer, might be derived from plant species not yet discovered.

Q Where in South America could you find places in which no rainfall has ever been recorded?

A The Atacama Desert in northern Chile. This barren land of sand, rocks, borax lakes and saline deposits is one of the driest regions in the world. In parts of the desert, no rainfall has ever been recorded, and the city of Arica, at the northern edge, endured more than 14 consecutive years of drought from October 1903 through January 1918.

Q What South American possession lies farthest from the mainland?

A Easter Island, situated 2,300 miles (3,700 km) west of Chile in the Pacific Ocean. This small volcanic island was discovered on Easter Sunday in 1722, and was annexed by Chile in 1888. Although it belongs to Chile, geographically Easter Island is considered to be part of Oceania, not South America. It is best known for its strange monuments: scattered over the island are more than 600 huge stone faces, the earliest dating back more than 1,500 years.

Ancient statues, Easter Island

Q Where are the pampas?

A These flat, grassy plains—which are much like the prairies of North America—are found in the temperate regions of southern South America, east of the Andes. The largest such plain, known simply as the Pampa, covers much of central and northern Argentina, and extends into Uruguay. Since the 1550s, when European colonists introduced cattle to the Pampa, livestock raising has been a thriving industry. For many people, gauchos, or Argentinean cowboys, are the enduring symbol of the Pampa, although in the last century farming has superseded cattle ranching in economic importance.

Questions and Answers

Europe

Q Where is the Black Forest?

A In southwestern Germany, between the Rhine and Neckar rivers. The Black Forest, or Schwarzwald in German, is a mountainous region that takes its name from the dark coniferous trees that cover its slopes. Its fertile valleys provide good pastureland and produce grapes for wine, and its trees supply the lumber and woodworking industries, as well as toy and cuckoo clock manufacturers. The region's scenic beauty, winter sports facilities, and mineral springs attract many tourists each year.

Old Town of Zagreb, Croatia

Q How many national capitals are located on the Danube River?

A Four. The capital cities of Bratislava (Slovakia), Budapest (Hungary), Belgrade (Serbia), and Vienna (Austria) are all found along the banks of the Danube. Five other capitals are located on tributaries of the Danube: Bucharest (Romania), Sofia (Bulgaria), Ljubljana (Slovenia), Zagreb (Croatia), and Sarajevo (Bosnia and Herzegovina).

Q What is killing the forests of Northern Europe?

A Acid rain. In the atmosphere, airborne pollutants—especially sulfur and nitrogen dioxides from automobile and industrial emissions—adhere to water droplets, and then fall back to Earth as acidified rain, snow, or hail. This precipitation poisons plant and animal life, erodes buildings, and contaminates soil and drinking water. As a result of acid rain, as many as one-half of the trees in Germany's Black Forest and Switzerland's central alpine region are dead or dying. At least 4,000 lakes in Sweden are so acidic that no fish survive in them. To combat acid rain, the countries of the European Union recently agreed to significantly reduce nitrogen oxide and sulfur dioxide emissions.

Q How many times did the name of St. Petersburg, Russia, change in the 20th century?

A Three times. St. Petersburg was founded in 1703 by Peter the Great. In 1914, its name was changed to Petrograd, Russian for "Peter's City," and then in 1924 it was changed again, this time to Leningrad, in honor of Vladimir Lenin, the founder of Russian Communism. In 1991, following the collapse of Communist rule, the city name was changed back to St. Petersburg. Older citizens joke about being born in St. Petersburg, attending school in Petrograd, working in Leningrad, and growing old in St. Petersburg—all while living in the same place.

Q What independent countries were once part of Yugoslavia?

A Prior to 1991, Yugoslavia was comprised of six republics: Bosnia and Herzegovina, Croatia, Macedonia, Montenegro, Serbia, and Slovenia. In 1991-92, four of the six republics—Croatia, Slovenia, Macedonia, and Bosnia and Herzegovina—declared their independence. In 2003, the remaining republics agreed to change the name from Yugoslavia to Serbia and Montenegro. Then, in 2006, Serbia and Montenegro dissolved their union and became two separate countries. Most recently, the province of Kosovo declared its independence from Serbia in 2008. However, many of the world's countries have so far refused to recognize Kosovo as an independent country.

Q What independent countries were once part of the U.S.S.R.?

A When the Union of Soviet Socialist Republics (U.S.S.R.) broke up in 1991, its 15 republics all became independent countries: Armenia, Azerbaijan, Belarus, Estonia, Georgia, Kazakhstan, Krygyzstan, Latvia, Lithuania, Moldova, Russia, Tajikistan, Turkmenistan, Ukraine, and Uzbekistan.

Q What is the Chunnel?

A "Chunnel" is a nickname for the English Channel Tunnel, which connects England and France via rail under the English Channel. There are actually three separate tunnels: two for trains and a parallel service tunnel. The tunnels run for 31 miles between Coquelles, France, and Folkestone, England, at an average depth of 150 feet (46 m) below the seafloor. Work on the tunnels began in 1987, and the first trains crossed under the Channel in 1994.

Q Where is "Europe's Grand Canyon"?

A Along the Verdon River in the Provence region of southeastern France. The Verdon has carved a deep, narrow gorge, known as the Grand Cañon du Verdon, through the limestone plateau between the town of Castellane and the artificial Lac de Ste-Croix. The gorge stretches for 13 miles (21 km) and reaches a depth of 3,170 feet (965 m). It is considered one of the natural wonders of Europe.

Q What is the only volcano on the European mainland that erupted in the 20th century?

A Mt. Vesuvius (Vesuvio), located in southern Italy nine miles (15 km) east of Naples. It was active through much of the century, with significant eruptions in 1906, 1929, and 1944. Two thousand years ago, most Romans did not recognize Vesuvius as a volcano, and numerous farming communities thrived on the fertile land around its base. Then, in August of A.D. 79, the volcano exploded in a mighty eruption, burying the cities of Pompeii, Herculaneum, and Stabiae under cinders, ash, and mud, and killing more than 3,500 people.

Q How many European countries fall partially within the Arctic Circle?

A Four: Finland, Norway, Russia, and Sweden. Technically, a fifth country could be added to this list: Iceland's mainland ends just short of the Arctic Circle, but one of the country's islands, Grimsey, straddles the line, its northern half sitting within the Circle.

A fishing village in the Lofoten Islands of Norway

Q Where is Waterloo, site of Napoleon's famous defeat?

A Today, Waterloo is a suburb of Brussels, Belgium, although at the time of the battle—June 18, 1815—it lay 12 miles (19 km) away from the city, which was then much smaller. At Waterloo, the troops of French emperor Napoleon I were defeated by British forces under the command of the Duke of Wellington and Prussian forces led by Gebhard Blücher. The French defeat ended the Napoleonic Wars, which had begun in 1803.

Is Venice, Italy, really sinking?

Yes, although at a much slower rate than previously. The city, which dates back to the 4th century A.D., is built on 118 small islands in a lagoon at the top of the Adriatic Sea. Its buildings sit on foundations of wooden

Gondola and canal, Venice

pilings driven deep into the underlying sand, silt and clay. Originally the buildings were safely above high tide level, but over the course of 15 centuries, natural compaction of the subsoil caused the city to sink more than 30 inches (76 cm). Earlier this century, groundwater was pumped out of the subsoil to satisfy water needs on the mainland. This proved disastrous for Venice: the city quickly sank another five inches (13 cm) at a time when the sea level was rising by four inches (10 cm). The pumping was stopped, and Venice's sinking has slowed to its earlier "natural" rate. Unfortunately, the foundations of many buildings have been severely damaged by high water.

Which independent European countries are smaller than Rhode Island, the smallest U.S. state?

Seven independent European countries cover a smaller area than Rhode Island's 1,545 square miles (4,002 sq km): Vatican City, Monaco, San Marino, Liechtenstein, Malta, Andorra, and Luxembourg.

How many official languages are recognized in Switzerland?

Four: German, French, Italian, and Romansch. German is the most widely spoken language: 65% of the Swiss speak a dialect known as *Schwyzerdütsch*, or Swiss German. French is spoken by 18% of the population, Italian by 10%, and Romansch by only 1%.

Why is Ukraine called "the breadbasket of Europe"?

Ukraine's topography—flat plains, or "steppes," cover most of the country—and extremely fertile soils combine to make it one of the world's most outstanding agricultural areas. In 1994, the country produced almost 36 million tons (33 metric tons) of grain. Major crops include wheat, rye, barley, corn, potatoes, sunflower seeds, sugar beets, and cotton. Ukraine also has thriving dairy and livestock industries, as well as many food-processing plants.

If the Caspian Sea is a sea, then how can it be the world's largest lake?

Actually, it is both a sea and a lake. The word "sea" is used most often to designate specific regions of the oceans that are more or less surrounded by land; however, it can also apply to inland bodies of water, especially if they are large and/or salty. The Caspian Sea is both large and salty, so it is called a sea. "Lake" is a general term for inland bodies of water of substantial size. The Caspian Sea lies inland and has a surface area of 143,240 square miles (370,990 sq km), so it is also considered to be a lake. Other "sea-lakes" in the world include the Aral Sea, the Dead Sea, the Sea of Galilee, and California's Salton Sea.

Where is Transylvania?

In northwestern Romania. The region is bounded by the Carpathian Mountains in the north and east, the Transylvanian Alps in the south, and by Romania's borders with Hungary and Serbia and Montenegro in the west. A high plateau, averaging 1,000 to 1,600 feet (300 to 500 m) in elevation, covers much of Transylvania. In Bram Stoker's 1897 novel *Dracula*, Transylvania is the home of the blood-sucking Count. Stoker based the story on local vampire legends, many of which persist today: in some parts of eastern Europe, peasants still wear garlic necklaces and hang garlic wreaths from their doors to ward off vampires.

What countries contain parts of the Carpathian Mountains?

Five: the Czech Republic, Slovakia, Poland, Ukraine, and Romania. Curving for more than 900 miles (1,450 km) along the north and east sides of the Danube plain in central and eastern Europe, the Carpathians roughly form a half-circle connecting the Alps and the Balkans. The mountain system consists of two main parts: the Northern Carpathians, which include the Beskid and the Tatra ranges, and the Southern Carpathians, also called the Transylvanian Alps. The Carpathians' highest peak is Gerlachovský stít in Slovakia, which rises to 8,711 feet (2,655 m).

Where is Lapland?

In northern Scandinavia. Lapland is home to the Lapps, a nomadic people who have traditionally engaged in hunting, fishing, and reindeer-herding. When the Finns arrived in the southern part of present-day Finland 2,000 years ago, they found the Lapps already settled there. Over the years, the Lapps have been pushed north, and their territory has expanded to cover parts of northern Norway, Sweden, Finland, and northwestern Russia. Today, there are approximately 42,000 Lapps, most of whom work in a variety of farming, construction, and service fields. The Finnish government has made many efforts to protect the Lapps' language, called Sami, and culture.

Not counting landlocked countries, which European country has the shortest coastline?

Monaco, whose coastline on the Mediterranean Sea is a mere 2.5 miles (4.1 km) long. Bosnia and Herzegovina ranks second in this category: its coast on the Adriatic Sea between Croatia and Montenegro is just 12.4 miles (20 km) long. In third place is Slovenia, whose Adriatic coast is 29 miles (46.6 km) long.

Harbor and coastline, Monaco

What European city is the largest city in the world north of the Arctic Circle?

Murmansk, Russia, a city of 472,900 people located on the Kola Gulf of the Barents Sea. Although Murmansk lies approximately 150 miles north of the Arctic Circle, its harbor remains ice-free throughout the year due to the moderating effect of a warm ocean current called the North Atlantic Drift. While there are thousands of cities and towns north of the Arctic Circle, there are none at all south of the Antarctic Circle at the opposite end of the world.

Questions and Answers

Africa

Q What is the East African Rift System?

A This term refers to a series of rift valleys running through East Africa from Mozambique to the southern end of the Red Sea. These valleys are part of the Great Rift Valley, a 4,000-mile (6,430-km)-long depression that also includes the Red Sea, the Dead Sea, and the rest of the Jordan Valley. The East African Rift System marks the line along which geological forces are splitting East Africa off from the rest of the continent. Eventually, everything east of the Rift System—including all or part of present-day Mozambique, Tanzania, Rwanda, Burundi, Uganda, Kenya, Ethiopia, Djibouti, and Somalia—will be a huge island off of Africa's eastern coast. Madagascar was attached to the African mainland before similar forces split it off into an island 175 million years ago.

Q What is the Serengeti?

A Located in northern Tanzania, east of Lake Victoria and west of Kilimanjaro, the Serengeti is a vast plain of grassland, acacia bushes, forest, and rocky outcrops. Serengeti National Park, established in 1951, covers an area of the plain about the size of Connecticut. The park is home to one of the last great concentrations of African wildlife, including antelope, buffalo, cheetahs, elephants, gazelles, giraffes, hyenas, leopards, lions, black rhinoceroses, wildebeests, and zebras. Tourists from all over the world visit the park to observe the wildlife and to witness the large-scale animal migrations that occur in May and June.

Giraffes on the Serengeti

Q How has the Aswan High Dam affected the Nile Valley?

A Before the dam was built in 1971, floodwaters inundated the Nile Valley each fall, depositing fresh, fertile silt across the valley floor. This annual replenishment of the soil helped agriculture to thrive in the valley for thousands of years. The dam ended the annual floods, and now much of the Nile's water-borne silt settles to the bottom of Lake Nassar, the enormous artificial lake behind the dam. Water evaporating from the lake's surface has increased the regional humidity, which has accelerated the decay of many of the valley's great tombs and monuments. On the positive side, the dam supplies more than 25% of Egypt's hydro-electric power, and desert irrigation projects using water from Lake Nassar have created 900,000 new acres of arable land.

Q What is remarkable about the delta of the Okavango River?

A It is the largest inland delta in the world. The Okavango originates in the mountains of central Angola and flows 1,000 miles (1,600 km) to the northwest corner of Botswana, where it spills over the Gomare fault and fans out into a swampy delta covering 4,000 square miles (10,350 sq km). Meandering through a myriad of shallow channels, the waters of the Okavango quickly evaporate. The small amount that eventually emerges from the southeastern end of the delta represents less than 5% of the river's pre-delta flow.

Q What African country was previously known as Upper Volta?

A Burkina Faso. The Volta River's three upper branches —the Volta Blanche (White Volta), Volta Rouge (Red Volta), and Volta Noire (Black Volta)—all originate within the country, hence the earlier name. Burkina Faso, the Mossi-dialect name adopted in 1984, translates roughly as "Country of Honest Men."

Q What are the most important crops grown in Africa?

A Africa is the world's leading producer of cocoa beans (55% of the world total) and cassava roots (45% of the world total). It is also a major producer of grain and millet sorghum (27%), coffee (20%), peanuts (20%), palm oil (14%), tea (12%), and olive oil (12%).

Woman in sorghum fields

Q What object found along the banks of the Orange River in 1867 changed the course of South African history?

A A 21-carat diamond. The discovery of this gem near Hopetown precipitated a huge diamond rush, and thousands of people from all over the continent and the world raced to southern Africa. The town of Kimberley, site of the famous open mine known as the Big Hole, became the diamond capital of the world. Between 1871 and 1914, more than 14 million carats of diamonds were removed from the mine, which eventually reached a depth of 4,000 feet (1,220 m) and a width of one mile (1.6 km).

Q What is Cabinda?

A A coastal province of Angola that lies north of the Congo River and is separated from the rest of the country by a 19-mile (31-km)-wide corridor belonging to the Democratic Republic of the Congo. Most of Cabinda is covered by tropical forest. Offshore lie rich oil fields which produce one million barrels annually.

Q What African country was founded in 1847 by freed American slaves?

A Liberia, whose name comes from the Latin word *liber*, meaning "free." It is the only country in sub-Saharan Africa that has never been ruled by a colonial power. Liberia's capital city, Monrovia, was named for James Monroe, the fifth U.S. president.

Q What two African countries border only a single other country?

A Lesotho and The Gambia. South Africa surrounds Lesotho, and The Gambia is bordered in the north, east, and south by Senegal; to its west lies the Atlantic Ocean.

Q What is the Ngorongoro Crater?

A Located in northern Tanzania, Ngorongoro is the crater of a volcano that has been extinct for several million years. It has a diameter of 9 miles (14.5 km) and its walls rise about 2,000 feet (610 m) above its floor. The crater supports an abundance of wildlife, including wildebeests, elephants, rhinoceroses, hippopotamuses, lions, leopards, and flamingoes. In 1956 Ngorongoro was established as a conservation area, but its ecological balance is threatened by growing numbers of tourists and the large cattle herds of the nomadic Masai people.

Q Why is it difficult to say how large Lake Chad is?

A The lake's size fluctuates dramatically throughout the year. Numerous rivers and streams flow into Lake Chad, but it has no outlet. During the summer rainy season, floodwaters swell the lake to 10,000 square miles (25,900 sq km) and occasionally to twice that size. Even at its maximum size the lake is extremely shallow; its greatest depth is only 25 feet (8 m). By the end of the following spring, evaporation has shrunk the lake by 60%, to about 4,000 square miles (10,360 sq km). In recent decades, Lake Chad's cyclical fluctuations have been greatly affected by recurring droughts, which have reduced the flow of water into the lake and accelerated evaporation. Its volume has dropped by 80% since 1970.

Q What is significant about the location of Khartoum, Sudan?

A Khartoum, the capital of Sudan, is located at the point where the White Nile and Blue Nile rivers meet to form the Nile. Capitalizing on its strategic location, the city has become Sudan's commercial center and transportation hub. It is built on a curving strip of land that resembles the trunk of an elephant: the name "Khartoum" comes from the Arabic *Ras-al-hartum*, which means "end of the elephant's trunk."

Q What is Africa's newest country?

A Eritrea, which officially became independent in 1993. An Italian colony from 1890 to 1941, Eritrea was captured by the British during World War II. In 1952, the United Nations awarded Eritrea to Ethiopia under the condition that it be ruled as a self-governing territory. Ethiopia violated this agreement by annexing Eritrea in 1962, touching off a civil war which lasted more than 30 years. Eritrea formally declared its independence in May 1993, two years after defeating Ethiopia's Marxist regime.

Q What is the Sahel?

A The Sahel (Sudan) is a semiarid region that separates the Sahara Desert from the tropical savanna and rain forests of central Africa. It stretches halfway across the continent, from Mauritania in the west to Chad in the east, in a band

Woman returning from a well in the Sahel

averaging more than 1,000 miles (1,600 km) in width. Most of the Sahel is semiarid savanna, with low grasses in the north and tall grasses in the south. Annual precipitation varies from 4 inches to 24 inches (100 to 600 mm). The 8-month dry season makes farming difficult, and the region has experienced several severe droughts in recent decades.

Q In what country would you find Africa's northernmost point?

A Tunisia. The northernmost point is Cape Ben Sekka, which lies just north of the continent's northernmost town, Bechater. Parts of five European countries—Greece, Italy, Malta, Portugal, and Spain—lie farther south than Cape Ben Sekka. From the tip of the cape, Africa stretches southward approximately 5,000 miles (8,000 km) to its southernmost point, Cape Agulhas in South Africa.

Q How has the Sahara Desert changed in the last 5,000 years?

A Scientists believe that 5,000 years ago the climate of the Sahara was more temperate and far less arid than it is today. Much of the region was grassland. Around 3000 B.C. global climate patterns began to shift, and the region entered an arid period which continues today. The desert currently covers 3,500,000 square miles (9,100,000 sq km), an area nearly as large as the United States, and its size is increasing. In recent decades, recurring droughts and overgrazing in the Sahel region have contributed to the Sahara's southward expansion.

Q What is the traditional mode of transportation in the Sahara Desert?

A The camel, or more specifically, the one-humped dromedary, which was domesticated at least 3,000 years ago. Dromedaries are extremely well-suited to desert conditions. They have the ability to store water in their hump, and can tolerate water losses equal to one-fourth of their body weight. Their heavy-lidded eyes and closeable nostrils offer protection in sandstorms. Today, as the Saharan road system expands, truck convoys are replacing camel caravans, although trucks require frequent refueling, often overheat in the desert sun, and grind to a halt when sand clogs their engines.

Camel eating leaves

Q Which African country can boast the greatest known deposits, variety, and output of minerals in the world?

A South Africa. It has the world's largest known deposits of chromite, gold, manganese, platinum, and vanadium. The country leads the world in production of gold, chromite, vanadium, and the platinum group metals: platinum, palladium, iridium, rhodium, and ruthenium. It is also one of the leading producers of manganese, antimony, and gem and industrial diamonds.

Q Where is the Horn of Africa?

A This term refers to the horn-shaped area of eastern Africa that juts into the Indian Ocean. Somalia and Ethiopia occupy most of the horn. The cape of Gees Gwardafuy and the city of Caluula sit at the northeastern tip of the horn, marking the entrance to the Gulf of Aden, which connects the Arabian Sea and the Red Sea.

Q What is the Valley of the Kings?

A This narrow valley, across the Nile River from the city of Luxor, contains the tombs of the pharaohs who ruled Egypt during the New Kingdom period, 1550 B.C. to 1200 B.C. The tombs are carved deep into the sandstone walls of the valley; most have five to fifteen rooms. Among the pharaohs buried in the valley are Ramses II, Ramses VI, and Seti I. Upon their death, the pharaohs were mummified and then entombed with all of the material things that they might need in the afterlife, including gold, jeweled ornaments, furniture, clothing, and food. Most of the tombs were soon looted by robbers, who removed all items of value. However, in 1922 the tomb of Tutankhamen—"King Tut"—was discovered with most of its riches untouched.

Questions and Answers

Asia

Q **What natural features form the physical boundary between Europe and Asia?**

A Europe and Asia share the same huge landmass, which is known as Eurasia. The imaginary line dividing this landmass into two continents runs through the Ural Mountains, the Ural River, the Caspian Sea, the Caucasus mountains, the Black Sea, the Bosporus strait, the Sea of Marmara, and the Dardanelles strait.

Q **How many countries lie partially within Europe and partially within Asia?**

A Four: Azerbaijan, which is traversed by the Caucasus Mountains; Kazakhstan, whose far western lands lie west of the Ural River; Russia, which is split by the Ural Mountains, and Turkey, which includes a small area on the northwestern side of the Sea of Marmara.

Q **Why was the Great Wall of China built?**

A To defend China against invasion by the Huns and other enemies. Defensive walls were built in China as early as the 6th century B.C. In 214 B.C., under Emperor Shih Huang-ti, the existing walls were connected to form a single continuous wall with watchtowers. This wall was extended during the Han Dynasty (202 B.C. – A.D. 220) and the Sui Dynasty (A.D. 581 – 618). Seven hundred years later the wall had mostly crumbled, and in the late 1400s, under the Ming Emperors, it was completely rebuilt. The portions of the wall that remain today are those that were constructed during this most recent period.

The Great Wall winding through a hilly region in northern China

Q **How has the Aral Sea changed in recent decades?**

A It has shrunk by about 55% since 1960. The sea once covered nearly 25,000 square miles (64,720 sq km) and was the fourth-largest inland body of water in the world. Today it covers only about 11,100 square miles (28,700 sq km), and the former port city of Muynak lies 30 miles (48 km) inland. The sea's shrinkage can be blamed on cotton farming in the surrounding desert. Soviet-era efforts to establish a profitable cotton industry led to the creation of an extensive network of irrigation canals. These huge canals drain large amounts of water from the Syr Darya and Amu Darya, the only two rivers that empty into the sea.

Q **What is the Ring of Fire?**

A "Ring of Fire" designates the narrow band of active volcanoes encircling the Pacific Ocean basin. Of the approximately 1,500 volcanoes in the world that have been active within the last 10,000 years, more than two-thirds are part of the Ring. Over half of the Ring's active volcanoes are found in its Asian portion, which passes through Russia's Kamchatka Peninsula, the Kuril Islands, Japan, and the Philippines. The Ring of Fire's most recent major volcanic event was the 1991 eruption of Pinatubo on the Philippine island of Luzon, which prompted the evacuation of 250,000 people.

Q **What part of Asia is called Indochina?**

A "Indochina" refers to the southeastern Asian peninsula situated south of China and east of India. Countries located on the peninsula are Cambodia, Laos, Myanmar (Burma), Thailand, Vietnam, and the western portion of Malaysia. The eastern part of the Indochinese peninsula, including Cambodia, Laos, and Vietnam, was formerly known as French Indochina because of France's strong colonial presence there.

Q **The Khyber Pass links which two countries?**

A Afghanistan and Pakistan. Approximately 33 miles (53 km) long and reaching a maximum elevation of about 3,500 feet (1,067 m), the pass cuts through the Safed Koh mountains just south of the Kabul River, connecting the high plateau of Afghanistan with the Indus Valley. It has been used for centuries as a caravan route and as an invasion route into India. Today it is also traversed by a paved highway and, in Pakistan, by a railroad. In the 1980s several million refugees fleeing Afghanistan's civil war crossed into Pakistan via the pass.

Q **What Persian Gulf country is a federation of seven Arab sheikdoms?**

A United Arab Emirates, formed in 1971 through the unification of the sheikdoms of Abu Dhabi, Ajman, Dubai, Fujeirah, Sharjah, and Umm al-Qawain. Ras al-Khaimah joined the federation in 1972. Underdeveloped a few decades ago, the U.A.E. has been transformed by oil wealth into a modern and affluent country.

Q **What Asian country contains, or is bordered by, six of the world's ten highest mountains?**

A Nepal. Within Nepal or along its borders with China and India are found the following peaks: Mt. Everest (highest in the world), Kanchenjunga (3rd), Makalu (4th), Dhawalāgiri (5th), Annapurna (7th), and Xixabangma Feng (9th). Nanda Devi (10th) lies only 50 miles (80 km) northwest of Nepal's western border.

Q **Where is the Empty Quarter?**

A This hostile desert is found in the southern third of the Arabian Peninsula. Called *Ar Rub' Al-Khālī*, or "the Empty Quarter" in Arabic, it covers 250,000 square miles (647,000 sq km) and is the world's largest continuous sand body. Few people live in the Empty Quarter, and much of the region has never been explored.

Q **What Asian volcanic eruption has been called the loudest natural explosion in recorded history?**

A The 1883 eruption of Krakatau (Krakatoa), an island volcano between Sumatra and Java. Krakatau exploded three times on August 26 and 27, 1883, shooting tremendous amounts of gas and ash 50 miles (80 km) into the atmosphere. The explosions were so violent that they were heard nearly 3,000 miles (4,653 km) away on Rodrigues Island in the western Indian Ocean. Krakatau collapsed into itself, and when the explosions were over most of the island was submerged under 900 feet of water. Tsunamis up to 130 feet (40 m) high slammed the coasts of Sumatra and Java, washing away hundreds of villages and killing more than 36,000 people.

Q At their closest point, how far apart are Asia and North America?

A At the narrowest point of the Bering Strait, Asia and North America are separated by only 56 miles (90 km). Russia's Big Diomede (Ratmanov) Island and the United States' Little Diomede Island, which lie in the middle of the strait, are only 2.5 miles (4 km) apart.

Q Where is the Fertile Crescent?

A This term refers to a crescent-shaped area of fertile land in the Middle East which runs along the eastern coast of the Mediterranean Sea, then turns southeast through Mesopotamia, the land between the Tigris and Euphrates rivers, and ends at the head of the Persian Gulf. The Fertile Crescent was the birthplace of some of the world's oldest civilizations, including the Sumerians, Babylonians, and Assyrians.

Q What country was Pakistan part of before it became independent?

A India. Conflicts between Hindus and Muslims in British India led to the creation of Pakistan as a separate Muslim state in 1947. Originally, Pakistan included the two main centers of Muslim population, which lay in northwest and east India. The two areas, West Pakistan and East Pakistan, were separated by 1,000 miles (1,600 km). In 1971, East Pakistan declared its independence and changed its name to Bangladesh. The name "Pakistan" comes from the Urdu words *pakh*, meaning "pure," and *stan*, meaning "land."

Q What was Sri Lanka called before 1972?

A Ceylon, which is the name the British had given to the island when they claimed it in 1796. The island became independent in 1948, and in 1972 was renamed Sri Lanka, which in the Sinhala language means "Resplendent Land."

Q What is India's most famous tomb?

A The Taj Mahal, located in the city of Agra. Often described as one of the world's most beautiful buildings, it

The Taj Mahal

was built by the Mogul emperor Shah Jahan to honor the memory of his wife, Mumtaz-i-Mahal. Construction began in 1631 and was completed in 1648.

Q What two seas are linked by the Suez Canal?

A The Red Sea and the Mediterranean Sea. Before the 101-mile (163-km) canal was built in the mid-1800s, ships traveling between Europe and the Far East had to sail all the way around the southern tip of Africa. Depending on the origin and destination of the ship, the canal could shorten its trip dramatically. For example, a ship sailing from London to Bombay would have to travel almost 11,000 miles (17,700 km) around the African continent. Using the Suez Canal, the trip could be shortened to 6,300 miles (10,140 km), a distance reduction of over 40%.

Q Which independent Asian country has the highest population density?

A The tiny republic of Singapore, with 17,814 people per square mile (6,879 per sq km). Singapore's 4,375,000 people occupy an island measuring only 26 miles east-to-west and 14 miles north-to-south. Mongolia has the lowest density: 4.4 people per square mile (1.7 per sq km). Mongolia's land area is 2,458 times larger than Singapore's, but it holds only 2,675,000 people.

Q How long is Japan, from north to south?

Landscape on Hokkaido, Japan's northernmost island

A The islands of Japan stretch approximately 1,900 miles (3,060 km) from Hokkaido in the north to the Sakishima Archipelago in the south. This is approximately equal to the distance between New York City and Denver.

Q What region is known as the "Roof of the World"?

A Tibet, the high plateau region which lies north of the Himalayas. Covering 471,000 square miles (1,220,000 sq km), and with an average elevation of 15,000 feet (4,600 m), the Tibetan Plateau is the largest and highest plateau in the world. Much of Tibet is uninhabited; the region's fewer than two million people are concentrated in the valleys of the Brahmaputra (Yarlung) River and its tributaries.

Q Which Asian country leads the world in number of earthquake-related deaths since 1900?

A China, where 48 deadly earthquakes have killed an estimated 967,420 people since 1900. During the same period Iran has lost 147,293 people in 57 earthquakes, and in Japan 32 earthquakes have killed 123,462 people.

Q What cities mark the endpoints of the Trans-Siberian Railway?

A The longest railway line in the world, the Trans-Siberian Railway stretches 5,764 miles (9,297 km) between Moscow in the west and the Pacific Coast port city of Nakhodka (near Vladivostok) in the east. The eight-day journey between the two cities includes stops in 92 Russian cities and towns.

Q How many people live on the Indonesian island of Java?

A Java is home to approximately 118 million people. It is the world's most populous island, although it is only the 13th-largest in area. By contrast, the island of Cuba is four-fifths the size of Java, but its population is only one-eleventh as large.

Q What was the name of Ho Chi Minh City, Vietnam, prior to 1975?

A Saigon. When the city fell to North Vietnamese forces in 1975, it was renamed for Ho Chi Minh, founder of the Indochina Communist Party and president of North Vietnam from 1945 until his death in 1969.

Questions and Answers

Oceania (including Australia and New Zealand)

Q What is Oceania?

A The name "Oceania" refers to the scattered islands of a vast area of the Pacific Ocean, from Palau in the west to Easter Island in the east, and from the Midway Islands in the north to New Zealand in the south. The three main island groups of Oceania are Melanesia, Micronesia, and Polynesia. The continent of Australia and the islands of New Zealand are sometimes considered part of Oceania.

Q What is the Outback?

A This nickname refers to Australia's vast, largely uninhabited interior. The Outback's harsh beauty and its remoteness from the rest of Australia have made it popular with adventurous explorers and travelers. Through depictions in literature, art, and film, the region has become an integral part of Australia's identity. However, it is difficult to characterize the Outback, for its boundaries are undefined and its landscape varies from hot deserts to lush wilderness.

Eucalyptus tree in the Outback, Northern Territory

Q Why is Australia sometimes referred to as "the Land Down Under"?

A This nickname originated with the British, who began colonizing Australia in the late 1700s. Because of its extreme southern location in relation to Britain, Australia was considered "Down." The "Under" part of the phrase refers to the continent's position "under" the Eurasian landmass. But while people from the Northern Hemisphere think of Australia as "Down Under," Australians do not.

Q How much of Australia is arid or semiarid?

A More than two-thirds of the continent is considered to be arid or semiarid. The arid areas comprise several large deserts, including the Great Victoria Desert, the Gibson Desert, the Great Sandy Desert, and the Simpson Desert.

Q What distinction does Wellington, New Zealand have among national capitals of independent countries?

A Located at 41°18' south latitude, Wellington is the world's southernmost national capital. In second place is Canberra, Australia, which lies at 35°17' south latitude.

Q What is unusual about how the island of Nauru was formed?

A Nauru, the world's smallest republic, began as a coral atoll. Over the millennia, accumulated bird droppings filled in the central lagoon and created an 8-square-mile (21-sq-km) island whose highest point rises 210 feet (64 m) above sea level. The droppings are a rich source of phosphate, which is used in making fertilizers. Phosphate mining has long been Nauru's economic mainstay, but the resource will soon be exhausted.

Q What are the principal islands of New Zealand?

A Two islands, North Island and South Island, account for more than 98% of New Zealand's total land area. The country also includes Stewart Island, the Chatham Islands, the Antipodes Islands, the Auckland Islands, and hundreds of tiny islets.

Q What is Ayers Rock?

A Ayers Rock, now called by its Aboriginal name, Uluru, is a huge, red, oval-shaped rock outcropping that rises 1,143 feet (349 m) above the plains of central Australia. One of the largest monoliths in the world, Uluru is actually the summit of a massive sandstone hill, most of which is hidden underground. Aborigines consider Uluru sacred and incorporate numerous places around it into their ceremonial life.

Q What is the ratio of sheep to humans in Australia and New Zealand?

A Because both countries are major wool, mutton, and lamb producers, Australia and New Zealand each have a high ratio of sheep to humans. In Australia, there are 132 million sheep, or seven sheep for each human in the country. In New Zealand, the ratio is even greater: the country's 50 million sheep translate into 14 sheep for each human.

Q How many of Oceania's countries have become independent since 1975?

A Eight. Papua New Guinea became independent in 1975, the Solomon Islands and Tuvalu in 1978, Kiribati in 1979, Vanuatu in 1980, the Marshall Islands and the Federated States of Micronesia in 1986, and Palau (Belau) in 1994.

Q What is the Great Barrier Reef?

A This vast coral reef system is the longest in the world, stretching 1,250 miles (2,000 km) along Australia's northeast coast. It is composed of reefs, shoals, and hundreds of islands. Popular with divers, the Great Barrier Reef is home to a myriad of aquatic creatures.

Q On what island is Robert Louis Stevenson buried?

A Stevenson, author of *Dr. Jekyll and Mr. Hyde, Kidnapped,* and *Treasure Island,* is buried on the island of Upolu in Western Samoa. Born in Edinburgh, Scotland in 1850, Stevenson sailed to the South Pacific in 1888 and settled permanently in Samoa in 1890. He died there in 1894.

Q Where does Sydney rank among Australia's most populous cities?

A Measured by actual city population, Sydney is not even ranked in the top hundred: only 13,501 people live within its tiny city limits. Brisbane is Australia's largest city, with 751,115 people. The Sydney metropolitan area, however, is by far the largest in Australia, with 3,538,749 people.

Harbor and skyline of Sydney

Q What is Australia's only island state?

A Tasmania, which lies about 150 miles (240 km) south of the Australian mainland. Measuring 26,200 square miles (67,800 sq km) in area, it is the smallest of Australia's six states and accounts for less than 1% of the country's area. Originally part of New South Wales, Tasmania became a separate colony in 1825 and a state in 1901. Hobart, its capital, is home to 45% of the state's population.

Countries and Flags

This 12-page section presents basic information about each of the world's countries, along with an illustration of each country's flag. A total of 199 countries are listed: the world's 192 fully independent countries, and 7 internally independent countries which are under the protection of other countries in matters of defense and foreign affairs. Colonies and other dependent political entities are not listed.

The categories of information provided for each country are as follows.

Flag: In many countries two or more versions of the national flag exist. For example, there is often a "civil" version which the average person flies, and a "state" version which is flown only at government buildings and government functions. A common difference between the two is the inclusion of a coat of arms on the state version.

Country name: The short form of the English translation of the official country name.

Population: The population figures listed are 2006 estimates based on U.S. census bureau figures and other available information.

Area: Figures provided represent total land area and all inland water. They are based on official data or U.N. data.

Population density: The number of people per square mile and square kilometer, calculated by dividing the country's population figure by its area figure.

Capital: The city that serves as the official seat of government. Population figures follow the capital name. These figures are based upon the latest official data.

Afghanistan
Official name: Islamic State of Afghanistan
Population: 33,170,000
Area: 251,773 sq mi (652,090 sq km)
Pop. density: 132/sq mi (51/sq km)
Capital: Kābul, 1,424,400

Albania
Official name: Republic of Albania
Population: 3,630,000
Area: 11,100 sq mi (28,748 sq km)
Density: 327/sq mi (126/sq km)
Capital: Tiranë, 243,000

Algeria
Official name: People's Democratic Republic of Algeria
Population: 33,975,000
Area: 919,595 sq mi (2,381,741 sq km)
Density: 37/sq mi (14/sq km)
Capital: Algiers (El Djazaïr), 1,507,241

Andorra
Official name: Principality of Andorra
Population: 83,000
Area: 181 sq mi (468 sq km)
Density: 459/sq mi (177/sq km)
Capital: Andorra, 20,437

Angola
Official name: Republic of Angola
Population: 12,665,000
Area: 481,354 sq mi (1,246,700 sq km)
Density: 26/sq mi (10/sq km)
Capital: Luanda, 1,459,900

Anguilla
Official name: Anguilla
Population: 14,000
Area: 37 sq mi (96 sq km)
Density: 378/sq mi (146/sq km)
Capital: The Valley, 1,169

Antigua and Barbuda
Official name: Antigua and Barbuda
Population: 85,000
Area: 171 sq mi (442 sq km)
Density: 497/sq mi (192/sq km)
Capital: St. John's, 24,359

Argentina
Official name: Argentine Republic
Population: 40,700,000
Area: 1,073,519 sq mi (2,780,400 sq km)
Pop. density: 38/sq mi (15/sq km)
Capital: Buenos Aires, 2,776,138

Armenia
Official name: Republic of Armenia
Population: 2,965,000
Area: 11,506 sq mi (29,800 sq km)
Pop. density: 258/sq mi (99/sq km)
Capital: Yerevan, 1,103,488

Australia
Official name: Commonwealth of Australia
Population: 21,135,000
Area: 2,969,910 sq mi (7,692,030 sq km)
Pop. density: 7.1/sq mi (2.7/sq km)
Capital: Canberra, 311,518

Austria
Official name: Republic of Austria
Population: 8,210,000
Area: 32,378 sq mi (83,858 sq km)
Pop. density: 254/sq mi (98/sq km)
Capital: Vienna (Wien), 1,609,631

Azerbaijan
Official name: Azerbaijani Republic
Population: 8,205,000
Area: 33,437 sq mi (86,600 sq km)
Pop. density: 245/sq mi (95/sq km)
Capital: Baku (Bakı), 1,080,500

Bahamas
Official name: Commonwealth of The Bahamas
Population: 310,000
Area: 5,382 sq mi (13,939 sq km)
Pop. density: 58/sq mi (22/sq km)
Capital: Nassau, 173,300

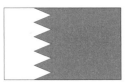

Bahrain
Official name: Kingdom of Bahrain
Population: 725,000
Area: 267 sq mi (691 sq km)
Pop. density: 2,715/sq mi (1,049/sq km)
Capital: Al Manāmah, 153,395

Bangladesh
Official name: People's Republic of Bangladesh
Population: 155,045,000
Area: 55,598 sq mi (143,998 sq km)
Pop. density: 2,789/sq mi (1,077/sq km)
Capital: Dhaka (Dacca), 3,637,892

Barbados
Official name: Barbados
Population: 285,000
Area: 166 sq mi (430 sq km)
Pop. density: 1,717/sq mi (663/sq km)
Capital: Bridgetown, 5,928

Belarus
Official name: Republic of Belarus
Population: 9,665,000
Area: 80,155 sq mi (207,600 sq km)
Pop. density: 121/sq mi (47/sq km)
Capital: Minsk, 1,661,000

Belgium
Official name: Kingdom of Belgium
Population: 10,410,000
Area: 11,787 sq mi (30,528 sq km)
Pop. density: 883/sq mi (341/sq km)
Capital: Brussels (Bruxelles), 133,845

Belize
Official name: Belize
Population: 305,000
Area: 8,867 sq mi (22,966 sq km)
Pop. density: 34/sq mi (13/sq km)
Capital: Belmopan, 8,130

Benin
Official name: Republic of Benin
Population: 8,660,000
Area: 43,484 sq mi (112,622 sq km)
Pop. density: 199/sq mi (77/sq km)
Capital: Porto-Novo (designated), 179,138, and Cotonou (de facto), 536,827

Bhutan
Official name: Kingdom of Bhutan
Population: 685,000
Area: 17,954 sq mi (46,500 sq km)
Pop. density: 38/sq mi (15/sq km)
Capital: Thimphu, 12,000

Bolivia
Official name: Republic of Bolivia
Population: 9,690,000
Area: 424,165 sq mi (1,098,581 sq km)
Pop. density: 23/sq mi (8.8/sq km)
Capital: La Paz (seat of government), 789,585, and Sucre (designated), 194,888

Bosnia and Herzegovina
Official name: Republic of Bosnia and Herzegovina
Population: 4,605,000
Area: 19,767 sq mi (51,197 sq km)
Pop. density: 233/sq mi (90/sq km)
Capital: Sarajevo, 367,703

Botswana
Official name: Republic of Botswana
Population: 1,970,000
Area: 224,607 sq mi (581,730 sq km)
Pop. density: 8.8/sq mi (3.4/sq km)
Capital: Gaborone, 186,007

Brazil
Official name: Federative Republic of Brazil
Population: 197,550,000
Area: 3,300,172 sq mi (8,547,404 sq km)
Pop. density: 60/sq mi (23/sq km)
Capital: Brasília, 1,947,133

Brunei
Official name: Negara Brunei Darussalam
Population: 385,000
Area: 2,226 sq mi (5,765 sq km)
Pop. density: 173/sq mi (67/sq km)
Capital: Bandar Seri Begawan, 45,867

Bulgaria
Official name: Republic of Bulgaria
Population: 7,235,000
Area: 42,855 sq mi (110,994 sq km)
Pop. density: 169/sq mi (65/sq km)
Capital: Sofia (Sofiya), 1,190,126

Burkina Faso
Official name: Burkina Faso
Population: 15,500,000
Area: 105,869 sq mi (274,200 sq km)
Pop. density: 146/sq mi (57/sq km)
Capital: Ouagadougou, 709,700

Burundi
Official name: Republic of Burundi
Population: 8,840,000
Area: 10,745 sq mi (27,830 sq km)
Pop. density: 823/sq mi (318/sq km)
Capital: Bujumbura, 226,628

Cambodia
Official name: Kingdom of Cambodia
Population: 14,365,000
Area: 69,898 sq mi (181,035 sq km)
Pop. density: 206/sq mi (79/sq km)
Capital: Phnom Penh (Phnum Pénh), 570,155

Cameroon
Official name: Republic of Cameroon
Population: 18,670,000
Area: 183,568 sq mi (475,440 sq km)
Pop. density: 102/sq mi (39/sq km)
Capital: Yaoundé, 560,785

Canada
Official name: Canada
Population: 33,350,000
Area: 3,855,103 sq mi (9,984,670 sq km)
Pop. density: 8.7/sq mi (3.3/sq km)
Capital: Ottawa, 648,480

Cape Verde
Official name: Republic of Cape Verde
Population: 430,000
Area: 1,557 sq mi (4,033 sq km)
Pop. density: 276/sq mi (107/sq km)
Capital: Praia, 61,644

Central African Republic
Official name: Central African Republic
Population: 4,480,000
Area: 240,536 sq mi (622,984 sq km)
Pop. density: 19/sq mi (7.2/sq km)
Capital: Bangui, 451,690

Chad
Official name: Republic of Chad
Population: 10,220,000
Area: 495,755 sq mi (1,284,000 sq km)
Pop. density: 21/sq mi (8/sq km)
Capital: N'Djamena, 546,572

Chile
Official name: Republic of Chile
Population: 16,530,000
Area: 291,930 sq mi (756,096 sq km)
Pop. density: 57/sq mi (22/sq km)
Capital: Santiago, 4,295,593

China
Official name: People's Republic of China
Population: 1,341,820,000
Area: 3,689,613 sq mi (9,556,054 sq km)
Pop. density: 364/sq mi (140/sq km)
Capital: Beijing (Peking), 6,690,000

Colombia
Official name: Republic of Colombia
Population: 45,330,000
Area: 439,737 sq mi (1,138,914 sq km)
Pop. density: 103/sq mi (40/sq km)
Capital: Bogotá, 4,931,796

Comoros
Official name: Union of the Comoros
Population: 740,000
Area: 863 sq mi (2,235 sq km)
Pop. density: 857/sq mi (331/sq km)
Capital: Moroni, 23,432

Congo
Official name: Republic of the Congo
Population: 3,960,000
Area: 132,047 sq mi (342,000 sq km)
Pop. density: 30/sq mi (12/sq km)
Capital: Brazzaville, 1,050,000

Congo, Democratic Republic of the
Official name: Democratic Republic of the Congo
Population: 67,590,000
Area: 905,446 sq mi (2,345,095 sq km)
Pop. density: 75/sq mi (29/sq km)
Capital: Kinshasa, 3,000,000

Costa Rica
Official name: Republic of Costa Rica
Population: 4,225,000
Area: 19,730 sq mi (51,100 sq km)
Pop. density: 214/sq mi (83/sq km)
Capital: San José, 309,672

Cote d'Ivoire
Official name: Republic of Cote d'Ivoire
Population: 20,395,000
Area: 124,504 sq mi (322,463 sq km)
Pop. density: 164/sq mi (63/sq km)
Capital: Abidjan (de facto), 1,929,079, and Yamoussoukro (designated), 106,786

Croatia
Official name: Republic of Croatia
Population: 4,490,000
Area: 21,829 sq mi (56,538 sq km)
Pop. density: 206/sq mi (79/sq km)
Capital: Zagreb, 867,865

Cuba
Official name: Republic of Cuba
Population: 11,440,000
Area: 42,804 sq mi (110,861 sq km)
Pop. density: 267/sq mi (103/sq km)
Capital: Havana (La Habana), 2,189,716

Cyprus
Official name: Republic of Cyprus
Population: 795,000
Area: 3,572 sq mi (9,251 sq km)
Pop. density: 223/sq mi (86/sq km)
Capital: Nicosia (Levkosía), 47,036

Czech Republic
Official name: Czech Republic
Population: 10,215,000
Area: 30,450 sq mi (78,866 sq km)
Pop. density: 335/sq mi (130/sq km)
Capital: Prague (Praha), 1,214,174

Denmark
Official name: Kingdom of Denmark
Population: 5,495,000
Area: 16,640 sq mi (43,096 sq km)
Pop. density: 330/sq mi (128/sq km)
Capital: Copenhagen (København), 449,148

Djibouti
Official name: Republic of Djibouti
Population: 510,000
Area: 8,958 sq mi (23,200 sq km)
Pop. density: 57/sq mi (22/sq km)
Capital: Djibouti, 329,337

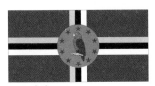

Dominica
Official name: Commonwealth of Dominica
Population: 73,000
Area: 290 sq mi (751 sq km)
Pop. density: 252/sq mi (97/sq km)
Capital: Roseau, 9,348

Dominican Republic
Official name: Dominican Republic
Population: 9,580,000
Area: 18,730 sq mi (48,511 sq km)
Pop. density: 511/sq mi (197/sq km)
Capital: Santo Domingo, 913,540

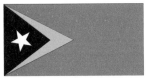

East Timor
Official name: Democratic Republic of Timor-Leste
Population: 1,120,000
Area: 5,743 sq mi (14,874 sq km)
Pop. density: 195/sq mi (75/sq km)
Capital: Dili, 50,000

Ecuador
Official name: Republic of Ecuador
Population: 14,465,000
Area: 109,484 sq mi (283,561 sq km)
Pop. density: 132/sq mi (51/sq km)
Capital: Quito, 1,399,378

Egypt
Official name: Arab Republic of Egypt
Population: 82,400,000
Area: 386,662 sq mi (1,001,449 sq km)
Pop. density: 213/sq mi (82/sq km)
Capital: Cairo (Al Qāhirah), 6,068,695

El Salvador
Official name: Republic of El Salvador
Population: 7,125,000
Area: 8,124 sq mi (21,041 sq km)
Pop. density: 877/sq mi (339/sq km)
Capital: San Salvador, 415,346

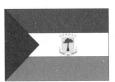

Equatorial Guinea
Official name: Republic of Equatorial Guinea
Population: 625,000
Area: 10,831 sq mi (28,051 sq km)
Pop. density: 58/sq mi (22/sq km)
Capital: Malabo, 31,630

Eritrea
Official name: State of Eritrea
Population: 5,575,000
Area: 45,406 sq mi (117,600 sq km)
Pop. density: 123/sq mi (47/sq km)
Capital: Asmera, 358,100

Estonia
Official name: Republic of Estonia
Population: 1,305,000
Area: 17,462 sq mi (45,227 sq km)
Pop. density: 75/sq mi (29/sq km)
Capital: Tallinn, 403,981

Ethiopia
Official name: Federal Democratic Republic of Ethiopia
Population: 83,870,000
Area: 426,373 sq mi (1,104,300 sq km)
Pop. density: 197/sq mi (76/sq km)
Capital: Addis Ababa (Adis Abeba), 2,084,588

Fiji
Official name: Republic of the Fiji Islands
Population: 940,000
Area: 7,056 sq mi (18,274 sq km)
Pop. density: 133/sq mi (51/sq km)
Capital: Suva, 77,366

Finland
Official name: Republic of Finland
Population: 5,250,000
Area: 130,559 sq mi (338,145 sq km)
Pop. density: 40/sq mi (16/sq km)
Capital: Helsinki (Helsingfors), 512,686

France
Official name: French Republic
Population: 62,260,000
Area: 208,482 sq mi (539,965 sq km)
Pop. density: 299/sq mi (115/sq km)
Capital: Paris, 2,125,246

Gabon
Official name: Gabonese Republic
Population: 1,500,000
Area: 103,347 sq mi (267,668 sq km)
Pop. density: 15/sq mi (5.6/sq km)
Capital: Libreville, 337,700

The Gambia
Official name: Republic of The Gambia
Population: 1,760,000
Area: 4,127 sq mi (10,689 sq km)
Pop. density: 426/sq mi (165/sq km)
Capital: Banjul, 42,407

Georgia
Official name: Republic of Georgia
Population: 4,625,000
Area: 26,911 sq mi (69,700 sq km)
Pop. density: 172/sq mi (66/sq km)
Capital: Tbilisi, 1,081,678

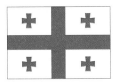

Germany
Official name: Federal Republic of Germany
Population: 82,350,000
Area: 137,847 sq mi (357,022 sq km)
Pop. density: 597/sq mi (231/sq km)
Capital: Berlin, 3,425,759

Ghana
Official name: Republic of Ghana
Population: 23,610,000
Area: 92,098 sq mi (238,533 sq km)
Pop. density: 256/sq mi (99/sq km)
Capital: Accra, 949,113

Greece
Official name: Hellenic Republic
Population: 10,730,000
Area: 50,949 sq mi (131,957 sq km)
Pop. density: 211/sq mi (81/sq km)
Capital: Athens (Athína), 772,072

Greenland
Official name: Greenland
Population: 58,000
Area: 836,331 sq mi (2,166,086 sq km)
Pop. density: 0.07/sq mi (0.03/sq km)
Capital: Godthåb (Nuuk), 13,445

Grenada
Official name: Grenada
Population: 91,000
Area: 133 sq mi (344 sq km)
Pop. density: 684/sq mi (265/sq km)
Capital: St. George's, 3,908

Guatemala
Official name: Republic of Guatemala
Population: 13,140,000
Area: 42,042 sq mi (108,889 sq km)
Pop. density: 313/sq mi (121/sq km)
Capital: Guatemala, 823,301

Guinea
Official name: Republic of Guinea
Population: 9,930,000
Area: 94,926 sq mi (245,857 sq km)
Pop. density: 105/sq mi (40/sq km)
Capital: Conakry, 950,000

Guinea-Bissau
Official name: Republic of Guinea-Bissau
Population: 1,520,000
Area: 13,948 sq mi (36,125 sq km)
Pop. density: 109/sq mi (42/sq km)
Capital: Bissau, 125,000

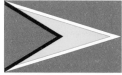

Guyana
Official name: Co-operative Republic of
   Guyana
Population: 770,000
Area: 83,000 sq mi (214,969 sq km)
Pop. density: 9.3/sq mi (3.6/sq km)
Capital: Georgetown, 70,100

Haiti
Official name: Republic of Haiti
Population: 8,955,000
Area: 10,714 sq mi (27,750 sq km)
Pop. density: 836/sq mi (323/sq km)
Capital: Port-au-Prince, 846,247

Honduras
Official name: Republic of Honduras
Population: 7,715,000
Area: 43,277 sq mi (112,088 sq km)
Pop. density: 178/sq mi (69/sq km)
Capital: Tegucigalpa, 769,061

Hungary
Official name: Republic of Hungary
Population: 9,920,000
Area: 35,919 sq mi (93,030 sq km)
Pop. density: 276/sq mi (107/sq km)
Capital: Budapest, 1,906,798

Iceland
Official name: Republic of Iceland
Population: 305,000
Area: 39,769 sq mi (103,000 sq km)
Pop. density: 7.7/sq mi (3.0/sq km)
Capital: Reykjavík, 100,850

India
Official name: Republic of India
Population: 1,157,055,000
Area: 1,222,510 sq mi (3,166,285 sq km)
Pop. density: 946/sq mi (365/sq km)
Capital: New Delhi, 294,783

Indonesia
Official name: Republic of Indonesia
Population: 238,910,000
Area: 735,310 sq mi (1,904,443 sq km)
Pop. density: 325/sq mi (125/sq km)
Capital: Jakarta, 8,347,083

Iran
Official name: Islamic Republic of Iran
Population: 66,135,000
Area: 636,372 sq mi (1,648,195 sq km)
Pop. density: 104/sq mi (40/sq km)
Capital: Tehrān, 6,758,845

Iraq
Official name: Republic of Iraq
Population: 28,585,000
Area: 169,235 sq mi (438,317 sq km)
Pop. density: 169/sq mi (65/sq km)
Capital: Baghdād, 3,841,268

Ireland
Official name: Ireland
Population: 4,180,000
Area: 27,133 sq mi (70,273 sq km)
Pop. density: 154/sq mi (59/sq km)
Capital: Dublin (Baile Átha Cliath), 481,854

Israel
Official name: State of Israel
Population: 7,175,000
Area: 8,019 sq mi (20,770 sq km)
Pop. density: 895/sq mi (345/sq km)
Capital: Jerusalem (Yerushalayim), 680,500

Italy
Official name: Italian Republic
Population: 58,140,000
Area: 116,342 sq mi (301,323 sq km)
Pop. density: 500/sq mi (193/sq km)
Capital: Rome (Roma), 2,649,765

Jamaica
Official name: Jamaica
Population: 2,815,000
Area: 4,244 sq mi (10,991 sq km)
Pop. density: 663/sq mi (256/sq km)
Capital: Kingston, 516,500

Japan
Official name: Japan
Population: 127,200,000
Area: 145,850 sq mi (377,750 sq km)
Pop. density: 872/sq mi (337/sq km)
Capital: Tōkyō, 8,025,508

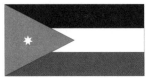

Jordan
Official name: Hashemite Kingdom of Jordan
Population: 6,270,000
Area: 34,495 sq mi (89,342 sq km)
Pop. density: 182/sq mi (70/sq km)
Capital: ʽAmmān, 963,490

Kazakhstan
Official name: Republic of Kazakhstan
Population: 15,370,000
Area: 1,049,156 sq mi (2,717,300 sq km)
Pop. density: 15/sq mi (5.7/sq km)
Capital: Astana, 286,000

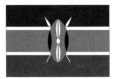

Kenya
Official name: Republic of Kenya
Population: 38,475,000
Area: 224,961 sq mi (582,646 sq km)
Pop. density: 171/sq mi (66/sq km)
Capital: Nairobi, 2,143,254

Kiribati
Official name: Republic of Kiribati
Population: 110,000
Area: 313 sq mi (811 sq km)
Pop. density: 351/sq mi (136/sq km)
Capital: Bairiki, 2,226

Korea, North
Official name: Democratic People's Republic of Korea
Population: 22,620,000
Area: 46,540 sq mi (120,538 sq km)
Pop. density: 486/sq mi (188/sq km)
Capital: Pʼyŏngyang, 2,741,260

Korea, South
Official name: Republic of Korea
Population: 48,445,000
Area: 38,328 sq mi (99,268 sq km)
Pop. density: 1,264/sq mi (488/sq km)
Capital: Seoul (Sŏul), 10,627,790

Kuwait
Official name: State of Kuwait
Population: 2,645,000
Area: 6,880 sq mi (17,818 sq km)
Pop. density: 384/sq mi (148/sq km)
Capital: Kuwait (Al Kuwayt), 28,747

Kyrgyzstan
Official name: Kyrgyz Republic
Population: 5,395,000
Area: 77,182 sq mi (199,900 sq km)
Pop. density: 70/sq mi (27/sq km)
Capital: Bishkek, 631,300

Laos
Official name: Lao People's Democratic Republic
Population: 6,755,000
Area: 91,429 sq mi (236,800 sq km)
Pop. density: 74/sq mi (29/sq km)
Capital: Viangchan (Vientiane), 464,000

Latvia
Official name: Republic of Latvia
Population: 2,240,000
Area: 24,942 sq mi (64,600 sq km)
Pop. density: 90/sq mi (35/sq km)
Capital: Rīga, 874,200

Lebanon
Official name: Republic of Lebanon
Population: 3,995,000
Area: 4,016 sq mi (10,400 sq km)
Pop. density: 995/sq mi (384/sq km)
Capital: Beirut (Bayrūt), 509,000

Lesotho
Official name: Kingdom of Lesotho
Population: 2,130,000
Area: 11,720 sq mi (30,355 sq km)
Pop. density: 182/sq mi (70/sq km)
Capital: Maseru, 137,837

Liberia
Official name: Republic of Liberia
Population: 3,395,000
Area: 43,000 sq mi (111,369 sq km)
Pop. density: 79/sq mi (30/sq km)
Capital: Monrovia, 465,000

Libya
Official name: Great Socialist People's Libyan Arab Jamahiriya
Population: 6,240,000
Area: 679,362 sq mi (1,759,540 sq km)
Pop. density: 9.2/sq mi (3.5/sq km)
Capital: Tripoli (Tarābulus), 591,062

Liechtenstein
Official name: Principality of Liechtenstein
Population: 35,000
Area: 62 sq mi (160 sq km)
Pop. density: 565/sq mi (219/sq km)
Capital: Vaduz, 5,106

Lithuania
Official name: Republic of Lithuania
Population: 3,560,000
Area: 25,213 sq mi (65,300 sq km)
Pop. density: 141/sq mi (55/sq km)
Capital: Vilnius, 578,639

Luxembourg
Official name: Grand Duchy of Luxembourg
Population: 490,000
Area: 999 sq mi (2,586 sq km)
Pop. density: 490/sq mi (189/sq km)
Capital: Luxembourg, 81,800

Macedonia
Official name: Republic of Macedonia
Population: 2,065,000
Area: 9,928 sq mi (25,713 sq km)
Pop. density: 208/sq mi (80/sq km)
Capital: Skopje, 440,577

Madagascar
Official name: Republic of Madagascar
Population: 20,345,000
Area: 226,658 sq mi (587,041 sq km)
Pop. density: 90/sq mi (35/sq km)
Capital: Antananarivo, 1,103,304

Malawi
Official name: Republic of Malawi
Population: 14,100,000
Area: 45,747 sq mi (118,484 sq km)
Pop. density: 308/sq mi (119/sq km)
Capital: Lilongwe, 435,964

Malaysia
Official name: Malaysia
Population: 25,495,000
Area: 127,320 sq mi (329,758 sq km)
Pop. density: 200/sq mi (77/sq km)
Capital: Kuala Lumpur (legal), 1,297,526
and Putrajaya (administrative), 55,000

Maldives
Official name: Republic of Maldives
Population: 395,000
Area: 115 sq mi (298 sq km)
Pop. density: 3,435/sq mi (1,326/sq km)
Capital: Male', 74,069

Mali
Official name: Republic of Mali
Population: 12,490,000
Area: 478,841 sq mi (1,240,192 sq km)
Pop. density: 26/sq mi (10/sq km)
Capital: Bamako, 658,275

Malta
Official name: Republic of Malta
Population: 405,000
Area: 122 sq mi (316 sq km)
Pop. density: 3,320/sq mi (1,282/sq km)
Capital: Valletta, 6,315

Marshall Islands
Official name: Republic of the Marshall
Islands
Population: 64,000
Area: 70 sq mi (181 sq km)
Pop. density: 914/sq mi (354/sq km)
Capital: Majuro (island)

Mauritania
Official name: Islamic Republic of
Mauritania
Population: 3,090,000
Area: 397,956 sq mi (1,030,700 sq km)
Pop. density: 7.8/sq mi (3.0/sq km)
Capital: Nouakchott, 558,195

Mauritius
Official name: Republic of Mauritius
Population: 1,280,000
Area: 788 sq mi (2,040 sq km)
Pop. density: 1,624/sq mi (627/sq km)
Capital: Port Louis, 144,303

Mexico
Official name: United Mexican States
Population: 110,585,000
Area: 758,452 sq mi (1,964,382 sq km)
Pop. density: 146/sq mi (56/sq km)
Capital: Mexico City (Ciudad de México),
8,720,916

Micronesia, Federated States of
Official name: Federated States of
Micronesia
Population: 110,000
Area: 271 sq mi (702 sq km)
Pop. density: 406/sq mi (157/sq km)
Capital: Palikir, 5,047

Moldova
Official name: Republic of Moldova
Population: 4,320,000
Area: 13,070 sq mi (33,851 sq km)
Pop. density: 331/sq mi (128/sq km)
Capital: Chişinău (Kishinev), 676,700

Monaco
Official name: Principality of Monaco
Population: 33,000
Area: 0.8 sq mi (2.0 sq km)
Pop. density: 41,250/sq mi (16,500/sq km)
Capital: Monaco, 33,000

Mongolia
Official name: Mongolia
Population: 3,020,000
Area: 604,829 sq mi (1,566,500 sq km)
Pop. density: 5.0/sq mi (1.9/sq km)
Capital: Ulan Bator (Ulaanbaatar), 649,797

Montenegro
Official name: Republic of Montenegro
Population: 675,000
Area: 5,333 sq mi (13,812 sq km)
Pop. density: 127/sq mi (49/sq km)
Capital: Podgorica, 118,059

Morocco
Official name: Kingdom of Morocco
Population: 34,600,000
Area: 172,414 sq mi (446,550 sq km)
Pop. density: 201/sq mi (77/sq km)
Capital: Rabat, 623,457

Mozambique
Official name: Republic of Mozambique
Population: 21,475,000
Area: 309,496 sq mi (801,590 sq km)
Pop. density: 69/sq mi (27/sq km)
Capital: Maputo, 966,837

Myanmar
Official name: Union of Myanmar
Population: 47,950,000
Area: 261,228 sq mi (676,578 sq km)
Pop. density: 184/sq mi (71/sq km)
Capital: Rangoon (Yangon), 2,705,039, and
   Nay Pyi Taw, 10,000

Namibia
Official name: Republic of Namibia
Population: 2,100,000
Area: 317,818 sq mi (823,144 sq km)
Pop. density: 6.6/sq mi (2.6/sq km)
Capital: Windhoek, 147,056

Nauru
Official name: Republic of Nauru
Population: 14,000
Area: 8.1 sq mi (21 sq km)
Pop. density: 1,728/sq mi (667/sq km)
Capital: Yaren District

Nepal
Official name: Kingdom of Nepal
Population: 28,380,000
Area: 56,827 sq mi (147,181 sq km)
Pop. density: 499/sq mi (193/sq km)
Capital: Kathmandu, 671,846

Netherlands
Official name: Kingdom of the Netherlands
Population: 16,680,000
Area: 16,164 sq mi (41,864 sq km)
Pop. density: 1,032/sq mi (398/sq km)
Capital: Amsterdam (designated), 727,053,
   and The Hague ('s-Gravenhage) (seat of
   government), 440,743

New Zealand
Official name: New Zealand
Population: 4,195,000
Area: 104,454 sq mi (270,534 sq km)
Pop. density: 40/sq mi (16/sq km)
Capital: Wellington, 167,190

Nicaragua
Official name: Republic of Nicaragua
Population: 5,840,000
Area: 50,054 sq mi (129,640 sq km)
Pop. density: 117/sq mi (45/sq km)
Capital: Managua, 864,201

Niger
Official name: Republic of Niger
Population: 15,025,000
Area: 489,192 sq mi (1,267,000 sq km)
Pop. density: 31/sq mi (12/sq km)
Capital: Niamey, 392,165

Nigeria
Official name: Federal Republic of Nigeria
Population: 147,735,000
Area: 356,669 sq mi (923,768 sq km)
Pop. density: 414/sq mi (160/sq km)
Capital: Abuja, 250,000

Niue
Official name: Niue
Population: 1,500
Area: 100 sq mi (259 sq km)
Pop. density: 15/sq mi (5.8/sq km)
Capital: Alofi, 682

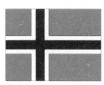

Northern Mariana Islands
Official name: Commonwealth of the
   Northern Mariana Islands
Population: 88,000
Area: 179 sq mi (464 sq km)
Pop. density: 492/sq mi (190/sq km)
Capital: Saipan (island)

Norway
Official name: Kingdom of Norway
Population: 4,655,000
Area: 125,050 sq mi (323,877 sq km)
Pop. density: 37/sq mi (14/sq km)
Capital: Oslo, 504,040

Oman
Official name: Sultanate of Oman
Population: 3,365,000
Area: 119,499 sq mi (309,500 sq km)
Pop. density: 28/sq mi (11/sq km)
Capital: Muscat (Masqaṭ), 34,683

Pakistan
Official name: Islamic Republic of Pakistan
Population: 174,525,000
Area: 339,732 sq mi (879,902 sq km)
Pop. density: 514/sq mi (198/sq km)
Capital: Islāmābād, 529,180

Palau
Official name: Republic of Palau
Population: 21,000
Area: 188 sq mi (487 sq km)
Pop. density: 112/sq mi (43/sq km)
Capital: Melekeok, 391

Panama
Official name: Republic of Panama
Population: 3,335,000
Area: 29,157 sq mi (75,517 sq km)
Pop. density: 114/sq mi (44/sq km)
Capital: Panamá, 415,964

Papua New Guinea
Official name: Independent State of Papua New Guinea
Population: 5,995,000
Area: 178,704 sq mi (462,840 sq km)
Pop. density: 34/sq mi (13/sq km)
Capital: Port Moresby, 246,664

Paraguay
Official name: Republic of Paraguay
Population: 6,915,000
Area: 157,048 sq mi (406,752 sq km)
Pop. density: 44/sq mi (17/sq km)
Capital: Asunción, 502,426

Peru
Official name: Republic of Peru
Population: 29,365,000
Area: 496,225 sq mi (1,285,216 sq km)
Pop. density: 59/sq mi (23/sq km)
Capital: Lima, 340,422

Philippines
Official name: Republic of the Philippines
Population: 97,020,000
Area: 115,831 sq mi (300,000 sq km)
Pop. density: 838/sq mi (323/sq km)
Capital: Manila, 1,654,761

Poland
Official name: Republic of Poland
Population: 38,490,000
Area: 120,728 sq mi (312,685 sq km)
Pop. density: 319/sq mi (123/sq km)
Capital: Warsaw (Warszawa), 1,707,147

Portugal
Official name: Portuguese Republic
Population: 10,695,000
Area: 35,516 sq mi (91,985 sq km)
Pop. density: 301/sq mi (116/sq km)
Capital: Lisbon (Lisboa), 663,394

Puerto Rico
Official name: Commonwealth of Puerto Rico
Population: 3,965,000
Area: 3,515 sq mi (9,104 sq km)
Pop. density: 1,128/sq mi (436/sq km)
Capital: San Juan, 421,958

Qatar
Official name: State of Qatar
Population: 830,000
Area: 4,412 sq mi (11,427 sq km)
Pop. density: 188/sq mi (73/sq km)
Capital: Ad Dawḩah (Doha), 361,540

Romania
Official name: Romania
Population: 22,230,000
Area: 91,699 sq mi (237,500 sq km)
Pop. density: 242/sq mi (94/sq km)
Capital: Bucharest (București), 2,067,545

Russia
Official name: Russian Federation
Population: 140,370,000
Area: 6,592,849 sq mi (17,075,400 sq km)
Pop. density: 21/sq mi (8.2/sq km)
Capital: Moscow (Moskva), 10,126,424

Rwanda
Official name: Republic of Rwanda
Population: 10,330,000
Area: 10,169 sq mi (26,338 sq km)
Pop. density: 1,016/sq mi (392/sq km)
Capital: Kigali, 603,049

St. Kitts and Nevis
Official name: Federation of St. Kitts and Nevis
Population: 40,000
Area: 101 sq mi (261 sq km)
Pop. density: 396/sq mi (153/sq km)
Capital: Basseterre, 11,295

St. Lucia
Official name: St. Lucia
Population: 160,000
Area: 238 sq mi (616 sq km)
Pop. density: 672/sq mi (260/sq km)
Capital: Castries, 11,846

St. Vincent and the Grenadines
Official name: St. Vincent and the Grenadines
Population: 105,000
Area: 150 sq mi (388 sq km)
Pop. density: 700/sq mi (271/sq km)
Capital: Kingstown, 15,466

Samoa
Official name: Independent State of Samoa
Population: 220,000
Area: 1,093 sq mi (2,831 sq km)
Pop. density: 201/sq mi (78/sq km)
Capital: Apia, 34,126

San Marino
Official name: Republic of San Marino
Population: 30,000
Area: 24 sq mi (61 sq km)
Pop. density: 1,250/sq mi (492/sq km)
Capital: San Marino, 2,294

Sao Tome and Principe
Official name: Democratic Republic of Sao Tome and Principe
Population: 210,000
Area: 372 sq mi (964 sq km)
Pop. density: 565/sq mi (218/sq km)
Capital: São Tomé, 5,245

Saudi Arabia
Official name: Kingdom of Saudi Arabia
Population: 28,420,000
Area: 830,000 sq mi (2,149,690 sq km)
Pop. density: 34/sq mi (13/sq km)
Capital: Riyadh (Ar Riyāḑ), 2,950,000

Senegal
Official name: Republic of Senegal
Population: 13,525,000
Area: 75,951 sq mi (196,712 sq km)
Pop. density: 178/sq mi (69/sq km)
Capital: Dakar, 1,490,450

Serbia
Official name: Republic of Serbia
Population: 9,195,000
Area: 34,116 sq mi (88,361 sq km)
Pop. density: 247/sq mi (95/sq km)
Capital: Belgrade (Beograd), 1,136,786

Seychelles
Official name: Republic of Seychelles
Population: 87,000
Area: 176 sq mi (455 sq km)
Pop. density: 494/sq mi (191/sq km)
Capital: Victoria, 24,907

Sierra Leone
Official name: Republic of Sierra Leone
Population: 6,365,000
Area: 27,699 sq mi (71,740 sq km)
Pop. density: 230/sq mi (89/sq km)
Capital: Freetown, 469,776

Singapore
Official name: Republic of Singapore
Population: 4,635,000
Area: 264 sq mi (683 sq km)
Pop. density: 17,557/sq mi (6,786/sq km)
Capital: Singapore, 4,185,200

Slovakia
Official name: Slovak Republic
Population: 5,460,000
Area: 18,924 sq mi (49,012 sq km)
Pop. density: 289/sq mi (111/sq km)
Capital: Bratislava, 451,395

Slovenia
Official name: Republic of Slovenia
Population: 2,005,000
Area: 7,821 sq mi (20,256 sq km)
Pop. density: 256/sq mi (99/sq km)
Capital: Ljubljana, 273,843

Solomon Islands
Official name: Solomon Islands
Population: 590,000
Area: 10,954 sq mi (28,370 sq km)
Pop. density: 54/sq mi (21/sq km)
Capital: Honiara, 30,413

Somalia
Official name: Somalia
Population: 9,695,000
Area: 246,201 sq mi (637,657 sq km)
Pop. density: 39/sq mi (15/sq km)
Capital: Mogadishu (Muqdisho), 600,000

South Africa
Official name: Republic of South Africa
Population: 48,985,000
Area: 470,693 sq mi (1,219,090 sq km)
Pop. density: 104/sq mi (40/sq km)
Capital: Pretoria (administrative), 525,583,
   Cape Town (legislative), 854,616, and
   Bloemfontein (judicial), 126,867

Spain
Official name: Kingdom of Spain
Population: 40,510,000
Area: 194,885 sq mi (504,750 sq km)
Pop. density: 208/sq mi (80/sq km)
Capital: Madrid, 2,882,860

Sri Lanka
Official name: Democratic Socialist
   Republic of Sri Lanka
Population: 21,230,000
Area: 25,332 sq mi (65,610 sq km)
Pop. density: 838/sq mi (324/sq km)
Capital: Colombo (designated), 642,163,
   and Sri Jayewardenepura Kotte (seat of
   government), 115,826

Sudan
Official name: Republic of the Sudan
Population: 40,650,000
Area: 967,500 sq mi (2,505,813 sq km)
Pop. density: 42/sq mi (16/sq km)
Capital: Khartoum (Al Kharṭūm), 947,483

Suriname
Official name: Republic of Suriname
Population: 480,000
Area: 63,037 sq mi (163,265 sq km)
Pop. density: 7.6/sq mi (2.9/sq km)
Capital: Paramaribo, 241,000

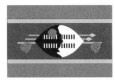

Swaziland
Official name: Kingdom of Swaziland
Population: 1,125,000
Area: 6,704 sq mi (17,364 sq km)
Pop. density: 168/sq mi (65/sq km)
Capital: Mbabane (administrative), 57,992,
   and Lobamba (legislative)

Sweden
Official name: Kingdom of Sweden
Population: 9,050,000
Area: 173,732 sq mi (449,964 sq km)
Pop. density: 52/sq mi (20/sq km)
Capital: Stockholm, 674,452

Switzerland
Official name: Swiss Confederation
Population: 7,595,000
Area: 15,943 sq mi (41,293 sq km)
Pop. density: 476/sq mi (184/sq km)
Capital: Bern (Berne), 136,338

Syria
Official name: Syrian Arab Republic
Population: 19,965,000
Area: 71,498 sq mi (185,180 sq km)
Pop. density: 279/sq mi (108/sq km)
Capital: Damascus (Dimashq), 1,549,932

Taiwan
Official name: Republic of China
Population: 22,950,000
Area: 13,901 sq mi (36,002 sq km)
Pop. density: 1,651/sq mi (637/sq km)
Capital: T'aipei, 2,641,856

Tajikistan
Official name: Republic of Tajikistan
Population: 7,280,000
Area: 55,251 sq mi (143,100 sq km)
Pop. density: 132/sq mi (51/sq km)
Capital: Dushanbe, 562,000

Tanzania
Official name: United Republic of Tanzania
Population: 40,630,000
Area: 364,900 sq mi (945,087 sq km)
Pop. density: 111/sq mi (43/sq km)
Capital: Dar es Salaam (de facto), 2,497,940, and Dodoma (legislative), 149,180

Thailand
Official name: Kingdom of Thailand
Population: 65,705,000
Area: 198,115 sq mi (513,115 sq km)
Pop. density: 332/sq mi (128/sq km)
Capital: Bangkok (Krung Thep), 6,355,144

Togo
Official name: Republic of Togo
Population: 5,940,000
Area: 21,925 sq mi (56,785 sq km)
Pop. density: 271/sq mi (105/sq km)
Capital: Lomé, 450,000

Tonga
Official name: Kingdom of Tonga
Population: 120,000
Area: 251 sq mi (650 sq km)
Pop. density: 478/sq mi (185/sq km)
Capital: Nuku'alofa, 22,400

Trinidad and Tobago
Official name: Republic of Trinidad and Tobago
Population: 1,230,000
Area: 1,980 sq mi (5,128 sq km)
Pop. density: 621/sq mi (240/sq km)
Capital: Port of Spain, 50,878

Tunisia
Official name: Republic of Tunisia
Population: 10,435,000
Area: 63,170 sq mi (163,610 sq km)
Pop. density: 165/sq mi (64/sq km)
Capital: Tunis, 702,330

Turkey
Official name: Republic of Turkey
Population: 76,300,000
Area: 302,541 sq mi (783,577 sq km)
Pop. density: 252/sq mi (97/sq km)
Capital: Ankara, 2,559,471

Turkmenistan
Official name: Turkmenistan
Population: 4,855,000
Area: 188,457 sq mi (488,100 sq km)
Pop. density: 26/sq mi (9.9/sq km)
Capital: Ashgabat, 557,600

Tuvalu
Official name: Tuvalu
Population: 12,000
Area: 10 sq mi (26 sq km)
Pop. density: 1,200/sq mi (462/sq km)
Capital: Funafuti, 2,191

Uganda
Official name: Republic of Uganda
Population: 31,935,000
Area: 93,065 sq mi (241,038 sq km)
Pop. density: 343/sq mi (132/sq km)
Capital: Kampala, 1,208,544

Ukraine
Official name: Ukraine
Population: 45,845,000
Area: 233,090 sq mi (603,700 sq km)
Pop. density: 197/sq mi (76/sq km)
Capital: Kiev (Kyyiv), 2,630,000

United Arab Emirates
Official name: United Arab Emirates
Population: 4,710,000
Area: 32,278 sq mi (83,600 sq km)
Pop. density: 146/sq mi (56/sq km)
Capital: Abū Ẓaby (Abu Dhabi), 552,000

United Kingdom
Official name: United Kingdom of Great Britain and Northern Ireland
Population: 61,030,000
Area: 93,788 sq mi (242,910 sq km)
Pop. density: 651/sq mi (251/sq km)
Capital: London, 7,650,944

United States
Official name: United States of America
Population: 305,710,000
Area: 3,794,083 sq mi (9,826,630 sq km)
Pop. density: 81/sq mi (31/sq km)
Capital: Washington, 572,059

Uruguay
Official name: Oriental Republic of Uruguay
Population: 3,485,000
Area: 67,574 sq mi (175,016 sq km)
Pop. density: 52/sq mi (20/sq km)
Capital: Montevideo, 1,269,552

Uzbekistan
Official name: Republic of Uzbekistan
Population: 27,475,000
Area: 172,742 sq mi (447,400 sq km)
Pop. density: 159/sq mi (61/sq km)
Capital: Tashkent, 2,113,300

Vanuatu
Official name: Republic of Vanuatu
Population: 215,000
Area: 4,707 sq mi (12,190 sq km)
Pop. density: 46/sq mi (18/sq km)
Capital: Port Vila, 19,311

Vatican City
Official name: State of the Vatican City
Population: 800
Area: 0.2 sq mi (0.4 sq km)
Pop. density: 4,000/sq mi (2,000/sq km)
Capital: Vatican City, 800

Venezuela
Official name: Bolivarian Republic of
Venezuela
Population: 26,615,000
Area: 352,145 sq mi (912,050 sq km)
Pop. density: 76/sq mi (29/sq km)
Capital: Caracas, 1,822,465

Vietnam
Official name: Socialist Republic of Vietnam
Population: 86,545,000
Area: 128,066 sq mi (331,689 sq km)
Pop. density: 676/sq mi (261/sq km)
Capital: Hanoi, 905,939

Yemen
Official name: Republic of Yemen
Population: 23,410,000
Area: 203,850 sq mi (527,968 sq km)
Pop. density: 115/sq mi (44/sq km)
Capital: Şan'ā', 427,150

Zambia
Official name: Republic of Zambia
Population: 11,765,000
Area: 290,586 sq mi (752,614 sq km)
Pop. density: 40/sq mi (16/sq km)
Capital: Lusaka, 1,084,703

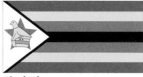

Zimbabwe
Official name: Republic of Zimbabwe
Population: 11,305,000
Area: 150,873 sq mi (390,759 sq km)
Pop. density: 75/sq mi (29/sq km)
Capital: Harare (Salisbury), 1,189,103

Introduction to the Maps and Legend

Continental and regional coverage of the world's land areas is provided by the following section of thematic maps and physical-political reference maps. The reference map section falls into a continental arrangement: North America, South America, Europe, Africa, Asia, and Oceania. Introducing each regional reference map section are several basic thematic maps.

To aid the reader in understanding the relative sizes of continents and of some of the countries and regions, uniform scales for comparable areas were used as far as possible. Most of the world is covered by a series of regional maps at scales of 1:16,000,000 and 1:12,000,000. Maps at 1:10,000,000 provide even greater detail for parts of Europe. The United States and parts of South America are mapped at 1:4,000,000.

Many of the symbols used are self-explanatory. A complete legend below provides a key to the symbols on the reference maps in the atlas.

The color tints on the maps depict the varying elevations and depths of land areas and bodies of water. The Relief legend that accompanies each map shows the specific elevation or depth that each color tint represents.

The surface configuration is represented by hill-shading, which gives the three-dimensional impression of landforms. This terrain representation is superimposed on the layer tints to convey a realistic and readily visualized impression of the surface. The combination of altitudinal tints and hill-shading best shows elevation, relief, steepness of slope, and ruggedness of terrain.

If the world used one alphabet and language, no particular difficulty would arise in understanding place-names. However, some of the people of the world, the Chinese and the Japanese, for example, use nonalphabetic languages. Their symbols are transliterated into the Roman alphabet. In this atlas, a "local-name" policy generally was used for naming cities, towns, and all local topographic and water features. However, for a few major cities the Anglicized name was preferred and the local name given in parentheses: for instance, Moscow (Moskva), Vienna (Wien), Bangkok (Krung Thep). In countries where more than one official language is used, a name appears in the dominant local language. The generic parts of local names for topographic and water features are self-explanatory in many cases because of the associated map symbols or type styles. A complete list of foreign generic names is given in the Glossary.

Physical-Political Reference Map Legend

Cultural Features

Political Boundaries

(over water)	International (Demarcated, Undemarcated, and Administrative)
	Disputed de facto
	Claim Boundary
	Indefinite or Undefined
(over water)	Secondary, State, Provincial, etc.
	Parks, Indian Reservations
	City Limits — Urbanized Areas
□	Neighborhoods, Sections of City

Populated Places

◉	1,000,000 and over
◎	250,000 to 1,000,000
⊙	100,000 to 250,000
•	25,000 to 100,000
○	0 to 25,000
TŌKYŌ	National Capitals
Boise	Secondary Capitals

Note: On maps at 1:20,000,000 and smaller the town symbols do not follow the specific population classification shown above. On all maps, type size indicates the relative importance of the city.

Transportation

	Railroads
	Railroads On 1:1,000,000 scale maps
	Railroad Ferries
	Roads On 1:1,000,000 scale maps
Major	
Other	
Major	On 1:4,000,000 scale maps
Other	
	On other scale maps
	Caravan Routes
✈	Airports

Other Cultural Features

	Dams
	Pipelines
▲	Points of Interest
∴	Ruins

Land Features

△	Peaks, Spot Heights
⹀	Passes
	Sand
	Contours

Water Features

Lakes and Reservoirs

	Fresh Water
	Fresh Water: Intermittent
	Salt Water
	Salt Water: Intermittent

Other Water Features

	Salt Basins, Flats
	Swamps
	Ice Caps and Glaciers
	Rivers
	Intermittent Rivers
	Aqueducts and Canals
	Ship Channels
	Falls
	Rapids
	Springs
△	Water Depths
	Sand Bars
	Reefs

Note: Country populations used throughout the atlas are 2002 estimates based on 2001 U.S. Census Bureau figures and other available information. City populations in the continent "At a Glance" sections reflect the latest available official data.

West of Greenwich

Arctic Ocean

QUEEN ELIZABETH ISLANDS

GREENLAND

RUSSIA
UNITED
STATES

MACKENZIE

C A N A D A

BAFFIN
ISLAND

Arctic Circle

ICELAND

N O R T H

A M E R I C A

UNITED STATES

Chicago

New York

ROCKY MOUNTAINS

GREAT PLAINS

APPALACHIAN MOUNTAINS

PORTUGAL

Atlantic

GREAT
BASIN

Los Angeles

MISSISSIPPI

WESTERN
SAHARA

S

Pacific

Tropic of Cancer

MEXICO

Mexico City

WEST INDIES

Ocean

MAURI-
TANIA

Ocean

GUINEA

VENEZUELA

COLOMBIA

Equator

Equator

ARCHIPIÉLAGO DE COLÓN
GALÁPAGOS ISLANDS

Amazon

S O U T H

B R A Z I L

Pacific

A N D E S

PERU

A M E R I C A

BOLIVIA

Atlanti

Tropic of Capricorn

PARAGUAY

Ocean

Rio de Janeiro

A R G E N T I N A

URUGUAY

PAMPA

Buenos Aires

Ocean

A

Antarctic Circle

Southern   *Ocean*

150°   120°   90°   60°   30°

Terrain

Land Elevations in Profile

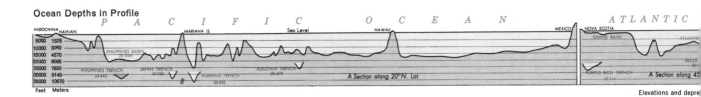

| OCEANIA | NORTH AMERICA | SOUTH AMERICA | AFRICA |

LOS ANDES

ATLAS

30000 9145

NEW ZEALAND   ALASKA RANGE   SIERRA NEVADA   Aconcagua (Vol.)
25000 7620

HAWAII   Mt. McKinley   CASCADE RANGE   Mt. Whitney   ROCKY MTS.   Pico de Orizaba   Chimborazo 20 702   Nev. Illimani   Jebel Toubkal 13 665   Ras Dashen 15 158
20000 6095   20 320   Mt. Rainier 14 410   14 494   Pikes Peak   18 406   Irazú (Vol.)   Nev. Illimani 20 741   Pico da Bandeira   Cameroon Mtn. 13 451

Aoraki Mauna Kea (Vol.)   14 110   Mt.   11 200   PLATEAU OF BOLIVIA   Nev. 482   IS. CANARIAS
15000 4570   12 316   13 796   GREAT   Mitchell HISPANIOLA   Pico de Teide
                TAHITI   BASIN   0 684 Pico Duarte   12 188
10000 3050   10 417
5000 1525   7 352
Feet Meters

Ocean Depths in Profile

P A C I F I C   O C E A N   A T L A N T I C

INDOCHINA HAINAN   MARIANA IS.   Sea Level   HAWAII   MEXICO   NOVA SCOTIA

5000 1525   GRAND BANK   ATLANTIC
10000 3050   PHILIPPINES BASIN
15000 4570   20 344
20000 6095   A Section along 20°N. Lat.   BRAZIL
25000 7620   PHILIPPINES TRENCH   JAPAN TRENCH   ALEUTIAN TRENCH
30000 9145   34 440   34 038   MARIANA TRENCH   26 574   PUERTO RICO TRENCH   A Section along 45
35000 10670   35 810   26 374
Feet Meters

Elevations and depre

Map Labels

Arctic Ocean

NORWAY
SWEDEN
FINLAND
Berlin
POLAND
BELARUS
GERMANY
Moscow
Volga
Ob'
RUSSIA
Arctic Circle
UKRAINE
EUROPE
ITALY
Rome
ROMANIA
Black Sea
TURKEY
Caspian Sea
KAZAKHSTAN
ASIA
MONGOLIA
GOBI
Mediterranean Sea
SYRIA
Tehran
TURKMENISTAN
Beijing
JAPAN
CHINA
Tokyo
LIBYA
Cairo
EGYPT
ISRAEL
IRAQ
IRAN
SAUDI ARABIA
PAKISTAN
HIMALAYAS
Shanghai
Pacific
Red Sea
Nile
Ganges
INDIA
BNGL.
Tropic of Cancer
Ocean
NIGER
CHAD
SUDAN
Kolkata
MYANMAR
THAILAND
VIETNAM
AFRICA
NIGERIA
CENTRAL AFRICAN REPUBLIC
ETHIOPIA
SOMALIA
Mumbai
CMBR.
PHILIPPINES
GABON
CONGO
Congo
DEM. REP. OF THE CONGO
ZAIRE
RIFT VALLEY
MT Victoria
TANZANIA
Equator
MALAYSIA
Equator
PAPUA NEW GUINEA
ANGOLA
ZAMBIA
Jakarta
INDONESIA
ZIMBABWE
MOZAMBIQUE
MADAGASCAR
SUMATRA
EAST TIMOR
TIMOR
NAMIBIA
KALAHARI DESERT
BOTSWANA
Indian
GREAT SANDY DESERT
GREAT DIVIDING RANGE
SOUTH AFRICA
Cape Town
Tropic of Capricorn
Ocean
GREAT VICTORIA DESERT
AUSTRALIA
Sydney
NEW ZEALAND

Southern Ocean
Antarctic Circle
ANTARCTICA

30° 60° 90° 120° 150°

A-510000-792

© Rand McNally & Co.

Scale

| 0 | 1000 | 2000 Mi. |
| 0 | 1000 | 2000 Km. |

Scale

Elevation Profile (Top)

EUROPE ASIA OCEANIA

	Meters	Feet
	9145	30000
	7620	25000
	6095	20000
	4570	15000
	3050	10000
	1525	5000

ALPS
Mt. Blanc 15,771
CAUCASUS
Gora El'brus 18,510
Qollah-ye Damavand 18,386
ELBURZ
K2 28,250
Everest 29,028
Kanchenjunga 28,208
Gongga Shan 24,790
PYRENEES
Pico de Aneto
KJÖLEN
PAMIRS
PLATEAU OF TIBET
SUMATRA
BORNEO
NEW GUINEA
AUSTRALIA
Glittertinden 8110
Etna (Vol.) 10,902
Dj. esh-Sheikh (Hermon) 9232
HIMALAYAS
Fuji-San (Vol.) 12,388
Klyuchevskaya 15,584
JAVA
Kinabalu 13,455
Mt. Apo 9692
Puncak Jaya 16,503
MADAGASCAR
Maromokoro 9436
Hekla (Vol.) 4892
Norodnaya 5217
IRAN
Pidurutalagala 8291
SRI LANKA
GOBI DESERT
Semeru 12,000
MYANMAR
12,467

Cross Section (Bottom)

MEDITERRANEAN SEA INDIAN OCEAN ARCTIC OCEAN PACIFIC OCEAN

FRANCE
GIBRALTAR
MALTA
ISRAEL
Sea Level
SOEMBA
NORTH POLE
65°N
65°S
LITTLE AMERICA
SOUTH POLE

A Section along 10°S. Lat.

in feet

Meters	Feet
1525	5000
3050	10000
4570	15000
6095	20000
7620	25000
9145	30000
10670	35000

Meters Feet

World Climate Map

World Climate Zones

Tropical
- Tropical rain forest
- Tropical savanna

Dry
- Steppe
- Desert

Temperate - Mild and rainy winter
- Mediterranean
- Humid subtropical
- Marine West Coast

Temperate - Cold and snowy winter
- Humid continental, warm summer
- Humid continental, cool summer
- Subarctic

Polar
- Tundra
- Ice cap
- Highlands

© Rand McNally & Co.
N-ANS10000-C1- - -1- -4

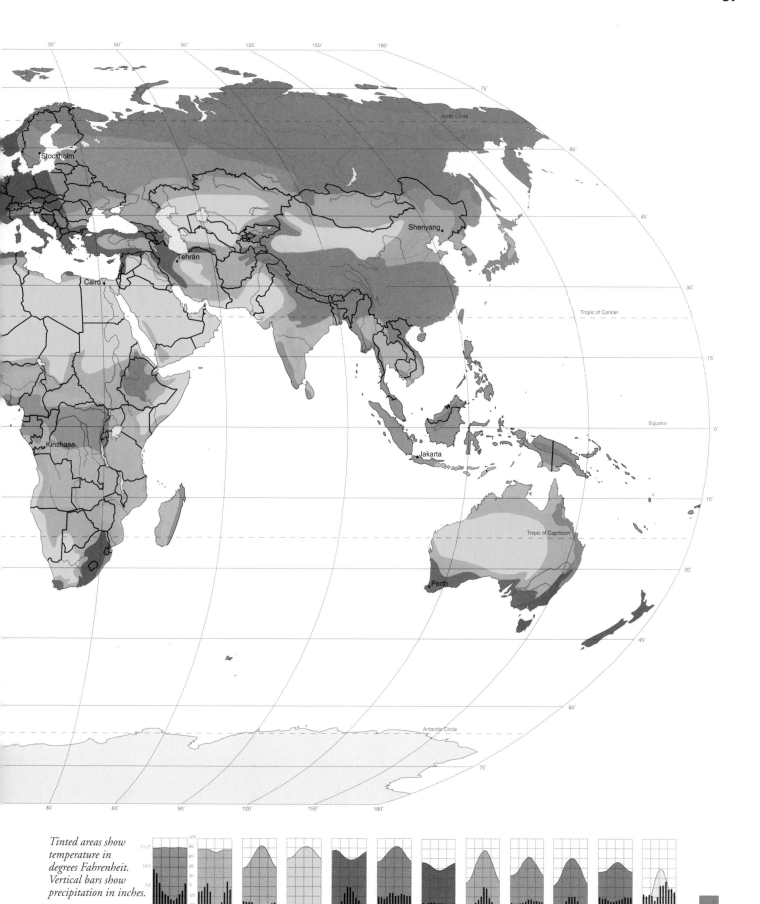

Tinted areas show temperature in degrees Fahrenheit. Vertical bars show precipitation in inches.

Jakarta
Hot and rainy

Kinshasa
Hot with rainy and dry seasons

Tehrān
Semiarid

Cairo
Very dry

Perth
Hot, dry summer / mild, rainy winter

Houston
Warm, humid summer / mild winter

Punta Arenas
Mild and rainy

Shenyang
Warm, humid summer / cold, snowy winter

Stockholm
Cool, humid summer / cold, snowy winter

Edmonton
Short, cool, humid summer / very cold, snowy winter

Reykjavík
Cold and dry

Nord
Very cold, perpetual frost

Extensive uplands
Climate varies with elevation and latitude

World Vegetation Map

180° 150° 120° 90° 60° 30°

75°

Arctic Circle

60°

45°

ROCKY MOUNTAINS

Great Plains

APPALACHIAN MTS.

New York

30°

Tropic of Cancer

15°

Mexico City

0° Equator

Amazon Basin

15°

ANDES MOUNTAINS

Tropic of Capricorn

Rio de Janeiro

30°

Buenos Aires

Patagonia

45°

© Rand McNally & Co.
N-ANS10000-E1- -1-2-4

60°

Antarctic Circle

75°

180° 150° 120° 90° 60° 30°

Vegetation Regions

| ■ Tropical and sub-tropical forests | ■ Savanna | □ Desert | ■ Mediterranean | ■ Temperate grassland |

Temperate forest

Taiga (northern forests)

Tundra (lichen and moss)

Mountain

Polar and high mountain

Map labels:

Siberia

URALS

Moscow

ALPS

Balkan Peninsula

Cairo

Arabian Peninsula

Congo Basin

MADAGASCAR

Johannesburg

Beijing

Tōkyō

HIMALAYAS

Great Sandy Desert

Sydney

Melbourne

Arctic Circle

Tropic of Cancer

Equator

Tropic of Capricorn

Antarctic Circle

30° 60° 90° 120° 150° 180°

75° 60° 45° 30° 15° 0° 15° 30° 45° 60° 75°

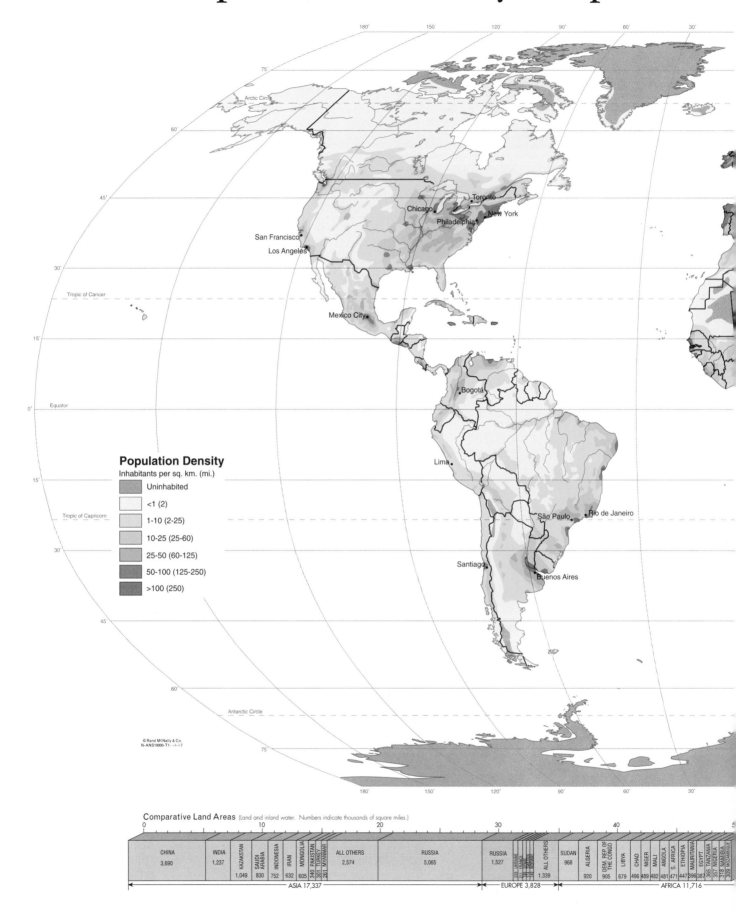

Population Density
Inhabitants per sq. km. (mi.)

	Uninhabited
	<1 (2)
	1-10 (2-25)
	10-25 (25-60)
	25-50 (60-125)
	50-100 (125-250)
	>100 (250)

© Rand McNally & Co.
N-ANS10000-T1-- --3-7

Comparative Land Areas (Land and inland water. Numbers indicate thousands of square miles.)

0		10							20		30				40		

| CHINA 3,690 | INDIA 1,237 | KAZAKSTAN 1,049 | SAUDI ARABIA 830 | INDONESIA 752 | IRAN 632 | MONGOLIA 605 | PAKISTAN 340 | TURKEY 301 | MYANMAR 261 | ALL OTHERS 2,574 | RUSSIA 5,065 | RUSSIA 1,527 | UKRAINE 233 | FRANCE | SPAIN | SWEDEN | GERMANY | FINLAND | ALL OTHERS 1,339 | SUDAN 968 | ALGERIA 920 | DEM. REP. OF THE CONGO 905 | LIBYA 679 | CHAD 496 | NIGER 489 | MALI 482 | ANGOLA 481 | S. AFRICA 471 | ETHIOPIA 447 | MAURITANIA 396 | EGYPT 387 | TANZANIA 365 | NIGERIA 357 | NAMIBIA 318 | MOZAMBIQUE 309 |

| ASIA 17,337 | EUROPE 3,828 | AFRICA 11,716 |

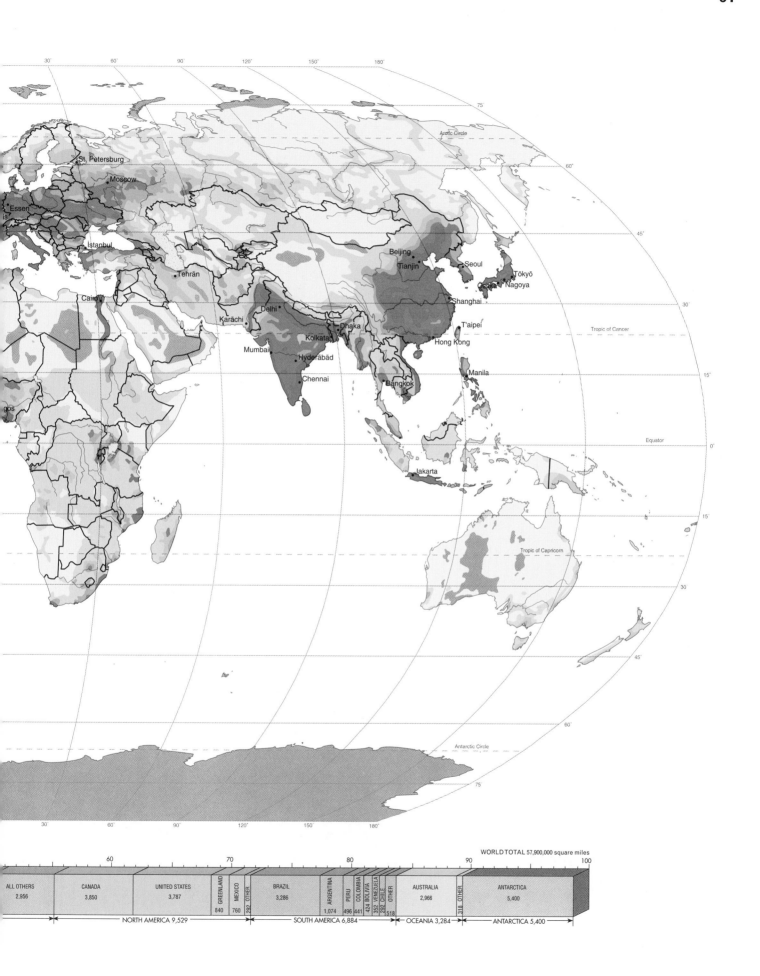

St. Petersburg
Moscow
Essen
is
İstanbul
Tehrān
Cairo
Karāchi
Delhi
Mumbai
Hyderābād
Chennai
Kolkata
Dhaka
Bangkok
Beijing
Tianjin
Seoul
Tōkyō
Osaka Nagoya
Shanghai
T'aipei
Hong Kong
Manila
Jakarta
gos

Arctic Circle
Tropic of Cancer
Equator
Tropic of Capricorn
Antarctic Circle

WORLD TOTAL 57,900,000 square miles

ALL OTHERS 2,956	CANADA 3,850	UNITED STATES 3,787	GREENLAND 840	MEXICO 760	OTHER 292	BRAZIL 3,286	ARGENTINA 1,074	PERU 496	COLOMBIA 441	BOLIVIA 424	VENEZUELA 352	CHILE 292	OTHER 518	AUSTRALIA 2,966	OTHER 318	ANTARCTICA 5,400

NORTH AMERICA 9,529
SOUTH AMERICA 6,884
OCEANIA 3,284
ANTARCTICA 5,400

World Environments Map

© Rand McNally & Co.
N-ANS10900-M1- -1-1-4

Environments

Urban

Cropland

Cropland, woodland

Cropland,
grazing land

Grassland,
grazing land

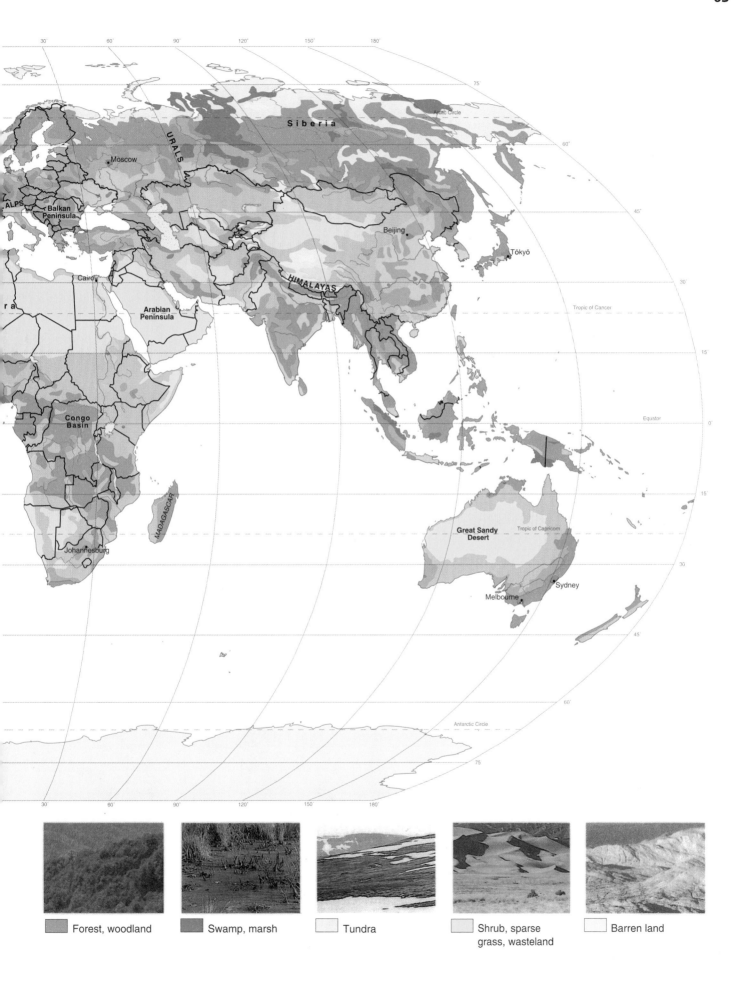

Forest, woodland	Swamp, marsh	Tundra	Shrub, sparse grass, wasteland	Barren land

World Time Zones Map

Time Zone variations

...h ...min	hours, minutes
	Time varies from the standard time zone by half an hour
	Time varies from the standard time zone by other than half an hour

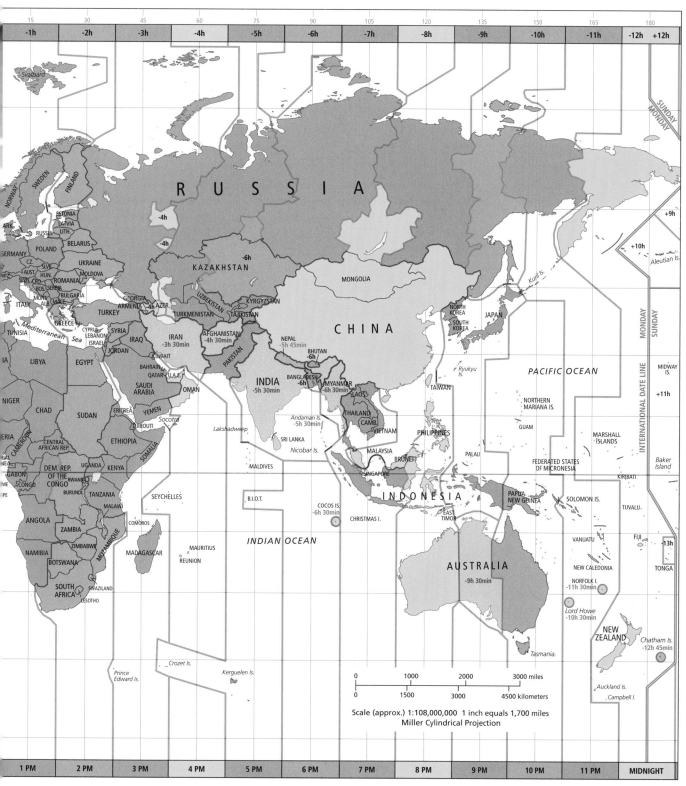

The standard time zone system, fixed by international agreement and by law in each country, is based on a theoretical division of the globe into 24 zones of 15° longitude each. The mid-meridian of each zone fixes the hour for the entire zone. The zero time zone extends 7½° east and 7½° west of the Greenwich meridian, 0° longitude. Since the earth rotates toward the east, time zones to the west of Greenwich are earlier, to the east, later. Plus and minus hours at the top of the map are added to or subtracted from local time to find Greenwich time.

Local standard time can be determined for any area in the world by adding one hour for each time zone counted in an easterly direction from one's own, or by subtracting one hour for each zone counted in a westerly direction. To separate one day from the next, the 180th meridian has been designated as the international date line. On both sides of the line the time of day is the same, but west of the line it is one day later than it is to the east. Countries that adhere to the international zone system adopt the zone applicable to their location. Some countries, however, establish time zones based on political boundaries, or adopt the time zone of a neighboring unit. For all or part of the year some countries also advance their time by one hour, thereby utilizing more daylight hours each day.

North America

North America is the world's third-largest continent, covering an area of 9.5 million square miles (24.7 million sq km). It lies primarily between the Arctic Circle and the Tropic of Cancer, and comes within 500 miles (800 km) of both the North Pole and the Equator. The continent's western flank is dominated by the spectacular Rocky Mountains. Covering vast stretches of the central United States and Canada are the fertile Great Plains, a large part of which is drained by the Mississippi River and its tributaries.

In the north, Hudson Bay is frozen for much of the year. Mexico, located in the continent's southern third, is mostly mountainous and dry, but farther south, the climate is wet. Many of the small Central American countries have volcanoes along the Pacific Coast.

North America at a glance

Land area:
9,500,000 square miles (24,700,000 sq km)

Estimated population:
531,180,000

Population density:
56/square mile (22/sq km)

Mean elevation:
2,000 feet (610 m)

Highest point:
Mt. McKinley, Alaska, U.S.,
20,320 feet (6,194 m)

Lowest point:
Death Valley, California, U.S.,
282 feet (86 m) below sea level

Longest river:
Mississippi-Missouri, 3,740 mi (6,019 km)

**Number of countries
(incl. dependencies):** 37

Largest independent country:
Canada, 3,855,103 square miles
(9,984,670 sq km)

Smallest independent country:
St. Kitts and Nevis, 101 square miles
(261 sq km)

Most populous independent country:
United States, 305,710,000

Least populous independent country:
St. Kitts and Nevis, 40,000

Most populous metropolitan area:
New York-Newark, United States,
population 19 million

Lake Louise in the Canadian Rockies

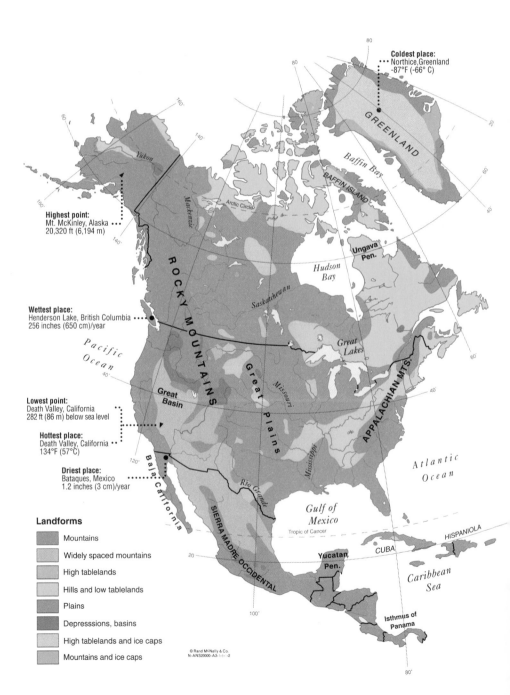

Coldest place:
Northice, Greenland
-87°F (-66° C)

Highest point:
Mt. McKinley, Alaska
20,320 ft (6,194 m)

Wettest place:
Henderson Lake, British Columbia
256 inches (650 cm)/year

Lowest point:
Death Valley, California
282 ft (86 m) below sea level

Hottest place:
Death Valley, California
134°F (57°C)

Driest place:
Bataques, Mexico
1.2 inches (3 cm)/year

Landforms

- Mountains
- Widely spaced mountains
- High tablelands
- Hills and low tablelands
- Plains
- Depresssions, basins
- High tablelands and ice caps
- Mountains and ice caps

© Rand McNally & Co.
N-ANS20000-A3-1-1--2

Climate

North America contains almost every type of climate that can be found in the world. Ice and tundra cover northern Canada and Greenland. Much of the central and eastern parts of the U.S. and Canada are temperate, with great seasonal changes marked by warm summers and cold winters. The Pacific Ocean moderates weather changes along the west coast, where it is cool and wet in the north and warm and dry in the south. Desert and semi-desert cover much of the southwestern U.S. and Mexico. The tropical southern region of the continent and the islands of the Caribbean Sea are hot and rainy.

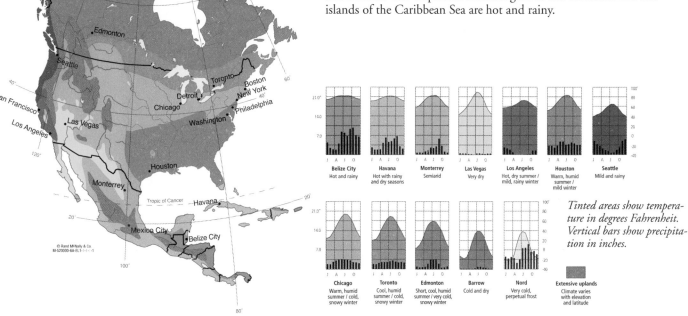

Belize City	Havana	Monterrey	Las Vegas	Los Angeles	Houston	Seattle
Hot and rainy	Hot with rainy and dry seasons	Semiarid	Very dry	Hot, dry summer / mild, rainy winter	Warm, humid summer / mild winter	Mild and rainy

Chicago	Toronto	Edmonton	Barrow	Nord	Extensive uplands
Warm, humid summer / cold, snowy winter	Cool, humid summer / cold, snowy winter	Short, cool, humid summer / very cold, snowy winter	Cold and dry	Very cold, perpetual frost	Climate varies with elevation and latitude

Tinted areas show temperature in degrees Fahrenheit. Vertical bars show precipitation in inches.

Population

About 60% of all North Americans live in the United States, the world's third most-populous country. Canada is the continent's largest country, but one of the world's least densely populated; most Canadians live within 100 miles (160 km) of the country's southern border. Mexico, with approximately 20% of North America's inhabitants, has one of the world's largest and fastest growing metropolitan areas, Mexico City, which is home to almost 20 million people.

Canada is populated mostly by descendants of French and British settlers, as well as native Americans, such as the Inuit (Eskimos) of the far north. The United States' populace reflects the country's diverse history of immigration, with European ancestry being the most common. The people of Mexico and Central America trace their origins to Spaniards and Native Americans. The population of the Caribbean islands includes many descendants of African slaves and European settlers.

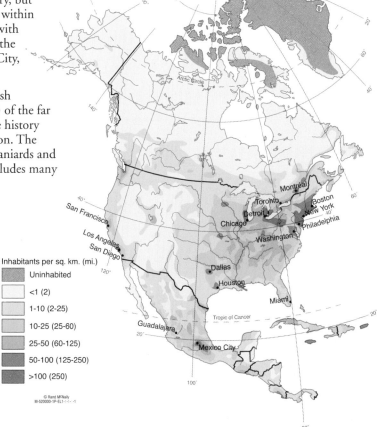

Inhabitants per sq. km. (mi.)

	Uninhabited
	<1 (2)
	1-10 (2-25)
	10-25 (25-60)
	25-50 (60-125)
	50-100 (125-250)
	>100 (250)

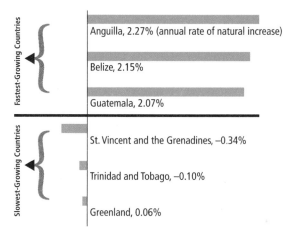

Fastest-Growing Countries

Anguilla, 2.27% (annual rate of natural increase)

Belize, 2.15%

Guatemala, 2.07%

Slowest-Growing Countries

St. Vincent and the Grenadines, −0.34%

Trinidad and Tobago, −0.10%

Greenland, 0.06%

Environments and Land Use

Although only 12% of the continent is suitable for agriculture, North America is the world's leading food producer. Unlike other parts of the world, famine is virtually unknown. Large quantities of food, such as grains from the central U.S. and Canada, are exported worldwide. Sixteen percent of the continent is used for grazing, and the livestock raised on these lands are also an important source of food at home and abroad.

Forests cover one-third of the land, and the timber and paper industries are important to the U.S. and Canada. The continent has an extremely long coastline, and many countries send great fishing fleets to sea. This is especially true of Canada, whose eastern-most provinces are fittingly known as the Maritime Provinces. However, sharp declines in catches due to overfishing have put the industry in economic turmoil.

Blue waters, sunny skies, and idyllic beaches draw millions of tourists to the Caribbean each year. While tourism provides income for island countries that have few other assets, the economic gap between the visitors and the people who serve them remains dramatic.

One of the greatest challenges facing North America in the coming decades is a familiar one: coping with a growing population and dwindling resources. Pollution and the environment are divisive issues. Although the United States has begun to clean up its air and water, economic pressures will continue to be an argument for a relaxation of policies. Meanwhile, in Mexico, environmental issues have been pushed aside by concerns about the economy and the exploding population.

Field of corn in the midwestern United States

Urban

Cropland

Cropland and woodland

Cropland and grazing land

Grassland, grazing land

Forest, woodland

Swamp, marsh

Tundra

Shrub, sparse grass, wasteland

Barren land

© Rand McNally & Co.
N-AMS20000-M1- -/-2-1

| 0 | 200 | 400 | 600 | 800 | 1000 Miles |

| 0 | 300 | 600 | 900 | 1200 | 1500 Kilometers |

Urbanization in North America

Seen from the air, large portions of North America still bear the checkerboard imprint left by the people who settled the continent: a vast array of small farms that could be worked by one man and a horse. As industrialization swept through the United States in the second half of the 19th century, many farmers left their farms. Great numbers moved to fast-growing cities such as Chicago and St. Louis. Many small towns saw their populations dwindle.

In the cities, change was continuous. The former farm families were joined by waves of European immigrants. Over the next 100 years, urban populations continued to grow, and cities that had once been separate became part of vast urban megalopolises. An example can be seen in the eastern United States, where a band of urban centers stretches almost continuously from Boston south through New York City to Washington D.C. (see map at right). After World War II, as the U.S. middle class expanded, large numbers of families moved out of the city centers into suburban communities of mass-produced, affordable homes. Many of those who remained were economically disadvantaged. A shrinking tax base meant that cities could not support their infrastructures, and conditions in the inner cities worsened. In the suburbs the opposite was true: vast sums were spent building new roads, houses, and shopping centers.

The same process that transformed the U.S. is now occurring in Mexico. In 1945, 25% of the population was considered urban, but today the figure surpasses 70% (see graph above). Not content to lead lives as subsistence farmers, scores of Mexicans arrive in the cities each day in search of jobs that will enable them to provide a better life for their families.

Sadly, these dreams are often elusive. Most of the people end up in low-paying jobs, with their meager wages going to pay for the food that they once grew themselves. City officials are hard-pressed to provide clean water to their ever-growing populations, let alone electricity, transportation, and education.

As elsewhere in the world, coping with the pressures of growing populations is one of the greatest challenges facing North Americans today.

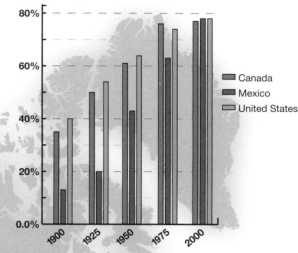

Rising Urban Population

Urban population as a percentage of total population, 1900-2000

Legend:
- Canada
- Mexico
- United States

(The definition of "urban" varies from country to country. In Canada, all towns with more than 1,000 people are considered urban, while in the U.S. and Mexico only towns with more than 2,500 people are defined as urban.)

Mexico City, whose metropolitan area population exceeds 20 million, sprawls toward the distant mountains.

Scale 1:40 000 000; one inch to 630 miles. Lambert's Azimuthal Equal Area Projection
Elevations and depressions are given in feet

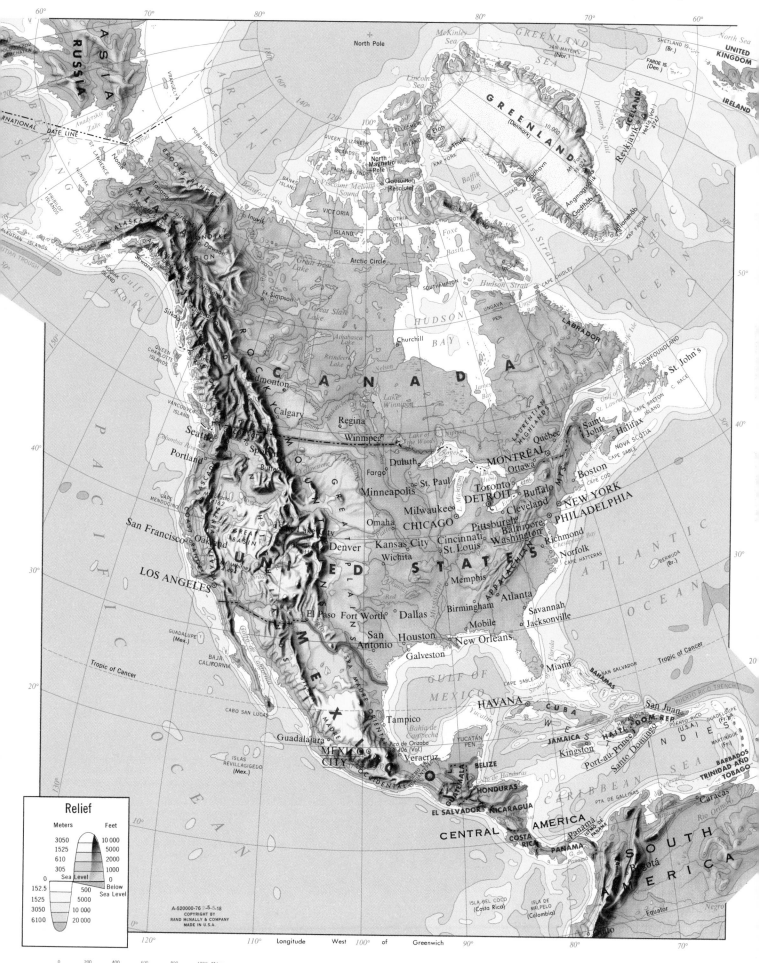

Relief

Meters	Feet
3050	10 000
1525	5000
610	2000
305	1000
0 Sea Level	0
152.5	500
1525	5000
3050	10 000
6100	20 000

Below Sea Level

A-520000-76 2-5-S-18
COPYRIGHT BY
RAND McNALLY & COMPANY
MADE IN U.S.A.

Scale 1:40 000 000; one inch to 630 miles. Lambert's Azimuthal Equal Area Projection
Elevations and depressions are given in feet

| 0 | 200 | 400 | 600 | 800 | 1000 Miles |
| 0 | 400 | 800 | 1200 | 1600 Kilometers |

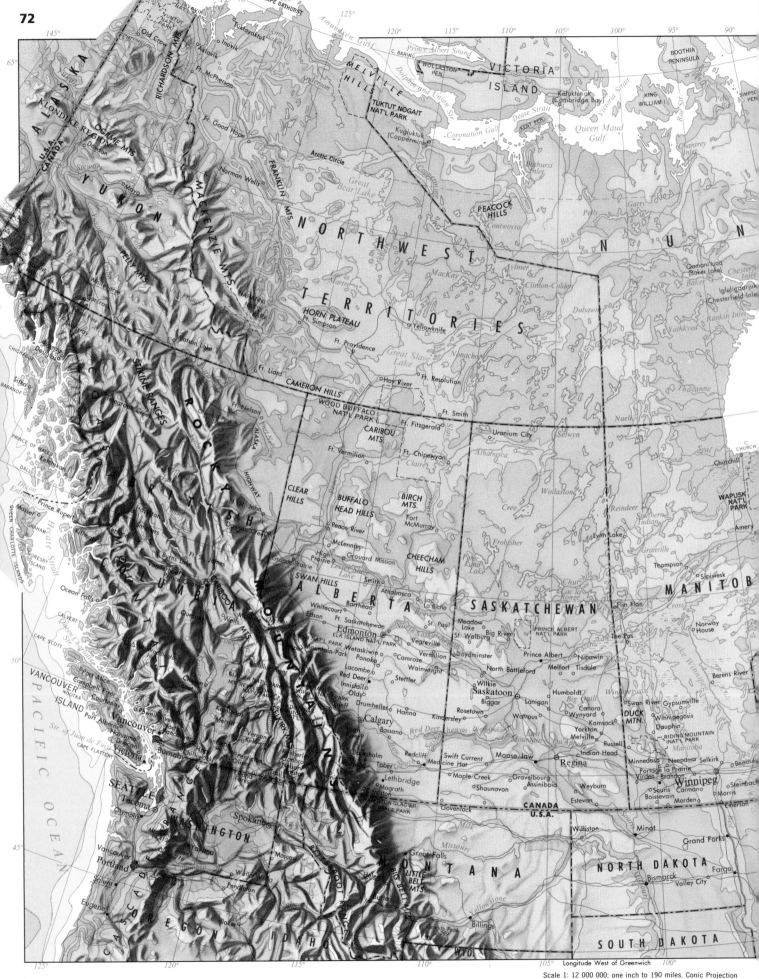

Scale 1: 12 000 000; one inch to 190 miles. Conic Projection
Elevations and depressions are given in feet

Longitude West of Greenwich

a

Longitude West of Greenwich

QUEBEC

NEWFOUNDLAND AND LABRADOR

Same scale as main map

CAPE BAULD

Gulf of St. Lawrence

GROS MORNE NAT'L PARK
Deer Lake
Corner Brook
Stephenville
Grand Falls
Botwood
Windsor
Gander
TERRA NOVA NAT'L PARK
Twillingate
Bonavista

NEWFOUNDLAND
St. George's
Trinity

Channel-Port-aux-Basques
Grand Bank
Burin

ST. PIERRE AND MIQUELON (Fr.)

St. John's

CAPE BRETON ISLAND

ATLANTIC OCEAN

Relief

Meters		Feet
3050		10 000
1525		5000
610		2000
305		1000
152.5		500
Sea Level		0
152.5		500
1525		5000
3050		10 000

A-520200-76
COPYRIGHT BY
RAND McNALLY & COMPANY
MADE IN U.S.A.

0   25 50 75 100   200   300   400   500 Miles
0   100   200   400   600   800 Kilometers

Scale 1:12 000 000; one inch to 190 miles. Polyconic Projection
Elevations and depressions are given in feet

PRINCE
EDWARD
ISLAND

O N T A R I O   Q U E B E C

NEW
BRUNSWICK

Kenora

Lake of the
Woods
QUETICO
PROV.
PARK

Cochrane

Chicoutimi

Chatham
Charlottetown

Campbellton

Moncton

NOVA
SCOTIA

Fredericton

Truro

International
Falls

Thunder Bay

ISLE ROYALE
NAT'L PARK

Sudbury

Roberval

LAURENTIDES
PROVINCIAL
PARK

Windsor
Halifax

C. SABLE

Hibbing   Virginia

Duluth

Superior

Ashland

Sault Ste. Marie

Sault Ste. Marie

North Bay

MONTAGNE
TREMBLANTE
PROVINCIAL
PARK

Québec

MONTRÉAL

Sherbrooke

St. Jean

M A I N E

Saint John

Calais

Bangor

ACADIA
NAT'L PARK

Yarmouth

MINNESOTA

St. Cloud

Hancock

Marquette
Escanaba

M I C H I G A N

Alpena

Owen
Sound

Georgian
Bay

Party Sound

ALGONQUIN
PROVINCIAL
PARK

Ottawa

Pembroke

Peterborough

TORONTO

Brockville
Kingston

Ogdensburg

Watertown

ADIRONDACK
MTS.

Champlain

Burlington

Montpelier

Plattsburgh

VT. N.H.

GREEN MTS.

Augusta

Washington
6288

Lewiston
Auburn

Portland

Portsmouth

Concord

Manchester

Nashua
Lynn

St. Paul

Eau
Claire

Wausau

Green
Bay

Marinette

Sheboygan

Saginaw
Bay

Bay City
Flint

Saginaw

Owen

Lake
Huron

Sarnia

Lake Ontario

Rochester
Syracuse

Utica

Troy

Schenectady
Albany

Springfield
Hartford

MASS.

Worcester
Providence

BOSTON

C. COD

New Bedford

NANTUCKET

MINNEAPOLIS

WISCONSIN

Appleton

Oshkosh

Fond du Lac

Madison

Muskegon
Grand
Rapids

Lansing

Pontiac

Port
Huron

Brantford

Hamilton

Niagara
Falls

BUFFALO

Jamestown

Binghamton

Ithaca

NEW YORK

CATSKILL
MTS.

Kingston

Poughkeepsie

Springfield

New
Haven

CONN. R.I.

Fall
River

Mankato
Winona

Rochester

La
Crosse

Beloit

Racine

Kenosha

Battle
Creek

Kalamazoo

Ann
Arbor

Jackson

Windsor

DETROIT

Lakewood

CLEVELAND

Erie

Youngstown

Scranton

Wilkes-
Barre

Allentown

Reading

Trenton

Jersey City
Newark

N.J.

NEW YORK

40°

Fort
Dodge

Mason City

I O W A

Waterloo
Dubuque

Cedar
Rapids

Rockford

Freeport
Waukegan

Elgin

Aurora

Gary

South
Bend

Toledo

Sandusky

Akron

Canton

PENN.

Johnstown
Altoona

Harrisburg

Lancaster

York

Wilmington

PHILADELPHIA

Camden

Atlantic City

Omaha

Des Moines

Iowa City

Davenport

CHICAGO

Hammond

Fort Wayne

Lima

O H I O

Columbus

Springfield

Dayton

Parkers-
burg

Cumberland

Hagerstown

BALTIMORE

Dover

Annapolis

MD.

DEL.

Delaware Bay

Council
Bluffs

Ottumwa

Burlington

Rock Island

Galesburg

Peoria

Bloomington

Logansport

Lafayette

Marion

Muncie

I N D I A N A

Indianapolis

Hamilton

CINCINNATI

WEST

WASHINGTON
D.C.

Alexandria

SHENANDOAH
NAT'L PARK

Kirksville

St. Joseph

Quincy

Hannibal

Decatur

Springfield

I L L I N O I S

Champaign

Terre Haute

Covington

Newport

Portsmouth

Huntington

VIRGINIA

Charleston

Frankfort

VIRGINIA

Lynchburg

Charlottes-
ville

Richmond

James

Kansas City

Moberly

Columbia

Jacksonville

Mattoon

Vincennes

Evansville

Lexington

Roanoke

Petersburg

Newport News

KANSAS
CITY

ST. LOUIS

Sedalia

Jefferson City

Alton

East St. Louis

Louisville

Owensboro

K E N T U C K Y

Danville

Bristol

Portsmouth

Norfolk

35°

Fort
Scott

Pittsburg

M I S S O U R I

Cape Girardeau

Cairo

MAMMOTH
CAVE
NAT'L PARK

Bowling
Green

Hopkinsville

Paducah

Nashville

Johnson City

Bristol
Kingsport

Winston-
Salem

Greensboro

Durham

Raleigh

New Bern

C. HATTERAS

Joplin

Springfield

OZARK
PLATEAU

Wappapello
Res.

Bull Shoals
Res.

Jonesboro

Memphis

T E N N E S S E E

Chattanooga

Jackson

Knoxville

GREAT SMOKY MTS.
NAT'L PARK

Asheville

Mt. Mitchell
6684

N O R T H   C A R O L I N A

Charlotte

Rock Hill

Wilmington

Muskogee

BOSTON MTS.

Fort Smith

Helena

Florence

Gadsden

Rome

Athens

Greenville

Anderson

Spartanburg

Greenville

Columbia

SOUTH
CAROLINA

McAlester

Paris

A R K A N S A S

Hot Springs

Little Rock

OUACHITA MTS. NAT'L PARK

Pine
Bluff

Birmingham

Anniston

ATLANTA

La
Grange

Macon

Augusta

Charleston

Texarkana

El Dorado

Tuscaloosa

Selma

Montgomery

Columbus

Americus

G E O R G I A

Savannah

Marshall

Tyler

Monroe

Vicksburg

Jackson

Meridian

A L A B A M A

Albany

Waycross

Brunswick

Palestine

L O U I S I A N A

Alexandria

Natchez

Laurel

Hattiesburg

Mobile

Dothan

Tallahassee

Jacksonville

St. Augustine

30°

Beaumont

Lake
Charles

Lafayette

Baton
Rouge

Biloxi

Pensacola

F L O R I D A

Gainesville

Daytona Beach

HOUSTON

Port Arthur

Galveston

New Orleans

C. SAN BLAS

Apalachee
Bay

St. Johns

Sanford

CAPE CANAVERAL

G U L F   O F   M E X I C O

Orlando

Tampa

St. Petersburg

Tampa Bay

Lakeland

Okeechobee

W. Palm Beach

GT. ABACO

BAHAMAS

40,000 SQ MI
AREA

0   100   200

Miles

EVERGLADES
NAT'L PARK

MIAMI

25°

C. SABLE

ANDROS

Key West

FLORIDA KEYS

Straits of Florida

25 50 75 100   200   300   400   500 Miles

100   200   300   400   500   600   800 Kilometers

**Cities
and
Towns**

0 to 50,000   500,000 to 1,000,000

50,000 to 500,000   1,000,000 and over

Scale 1:12 000 000; one inch to 190 miles. Polyconic Project
Elevations and depressions are given in feet

PRINCE EDWARD ISLAND

C A N A D A

NEW BRUNSWICK

NOVA SCOTIA

Q U E B E C

Chicoutimi
Roberval
Campbellton
Chatham
Moncton
Charlottetown
Fredericton
Windsor
Halifax
Truro
Yarmouth
C. SABLE

LAURENTIDES PROVINCIAL PARK
Trois-Rivières
Québec
Sherbrooke
St. Jean
Montréal
MONTAGNE TREMBLANTE PROVINCIAL PARK

Cochrane

North Bay
Sudbury

O N T A R I O

Kenora
Lake of the Woods
QUETICO PROV. PARK
Rainy
International Falls
Thunder Bay
ISLE ROYALE NAT'L PARK
LAKE SUPERIOR
Marquette
Sault Ste. Marie
Sault Ste. Marie
Escanaba

Nipigon

ALGONQUIN PROVINCIAL PARK
Pembroke
Parry Sound
Ottawa
Nipissing
Georgian Bay
Owen Sound
Peterborough
Guelph
TORONTO
Hamilton
Brantford
Niagara Falls

Brockville
Kingston
Watertown
ADIRONDACK MTS.
Ogdensburg
Burlington
Montpelier
Concord
Augusta
MT. WASHINGTON 6288
Lewiston
Auburn
Portland
Portsmouth
Manchester
Nashua
Lowell
Lynn
BOSTON
Worcester
Providence
New Bedford
NANTUCKET
C. COD

Chaleur Bay

M A I N E
Calais
Saint John
Bay of Fundy
ACADIA NAT'L PARK
Bangor

N. H.
VT.
MASS.
CONN.
R. I.

Joliette
Sorel

Chateaugay

Roverval

St. Jean

Hibbing
Virginia
Duluth
Superior
Ashland
Hancock

M I C H I G A N

Alpena

LAKE HURON

LAKE MICHIGAN

LAKE ERIE
LAKE ONTARIO

Rochester
Syracuse
Utica
Schenectady
Troy
Albany
Springfield
Hartford
New Haven
Bridgeport
New York
Poughkeepsie
CATSKILL MTS.
Kingston
Binghamton
Olean
Jamestown

Buffalo
N E W Y O R K
Oswego

LONG I.

Scranton
Wilkes-Barre
Allentown
Reading
Trenton
PHILADELPHIA
Camden
Atlantic City

I N N E S O T A
St. Cloud
St. Paul
NNEAPOLIS
Mankato
Winona
Rochester

W I S C O N S I N
Eau Claire
Wausau
Green Bay
Appleton
Oshkosh
Sheboygan
Fond du Lac
Madison
MILWAUKEE
Racine
Kenosha
Beloit
Waukegan

Saginaw
Bay City
Flint
Pontiac
DETROIT
Ann Arbor
Windsor
Lansing
Grand Rapids
Muskegon
Kalamazoo
Battle Creek
Jackson
Port Huron

Port Hamilton

Erie
Ashtabula
Lakewood
CLEVELAND
Sandusky
Toledo
Youngstown
Akron
Canton
Johnstown
Altoona

P E N N.
Harrisburg
Lancaster
York
Wilmington
Dover
DEL.
BALTIMORE
Annapolis
MD.
WASHINGTON D.C.
Alexandria
Frederick
Hagerstown
Cumberland

Mason City
Fort Dodge
Waterloo
Dubuque
I O W A
Cedar Rapids
Rockford
Freeport
Elgin
Aurora
CHICAGO
Gary
Hammond
South Bend
Fort Wayne

Green Bay
La Crosse

Des Moines
Iowa City
Davenport
Rock Island
Galesburg
Peoria
Bloomington

Ottumwa
Burlington
Keokuk

I L L I N O I S
Champaign
Decatur
Springfield
Lafayette
Muncie
I N D I A N A
Indianapolis
Terre Haute

O H I O
Lima
Marion
Dayton
Springfield
Columbus
Hamilton
CINCINNATI
Covington
Newport
Portsmouth
Parkersburg
Clarksburg
W E S T
V I R G I N I A
SHENANDOAH NAT'L PARK
Charlottesville
Richmond

Kirksville
St. Joseph
Hannibal
Quincy
Moberly
Jacksonville
Mattoon
Columbia
Alton
KANSAS CITY
Sedalia
Jefferson City
ST. LOUIS
East St. Louis
Vincennes
Evansville
Louisville
Frankfort
Lexington
Huntington

M I S S O U R I
Owensboro
Cape Girardeau
Cairo
Paducah
Hopkinsville
Bowling Green
MAMMOTH CAVE NAT'L PARK
K E N T U C K Y

eka
poria
Fort Scott
ffeyville
Pittsburg

Joplin
Springfield
OZARK PLATEAU
Cape Girardeau

Charleston
NAT'L PARK

APPALACHIAN

Lynchburg
Roanoke
Danville
Petersburg
Portsmouth
Norfolk
Newport News
V I R G I N I A
James
C. HATTERAS

Bristol
Johnson City
Salem
Winston-Salem
Greensboro
Durham
Raleigh
New Bern
N O R T H C A R O L I N A
Knoxville
Asheville
GREAT SMOKY MTS. NAT'L PARK
MT. MITCHELL 6684
Spartanburg
Charlotte
Rock Hill

ulsa
Muskogee
BOSTON MTS.
Jonesboro
Fort Smith
McAlester

A R K A N S A S
Hot Springs
HOT SPRINGS NAT'L PARK
OUACHITA MTS. NAT'L PARK
Little Rock
Pine Bluff

T E N N E S S E E
Jackson
Memphis
Nashville
Chattanooga

Florence
Gadsden
Anniston
Rome
Athens
Greenville
Anderson
Columbia
S O U T H
C A R O L I N A
Wilmington

Helena

M I S S I S S I P P I
Greenville
Vicksburg
Jackson
Meridian
Natchez
Laurel
Hattiesburg

Paris
Texarkana
Texarkana
El Dorado
Marshall
Tyler
Palestine
Toledo Bend Res.

A L A B A M A
Birmingham
Tuscaloosa
Selma
Montgomery
Mobile

L O U I S I A N A
Alexandria
Monroe
Shreveport
Bayou Bodcau Res.
Lake Charles
Lafayette
Baton Rouge
Biloxi
New Orleans

Beaumont
Port Arthur
HOUSTON
Galveston

A T L A N T I C   O C E A N

ATLANTIC CITY
Delaware Bay

Charleston
Savannah
Brunswick

G E O R G I A
Columbus
Americus
Macon
Augusta
La Grange
ATLANTA
Albany
Waycross
Valdosta
Dothan

F L O R I D A
Tallahassee
Pensacola
Gainesville
Jacksonville
St. Augustine
Daytona Beach
Sanford
Orlando
Lakeland
Tampa
St. Petersburg
Tampa Bay
Lake Okeechobee
W. Palm Beach
MIAMI
EVERGLADES NAT'L PARK
C. SABLE
Key West
FLORIDA KEYS
Straits of Florida

CAPE CANAVERAL

G U L F   O F   M E X I C O

BAHAMAS
GT. ABACO
ANDROS

Relief

Meters		Feet
3050		10 000
1525		5000
610		2000
305		1000
152.5		500
0	Sea Level	0
		Below Sea Level
152.5		500
1525		5 000
3050		10 000
6100		20 000

0   25   50   75   100   200   300   400   500 Miles
0   100   200   400   600   800 Kilometers

Cities and Towns

0 to 50,000 ○   500,000 to 1,000,000 ⊚
50,000 to 500,000 ⊙   1,000,000 and over

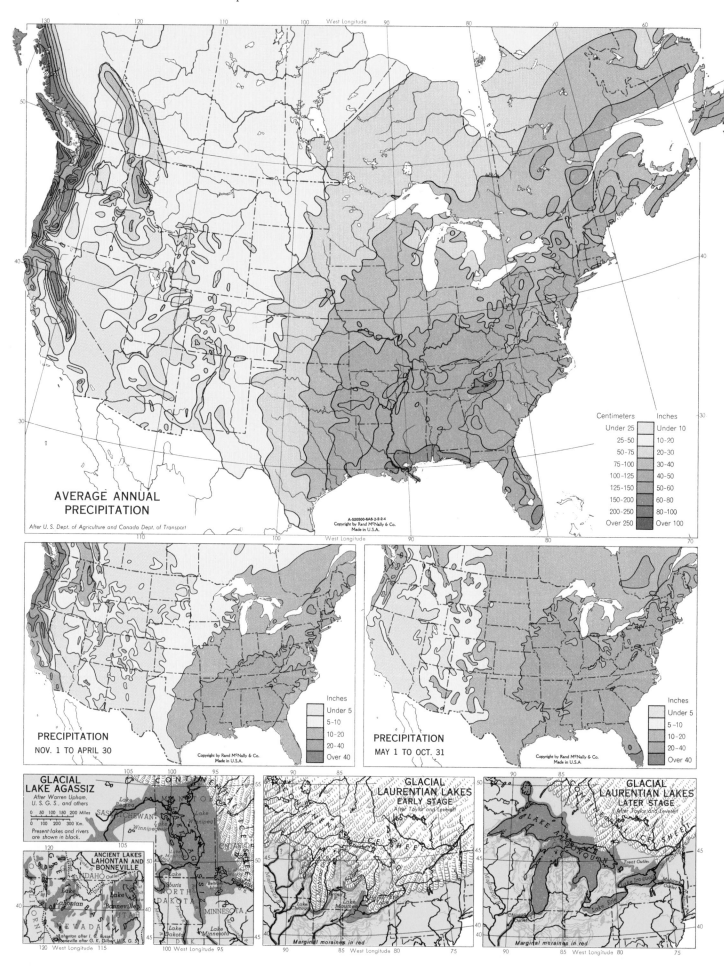

AVERAGE ANNUAL PRECIPITATION

After U. S. Dept. of Agriculture and Canada Dept. of Transport

A-520500-6A5-2-2-2-4
Copyright by Rand McNally & Co.
Made in U.S.A.

Centimeters	Inches
Under 25	Under 10
25-50	10-20
50-75	20-30
75-100	30-40
100-125	40-50
125-150	50-60
150-200	60-80
200-250	80-100
Over 250	Over 100

PRECIPITATION
NOV. 1 TO APRIL 30

Copyright by Rand McNally & Co.
Made in U.S.A.

Inches
Under 5
5-10
10-20
20-40
Over 40

PRECIPITATION
MAY 1 TO OCT. 31

Copyright by Rand McNally & Co.
Made in U.S.A.

Inches
Under 5
5-10
10-20
20-40
Over 40

GLACIAL LAKE AGASSIZ
*After Warren Upham,
U. S. G. S., and others*

0 50 100 150 200 Miles
0 100 200 300 Km.

*Present lakes and rivers
are shown in black.*

ANCIENT LAKES LAHONTAN AND BONNEVILLE

*Lahontan after I. C. Russell
Bonneville after G. K. Gilbert, U. S. G. S.*

GLACIAL LAURENTIAN LAKES
EARLY STAGE
After Taylor and Leverett

Marginal moraines in red

GLACIAL LAURENTIAN LAKES
LATER STAGE
After Taylor and Leverett

Marginal moraines in red

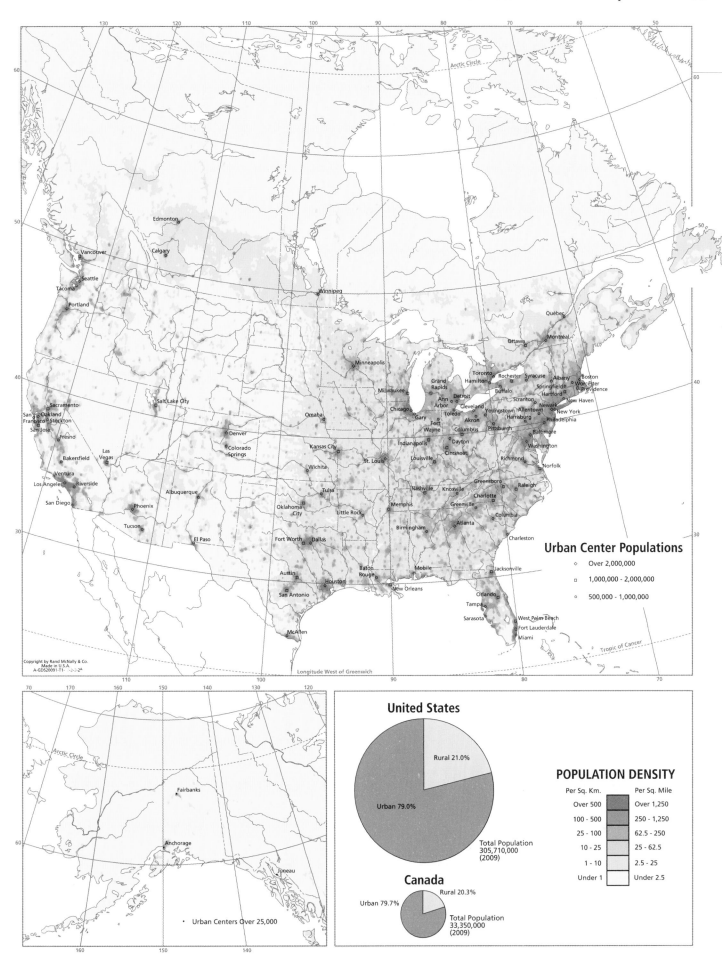

Urban Center Populations

◇ Over 2,000,000

▢ 1,000,000 - 2,000,000

○ 500,000 - 1,000,000

Copyright by Rand McNally & Co.
Made in U.S.A.
A-GDS20091-T1- -2-2-2^A

Longitude West of Greenwich

• Urban Centers Over 25,000

United States

Rural 21.0%

Urban 79.0%

Total Population
305,710,000
(2009)

Canada

Rural 20.3%

Urban 79.7%

Total Population
33,350,000
(2009)

POPULATION DENSITY

Per Sq. Km.	Per Sq. Mile
Over 500	Over 1,250
100 - 500	250 - 1,250
25 - 100	62.5 - 250
10 - 25	25 - 62.5
1 - 10	2.5 - 25
Under 1	Under 2.5

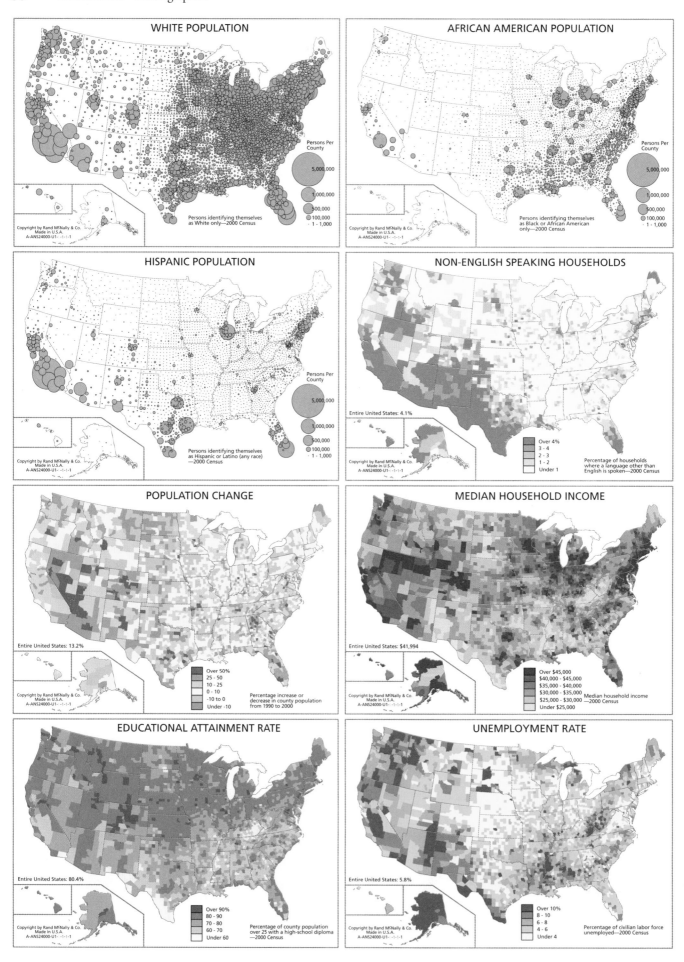

WHITE POPULATION

Persons Per County

5,000,000
1,000,000
500,000
100,000
1 - 1,000

Persons identifying themselves as White only—2000 Census

Copyright by Rand McNally & Co.
Made in U.S.A.
A-ANS24000-U1- -1-1-1

AFRICAN AMERICAN POPULATION

Persons Per County

5,000,000
1,000,000
500,000
100,000
1 - 1,000

Persons identifying themselves as Black or African American only—2000 Census

Copyright by Rand McNally & Co.
Made in U.S.A.
A-ANS24000-U1- -1-1-1

HISPANIC POPULATION

Persons Per County

5,000,000
1,000,000
500,000
100,000
1 - 1,000

Persons identifying themselves as Hispanic or Latino (any race) —2000 Census

Copyright by Rand McNally & Co.
Made in U.S.A.
A-ANS24000-U1- -1-1-1

NON-ENGLISH SPEAKING HOUSEHOLDS

Entire United States: 4.1%

Over 4%
3 - 4
2 - 3
1 - 2
Under 1

Percentage of households where a language other than English is spoken—2000 Census

Copyright by Rand McNally & Co.
Made in U.S.A.
A-ANS24000-U1- -1-1-1

POPULATION CHANGE

Entire United States: 13.2%

Over 50%
25 - 50
10 - 25
0 - 10
-10 to 0
Under -10

Percentage increase or decrease in county population from 1990 to 2000

Copyright by Rand McNally & Co.
Made in U.S.A.
A-ANS24000-U1- -1-1-1

MEDIAN HOUSEHOLD INCOME

Entire United States: $41,994

Over $45,000
$40,000 - $45,000
$35,000 - $40,000
$30,000 - $35,000
$25,000 - $30,000
Under $25,000

Median household income —2000 Census

Copyright by Rand McNally & Co.
Made in U.S.A.
A-ANS24000-U1- -1-1-1

EDUCATIONAL ATTAINMENT RATE

Entire United States: 80.4%

Over 90%
80 - 90
70 - 80
60 - 70
Under 60

Percentage of county population over 25 with a high-school diploma —2000 Census

Copyright by Rand McNally & Co.
Made in U.S.A.
A-ANS24000-U1- -1-1-1

UNEMPLOYMENT RATE

Entire United States: 5.8%

Over 10%
8 - 10
6 - 8
4 - 6
Under 4

Percentage of civilian labor force unemployed—2000 Census

Copyright by Rand McNally & Co.
Made in U.S.A.
A-ANS24000-U1- -1-1-1

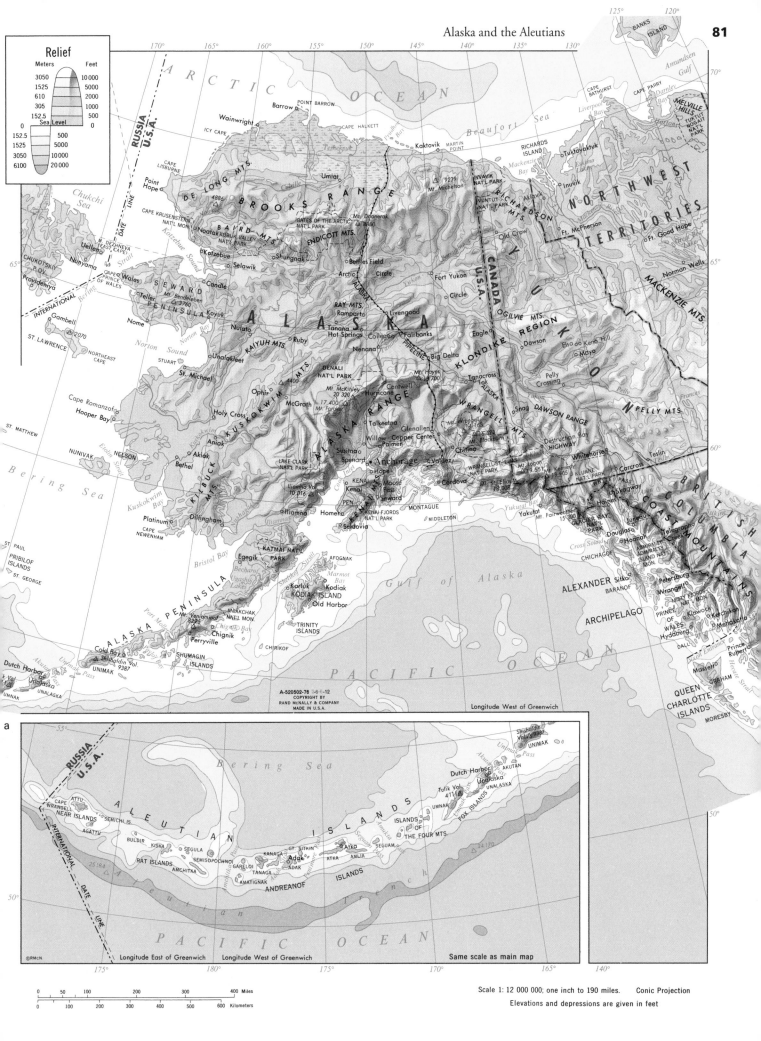

Relief

Meters	Feet
3050	10 000
1525	5000
610	2000
305	1000
152.5	500
0	Sea Level	0
152.5	500
1525	5000
3050	10 000
6100	20 000

ARCTIC OCEAN

RUSSIA
U.S.A.

Chukchi Sea

Beaufort Sea

Amundsen Gulf

NORTHWEST TERRITORIES

DE LONG MTS.
BROOKS RANGE
BAIRD MTS.
ENDICOTT MTS.

ALASKA

SEWARD PENINSULA

Bering Sea

KUSKOKWIM MTS.
KAIYUH MTS.
KILBUCK MTS.

ALASKA RANGE

DENALI NAT'L PARK
Mt. McKinley 20 320
17 400 Mt. Foraker

WRANGELL MTS.

Anchorage

KENAI MTS.

Gulf of Alaska

PACIFIC OCEAN

ALASKA PENINSULA

KODIAK ISLAND

KATMAI NAT'L PARK

SHUMAGIN ISLANDS

A-520502-76 3-6-8-12
COPYRIGHT BY
RAND McNALLY & COMPANY
MADE IN U.S.A.

Longitude West of Greenwich

YUKON
KLONDIKE REGION

DAWSON RANGE
PELLY MTS.

MACKENZIE MTS.

CANADA
U.S.A.

WRANGELL-ST. ELIAS NAT'L PARK

COAST MOUNTAINS

BRITISH COLUMBIA

ALEXANDER ARCHIPELAGO

PRINCE OF WALES

QUEEN CHARLOTTE ISLANDS

a

RUSSIA
U.S.A.

Bering Sea

ALEUTIAN ISLANDS

NEAR ISLANDS
RAT ISLANDS
ANDREANOF ISLANDS
FOX ISLANDS
ISLANDS OF THE FOUR MTS.

Aleutian Trench

PACIFIC OCEAN

INTERNATIONAL DATE LINE

Longitude East of Greenwich | Longitude West of Greenwich

Same scale as main map

| 0 | 50 | 100 | 200 | 300 | 400 Miles |
| 0 | 100 | 200 | 300 | 400 | 500 | 600 Kilometers |

Scale 1: 12 000 000; one inch to 190 miles.   Conic Projection

Elevations and depressions are given in feet

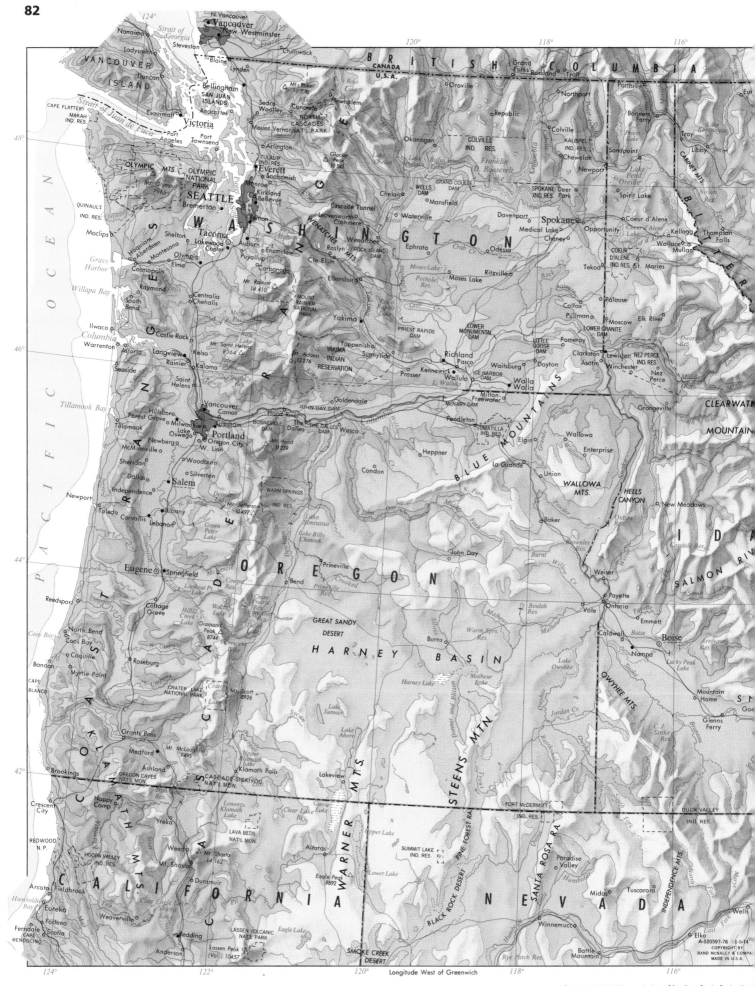

Scale 1: 4,000 000; one inch to 64 miles. Conic Projection
Elevations and depressions are given in feet

Longitude West of Greenwich

ALBERTA SASKATCHEWAN

CANADA
U.S.A.

WATERTON GLACIER
INTERNATIONAL
PEACE PARK

BLACKFEET
IND. RES.

Plentywood
Grenora

Morgan
Hogeland
Opheim
Scobey
Williston

Sunburst
Cut Bank
Shelby
Browning
Chinook
Harlem
Malta
Glasgow
Havre
Wolf Point
Poplar
Sidney
N. DAK.

FORT PECK
IND. RES.

Medicine
Lake

Kalispell
Whitefish
Lake Elwell
Marias
Valier
Conrad
Ft. Peck
Ft. Belknap
FT. BELKNAP
IND. RES.

ROCKY BOYS
IND. RES.

Fort Peck
Lake

HEAD
IAN
VATION
Ronan
NATIONAL
BISON RANGE

SWAN RANGE

Choteau
Teton
Fort Benton
Winifred
Brockway
Glendive
Beach

Blackfoot
Missoula
Lolo
Stevensville

Great
Falls
Belt
LITTLE BELT MTS.
Neihart
Lewistown
Winnett
Terry
Marmarth
Baker

M O N T A N A

Helena
East Helena
Canyon
White Sulphur
Spgs.
Harlowton
Roundup
Miles City
Forsyth

Deer Lodge
Townsend
Philipsburg
Anaconda
Walkerville

CRAZY
MTS.
Colstrip

R O C K Y   M O U N T A I N S

Hamilton
Butte
Three Forks
Bozeman
Big Timber
Livingston
Columbus
Laurel
Billings
Hardin
Huntley
Crow Agency
Tame Deer
NORTHERN CHEYENNE
IND. RES.

BIG HOLE NAT'L.
BATTLEFIELD
Twin Bridges

PIONEER MTS.
Homer
Youngs Peak
10,621
Dillon
Red Lodge
Granite Peak
12,799
Bear Creek

CROW IND. RES.

LITTLE
BIGHORN
BATTLEFIELD
NAT'L
MON.

Salmon
Electric Peak
10,992
Gardiner
Mt. Washburn
10,243

Sheridan
DEVILS TOWER
NAT'L. MON.
Sundance

BEAVERHEAD MTS.

Borah Pk.
12,662
Mackay
Mammoth
Hot Springs
Lovell
Powell
BIGHORN MOUNTAINS
Buffalo
Gillette
Moorcroft

YELLOWSTONE
NATIONAL
PARK
7733 ft. above
sea level

Cody
Greybull
Basin
Cloud Peak
13,167
Ten Sleep

LEMHI RANGE
LOST RIVER RA.
Hebgen Lake
Shoshone Lake

Worland
Kaycee

ABSAROKA RANGE

St. Anthony
Ashton
GRAND TETON
NAT'L PARK
Grand Teton
13,770
Jackson

Gebo
Thermopolis
Midwest

Rexburg
Rigby
WIND RIVER
IND.
RES.
Shoshoni
Powder River

Arco
CRATERS OF
THE MOON
NAT'L. MON.
Idaho Falls
Shelley
Garnett Peak
13,804
Fremont
Peak 13,745
WIND RIVER
IND.
Riverton
Lander

Glenrock
Casper
Douglas

S N A K E   R I V E R   P L A I N

Blackfoot
FORT HALL
IND. RES.
Pocatello

Orin

W Y O M I N G

American Falls
Rupert
Burley
Oakley

Soda Springs
Meade
Peak
9,957
Afton

WYOMING RANGE
Great Divide
Basin
Alcova Res.

Wheatland

Lava
Hot Spgs.
Montpelier

GREAT DIVIDE
BASIN

Pathfinder
Res.
Sweetwater
Seminoe
Res.
Hanna
Medicine Bow

Preston
Lewiston
Richmond
Smithfield
Logan
Providence
Kemmerer
Superior
Rawlins
Wheatland

Garland
Wellsville
Brigham

Granger
Green River
Rock Springs

GREAT
SALT LAKE
DESERT
Great
Salt
Lake
Lucin
Huntsville
Ogden
Morgan
Farmington

Flaming
Gorge
Res.

Steamboat Spgs.

Wendover
Bountiful
Salt Lake City
Murray
Midvale
Park City
Heber City

UINTA MTS.
Kings Peak
13,528
Mt. Emmons
13,440

DINOSAUR
NAT'L. MON.
Vernal
COLO.
Craig
Oak Creek

Tooele
UINTAH AND OURAY
IND. RES.

U T A H

PARK RANGE

Relief

Meters		Feet
3050		10000
1525		5000
610		2000
305		1000
152.5		500
0	Sea Level	0
1525		500

0 20 40 60 80 100 120 Miles
0 20 40 60 80 100 120 140 160 180 200 Kilometers

Scale 1:4 000 000; one inch to 64 miles. Conic Projection
Elevations and depressions are given in feet

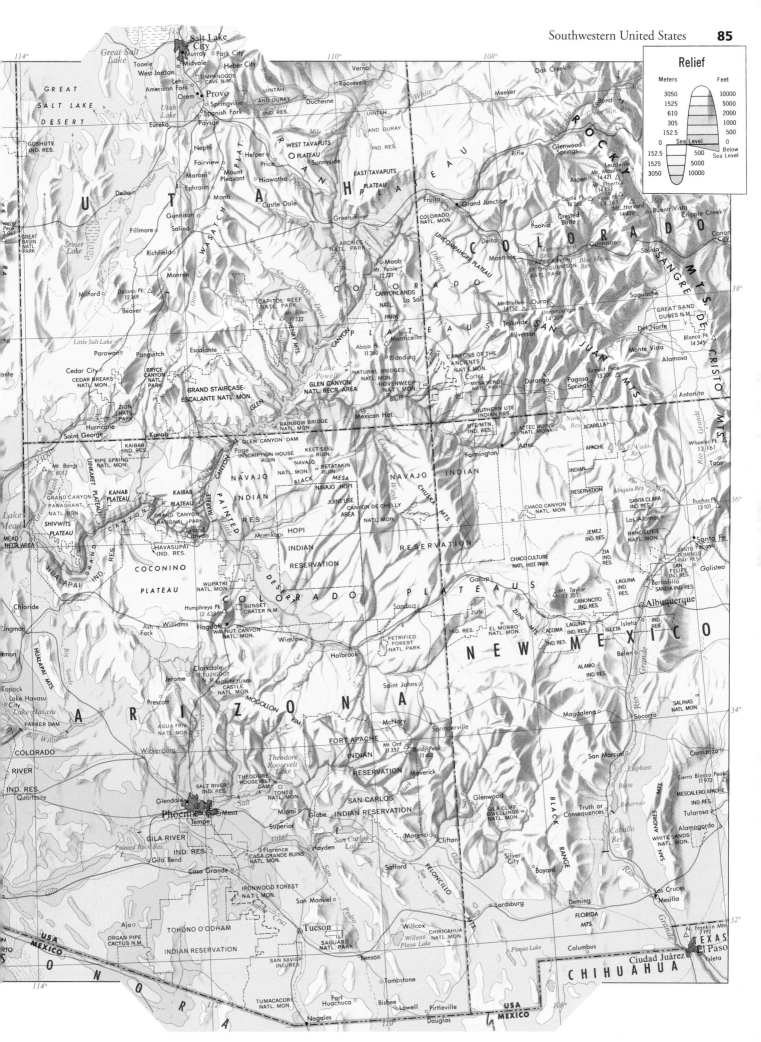

106° 104° 102° 100°

WYO. Cheyenne
Kimball Sidney Chappell Lake McConaughy Oshkosh Ord Sherman L
Julesburg Ogallala North Platte Broken Bow Loup City St. Paul Fullerton
North Platte South Loup Loup Central City

FRONT RANGE Steamboat Springs Oak Creek PARK RANGE MEDICINE BOW RANGE ROCKY MOUNTAIN NATIONAL PARK
Fort Collins Eaton Greeley Windsor Loveland Longmont Longs Peak 14,255 Boulder Louisville Golden Sterling Brush Fort Morgan Akron Yuma Wray Benkelman Haxtun Holyoke NEBRAS Hugh Butler Lake Curtis Cambridge Mc Cook Harry Strunk Lake Holdrege Minden Hastings Harva Frenchman Swanson Res. Beaver City Alma Red Cloud Franklin Superi

40°

Glenwood Springs Eagle Mt. Lincoln 14,286 Aspen Mt. Massive 14,421 La Plata Peak 14,361 Castle Peak 14,259 Crested Butte Gunnison Saguache Mt. Elbert 14,433 Mt. Harvard 14,420 Buena Vista Salida COLORADO
Fort Lupton Brighton DENVER Aurora Lakewood Englewood Littleton Limon Burlington Goodland Colby Oakley Wa Keeney Oberlin Norton Phillipsburg Smith Center Mankato Lovewell Res. Norton Res. North Fork Hill City Stockton Downs Beloit Osborne Waconda Lake Webster Res. Lincoln KANS Ellsworth

38°

Del Norte Monte Vista Alamosa Summit Peak 13,272 SANGRE DE CRISTO RANGE Manitou Springs Pikes Peak 14,110 Cripple Creek Canon City Florence Pueblo Ordway Sugar City Las Animas Lamar John Martin Res. Syracuse Garden City Dodge City Kinsley St. John Larned Great Bend Lyons Sterling Hutchinson Stafford Cheney Res. Kingman
Colorado Springs Kit Carson Cheyenne Wells Sharon Springs Scott City Ness City Cedar Bluffs Res. Hays Russell Wilson Res. Hoisington La Crosse Walnut Pawnee Smoky Hill Saline

Park View ROCKY MOUNTAINS Wheeler Pk. 13,160 Taos North Truchas Peak 13,110 Wagon Mound Mora Blanca Peak 14,345 Aguilar Delagua Trinidad Starkville Raton CAPULIN MOUNTAIN NAT'L MON. Folsom Des Moines Boise City Clayton GREAT SAND DUNES NAT'L MON. Walsenburg Fowler Rocky Ford La Junta Two Butte Springfield Elkhart Hugoton Liberal Meade Coldwater Ashland Kiowa Great Salt Plains Alva Cherokee Medford Anthony Harper Medicine Lodge

36°

Los Alamos BANDELIER NAT'L MON. UNITED PUEBLO IND. RES. Santa Fe Bernalillo Galisteo Albuquerque NEW MEXICO Las Vegas Ribera Springer Roy UNION NAT'L MON. Clayton Dalhart Guymon Beaver Perryton Hooker Woodward Fairview Seiling Okeene Watonga King
Tucumcari Dumas Borger Pampa Miami Canadian Lake Meredith Shattuck Elk City Sayre Weatherford El Reno Cordell OKL Foss Res. Clinton Geary Thomas

Vaughn Santa Rosa Puerto de Luna Fort Sumner GRAN QUIVIRA NAT'L MON. Clovis Farwell Portales Muleshoe Amarillo Canyon Hereford Tulia Plainview Memphis Clarendon Wellington Shamrock Erick Mangum Hobart Anadarko Cement Lindsa WICHITA MTS. Fort Sill Lawton Snyder Frederick Walters Duncan Marl Childress Quanah Grandfield Vernon Electra Burkburnett Iowa Park Wichita Falls Henrietta

34°

Carrizozo Roswell Artesia Dayton Hobbs McMillan Seagraves O'Donnell Lamesa Brownfield Lubbock Slaton Spur Post Tahoka LLANO ESTACADO TEXAS Floydada Paducah Pease Seymour Bow Olney Jacksboro Bridgepo Stamford Anson Haskell Graham Possum Kingdom Eagle N Snyder Rotan Hamlin Brazos Salt Fork Double Mountain Fork

Relief

Meters		Feet
3050		10 000
1525		5000
610		2000
305		1000
152.5		500
0	Sea Level	0

A-511006-76- -11 COPYRIGHT BY RAND McNALLY & COMPANY MADE IN U.S.A.

104° 102° 100° Longitude West of Greenwich 98°

Cities and Towns
0 to 50,000 ○ 50,000 to 500,000 ◉ 500,000 to 1,000,000 1,000,000 and over

Scale 1:4 000 000; one inch to 64 miles. Conic Projection
Elevations and depressions are given in feet.

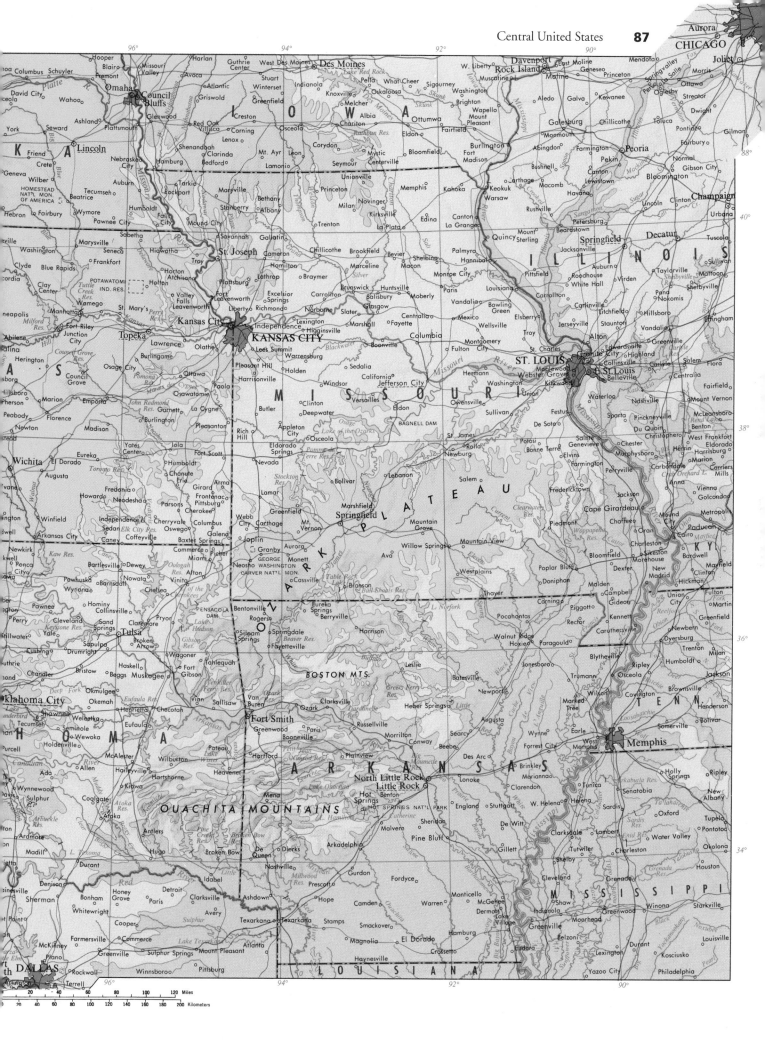

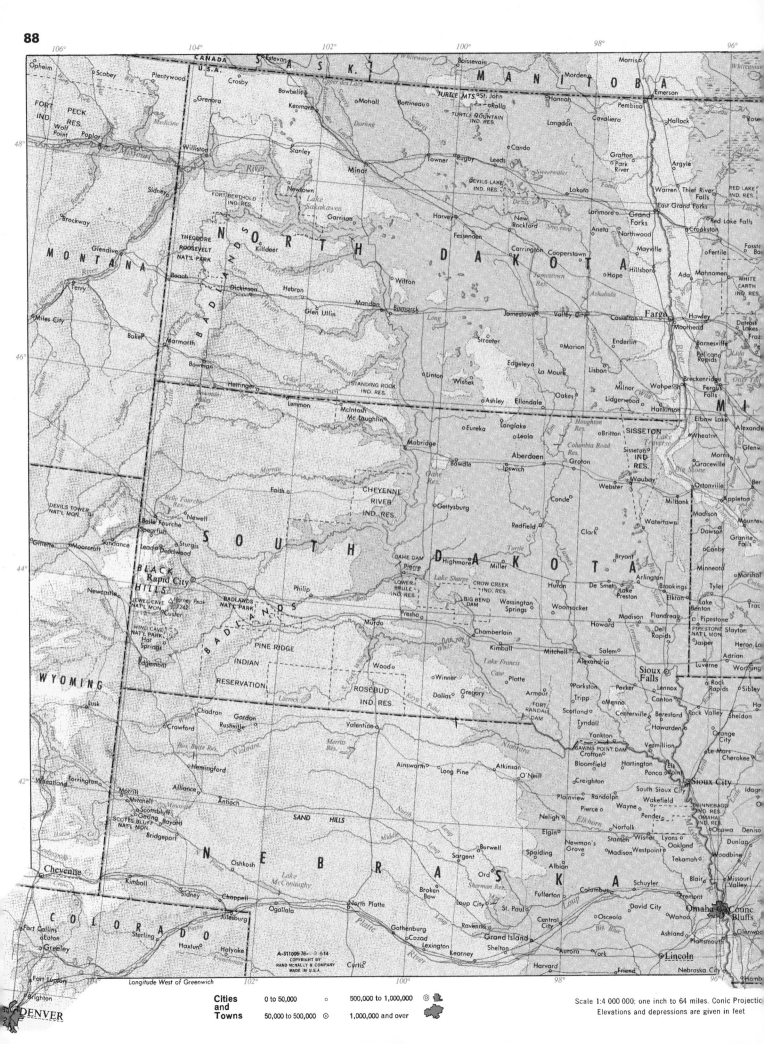

Scale 1:4 000 000; one inch to 64 miles. Conic Projection
Elevations and depressions are given in feet

Cities
and
Towns

0 to 50,000   o   500,000 to 1,000,000   ⊚

50,000 to 500,000   ⊙   1,000,000 and over

A-511005-76- 3 8-14
COPYRIGHT BY
RAND McNALLY & COMPANY
MADE IN U.S.A.

Longitude West of Greenwich

Lake of the Woods

Baudette

Fort Frances

International Falls

QUETICO PROVINCIAL PARK

VOYAGEURS PARK

Thunder Bay

GRAND PORTAGE NAT'L MON.

GRAND PORTAGE IND. RES.

ISLE ROYALE NAT'L PARK

CANADA
U.S.A.

Michipicoten Harbour

PUKASKWA NAT'NAL PARK

Upper Red Lake

Lower Red Lake

Blackduck

GREATER LEECH LAKE IND. RES.

Cass Lake

Deer River

Grand Rapids

Walker

Hill City

MESABI RANGE

VERMILION RANGE

Ely

Virginia Biwabik

Chisholm Buhl

Hibbing Keewatin

Nashwauk Coleraine

Eveleth Gilbert

Aurora

LAKE   SUPERIOR

Surface elev. 600 Feet above Sea Level
Maximum depth 1333 Feet

Copper Harbor

CARIBOU

Sault Ste. Marie

White Fish Bay

Sault Ste. Marie

BAY MILLS IND. RES.

Silver Bay

APOSTLE ISLANDS

OUTER

SAND STOCKTON

BED CLIFF IND. RES.

MADELINE

BAD RIVER IND. RES.

Two Harbors

Bayfield

Washburn

Ashland

Ontonagon

KEWEENAW

Calumet

Laurium Lake Linden

Hancock Houghton

L'ANSE AND VIEUX DESERT IND. RES.

HURON MTS.

Marquette

Munising

Newberry

Trout Lake

M I C H I

Proctor Duluth

Cloquet Superior

FOND DU LAC IND. RES.

Carlton

Bessemer Wakefield

Hurley Ironwood

GOGEBIC RANGE

Negaunee

Ishpeming

Champion

Princeton Gwinn

GRAND

Manistique

St. Ignace

GARDEN

HOG BEAVER I. IND. RES.

Cheboygan

Staples

Aitkin

Crosby

Brainerd

MILLE LACS IND. RES.

Mille Lacs

Sandstone

Hayward

LAC COURT OREILLE IND. RES.

LAC DU FLAMBEAU IND. RES.

MENOMINEE RANGE

Iron River Crystal Falls

Stambaugh

Iron Mountain Norway

Niagara

Pine

Escanaba

BIG BAY DE NOC

HIGH BEAVER

S FOX

Harbor Springs

Charlevoix

Petoskey

L. Charlevoix

Grand Travers Bay E. Jordan

Boyne City

Little Falls

Milaca

Pine City

Mora

Rush City

ST. CROIX IND. RES.

Cumberland

Spooner

Rice Lake

Park Falls

Phillips

Rhinelander

Crandon

Wausaukee

WASHINGTON

MANITOU ISLANDS

Manistee

Mancelona

Traverse City

Frankfort

Jennings

Cadillac

Sauk Centre

Sauk Rapids

St. Cloud

Princeton

Cambridge

Barron

Chetek

Ladysmith

Rib Lake

Tomahawk

Merrill

Antigo

DOOR PEN.

Algoma

Manistee

Reed City

Big Rapids

Paynesville

Monticello

Litchfield

Buffalo

Elk River

Anoka

Stillwater

New Richmond

Bloomer

Cornell

Medford

Stanley Owen

Wausau

Schofield

STOCKBRIDGE MUNSEE IND. RES.

Shawano

Oconto Oconto Falls

Peshtigo

Marinette

Menominee

Green Bay

Kewaunee

Two Rivers

Manitowoc

Sheboygan

Sheboygan Falls

Hart

Shelby

Whitehall

Fremont

Newaygo

Muskegon

Cokato

MINNEAPOLIS

St. Louis Park

St. Paul

Hutchinson

Glencoe

Shakopee

South St. Paul

Hastings

MORTON IND. RES.

Winthrop

Fairfax

New Ulm

New Prague

PRAIRIE ISLAND IND. RES.

Red Wing

Lake City

Wabasha

Hudson Menomonie

River Falls

Durand

Eau Claire

Augusta

Mondovi

Alma

Arcadia

Neillsville

Marshfield

Wisconsin Rapids

Stevens Point New London

Nekoosa

Waupaca

Appleton

Menasha Neenah

Oshkosh

Chilton

Kiel

Plymouth

Sturgeon Bay

WEST

Port Washington

Cedarburg

Grafton

Whitefish Bay Shorewood

Wauwatosa

MILWAUKEE

West Allis

Muskegon Heights

Grand Haven

Holland

Allegan

Otsego

Grand Rapids

Greenville

Belding

Hastings

Le Sueur

St. Peter

Faribault

Kenyon

Zumbrota

Plainview

Rochester

Kasson

Winona

Galesville

Sparta

Tomah

New Lisbon

Mauston

Princeton

Montello

Berlin

Ripon

Fond du Lac

Lake Winnebago

Waupun

Mayville

Horicon

Beaver Dam

Columbus

Watertown

Oconomowoc

Hartford

West Bend

Waukesha

South Milwaukee

Cudahy

Racine

Fairmont

Winnebago

Wells

Albert Lea

Austin

Blooming Prairie

Owatonna

Waseca

Waterville

Madelia

Lake Crystal

Mankato

St. James

Spring Valley

Chatfield

Preston

Caledonia

La Crosse

Westby

Viroqua

Hillsboro

Reedsburg

Baraboo

Wisconsin Dells

Portage

Adams

Omro

Estherville

Northwood

Lake Mills

Forest City

Osage

Cresco

Decorah

Lansing

Waukon

Richland Center

Sauk City

Jefferson

Fort Atkinson

Whitewater

Milton Elkhorn Burlington

Lake Geneva

Delavan

Kenosha

Emmetsburg

Algona

Britt

Clear Lake

Mason City

Charles City

New Hampton

Calmar

EFFIGY MOUNDS NAT'L MON.

Boscobel

Dodgeville

Madison

Stoughton

Edgerton

Evansville Janesville

Beloit

Walworth Harvard

Zion

North Chicago Lake Forest

Highland Park

St. Joseph

Benton Harbor

South Haven

Dowagiac

Pocahontas

Humboldt

Fonda

Rockwell City

Fort Dodge

Eagle Grove

Belmond

Clarion

Hampton

Waverly

Cedar Falls

Waterloo

Oelwein

Manchester

Guttenberg

Lancaster

Platteville

Darlington

Monroe

Woodstock

Rockford

Belvidere

Freeport

Galena

Dubuque

Dyersville

Libertyville

Fort Sheridan

Winnetka Wilmette

Evanston

Skokie

Niles

Three Rivers

Sturgis

Kalamazoo

Webster City

Iowa Falls

La Porte City

Grundy Center

Reinbeck

Independence

Maquoketa

Bellevue

Savanna

Mt. Carroll

Oregon

Sycamore

De Kalb

Geneva

St. Charles

Elgin

Des Plaines

CHICAGO

Oak Park

Cicero

E. Chicago

Michigan City

Elkhart

Lake City

Jefferson

Ogden

Boone

Nevada

Ames

Madrid

Perry

Marshalltown

Toledo

Tama

Belle Plaine

Marengo

Cedar Rapids

Marion

Anamosa

Clinton

Morrison

Sterling

Rock Falls

Dixon

Rochelle

Batavia

Aurora

Geneva Valley

Ottawa

Morris

Joliet

Chicago Heights

Crown Point

Lowell

Valparaiso

La Porte

W. Des Moines

Des Moines

Newton

Grinnell

Colfax

Guthrie Center

Stuart

Winterset

Indianola

Pella

Oskaloosa

What Cheer

Sigourney

Washington

Tipton

West Liberty

Muscatine

Davenport

Rock Island

Moline

Geneseo

Princeton

Kewanee

Galva

Oglesby

LaSalle

Marseilles

Mendota

Momence

Kankakee

N. Judson

Knoxville

Red Rock

Melcher

Brighton

Wapello

Aledo

Monmouth

Galesburg

Toluca

Minonk

Pontiac

Dwight

Gilman

Watseka

Kentland

Monticello

Fowler

Greenfield

Creston

Mt. Ayr

Lenox

Corydon

Leon

Mystic

Centerville

Seymour

Chariton

Albia

Osceola

Ottumwa

Fairfield

Mount Pleasant

Eldon

Bloomfield

Burlington

Fort Madison

Abingdon

Farmington

Peoria

Chillicothe

Fairbury

I L L I N O I S

I N D.

20 40 60 80 100 120 Miles
20 40 60 80 100 120 140 160 180 200 Kilometers

Relief

Meters	Feet
1525	5000
610	2000
305	1000
152.5	500
0 Sea Level	0
152.5	500

WISCONSIN

MICHIGAN

ILLINOIS

INDIANA

OHIO

KENTUCKY

WEST V...

LAKE HURON
Surface 579 Feet above Sea Level
maximum depth 750 Feet

LAKE ER...
Surface 570 Feet above Sea Level
maximum depth 210 Feet

Georgian Bay

North Channel

MANITOULIN ISLAND

CANADA
U.S.A.

Green Bay — Surface elevation 579 Feet above Sea Level maximum depth 870 Feet

MILWAUKEE
CHICAGO
DETROIT
CLEVELAND
CINCINNATI
ST. LOUIS

Sault Ste. Marie
Mackinac City
Straits of Mackinac
Petoskey
Charlevoix
Boyne City
Gaylord
Alpena
Traverse City
Cadillac
Grayling
Oscoda
Tawas City
Manistee
Ludington
Muskegon
Grand Rapids
Lansing
Battle Creek
Kalamazoo
Ann Arbor
Jackson
Flint
Saginaw
Bay City
Midland
Port Huron
Sarnia
Pontiac
Royal Oak
Warren
Dearborn
Windsor
Toledo
Lorain
Elyria
Akron
Canton
Youngstown
Columbus
Springfield
Dayton
Lima
Findlay
Fort Wayne
South Bend
Gary
Hammond
Joliet
Aurora
Elgin
Rockford
Madison
Green Bay
Appleton
Oshkosh
Fond du Lac
Sheboygan
Racine
Kenosha
Waukegan
Evanston
Peoria
Bloomington
Champaign
Urbana
Decatur
Springfield
Terre Haute
Indianapolis
Muncie
Anderson
Louisville
New Albany
Evansville
Lexington
Charleston
Huntington
Ashland
Portsmouth

Cities and Towns
0 to 50,000
50,000 to 500,000
500,000 to 1,000,000
1,000,000 and over

Longitude West of Greenwich

Scale 1:4 000 000; one inch to 64 miles. Conic Projection
Elevations and depressions are given in feet

GULF OF MEXICO

Scale 1:4 000 000; one inch to 64 miles. Conic Projection
Elevations and depressions are given in feet

Longitude West of Greenwich

A-520598-76
COPYRIGHT BY
RAND McNALLY & COMPANY
MADE IN U.S.A.

NEW MEXICO

Alamogordo
Alamo Pk.
9820
WHITE SANDS
NAT'L MON.
Artesia
Dayton
McMillan
Seagraves
O'Donnell
Haskell
Newcastle
Graham
Possum
Kingdom

N. Franklin Mtn.
7176
Hobbs
Lamesa
Snyder
Rotan
Hamlin
Stamford
Albany
Breckenridge
Strawn

Carlsbad
CARLSBAD
CAVERNS
NAT'L PARK
Seminole
Roscoe
Sweetwater
Merkel
Abilene
Ranger
Eastland
Cisco

Wind Mtn.
7278
Midland
Stanton
Big Spring
Colorado
City
Baird
Gorman
Desdemona
Stephe

El Paso
Ysleta
Ciudad Juárez
Guadalupe Pk.
8749
Red Bluff Res.
Odessa
Wink
Sterling City
Ballinger
Coleman
Santa Anna
Brownwood
Comanche
De Leon

Fabens
Winters
Brownwood
Hamilt

Guadalupe
Pecos
Toyah
Pecos
McCamey
San Angelo
Nasworthy
Eden
Brady
San Saba
Lometa
Lampa
Bur

Villa
Ahumada
Sierra Blanca
Van Horn
Eagle Pk.
7496
Fort Stockton
Sonora
Menard
Mason
Llano
Buchanan

DAVIS MTS.
Baldy Peak
8382
Marfa
Alpine
STOCKTON
PLATEAU
Big
Canyon
Sanderson
Junction
Rocksprings
Kerrville
Fredericksburg

SANTIAGO MTS.
Cathedral Mt.
8860
TEXAS
EDWARDS
PLATEAU

Chinati Pk.
7730
Presidio
BIG BEND
NAT'L PARK
Emory Pk.
7835
U.S.A.
MEXICO
SERRANIAS
DEL BURRO
Camp Wood
New Braunfels

Ojinaga
Coyame
Cuchillo Parado
San Antonio

Chihuahua
Aldama
Del Rio
Villa Acuña
Amistad
Res.
Brackettville
Sabinal
Hondo
Uvalde
Floresville

CHIHUAHUA
Meoqui
Jiménez
Piedras Negras
Fuente
Eagle Pass
Crystal City
Pearsall
Pleasanton

Naica
Zaragoza
Morelos
Nava
Carrizo Springs
Asherton
Cotulla
Fowlerton
George
West

SIERRA
Allende
Guerrero
Rosales
Encinal

Hidalgo
del Parral
Villa
Lopez
Jaco
Muzquiz
San Juan de Sabinas
Hidalgo
Dolores
San Diego

COAHUILA
MADRE
Progreso
Presa de
D. Martin
Nuevo Laredo
Laredo
Mirando City
Premont

Santa Barbara
Villa Coronado
Sierra Mojada
Laguna de
la Leche
Abasolo
Sacramento
San Buenaventura
Nadadores
Lampazos
Guerrero
Hebbronville
Falfurrias

Escalón
BOLSÓN
Cuatro Ciénegas
Monclova
Bustamante
Villaldama
Sabinas Hidalgo
Mier
Riogrande

Rosario
Villa
Ocampo
DE
ORIENTAL
Rey
Camargo
Mission
Ed

Inde
MAPIMI
NUEVO
Agualeguas
Reynosa

Santa Cruz
Mapimi
San Pedro de
las Colonias
Laguna de
Mayran
Paredón
Salinas Victoria
General Zuazua
Cerralvo
Los Herreros

DURANGO
Sacramento
Gómez Palacio
Torreón
Lerdo
Matamoros
Laguna de
Viesca
García
Monterrey
Santa Catarina
Cadereyta Jimenez
China

Rodeo
Nazas
Viesca
Parras
Ramos Arizpe
General Cepeda
Arteaga
Villa de Allende

San Luis del
Cordero
Gómez Farías
Saltillo
Montemorelos
LEON

San Juan del Rio
Cuencamé
San Bartolo
San Juan de
Guadalupe
Mazapil
Concepción
del Oro
Galeana
Linares
Burgos
San

Canatlán
Pánuco de
Coronado
Santa Clara
ZACATECAS
Juan Aldama
TAMAULI
Cruillas
San Carlos
Villagran

Durango

Longitude West of Greenwich

Scale 1:4 000 000; one inch to 64 miles. Conic Projection
Elevations and depressions are given in feet

Cities
and
Towns

0 to 50,000

50,000 to 500,000

500,000 to 1,000,000

1,000,000 and over

Scale 1:1 000 000

a

Scale 1:1 000 000
0 | 2 | 4 | 6 | 8 | 10 Miles
0 | 4 | 8 | 12 | 16 Kilometers

©RMCN.

A-530000-76-9 9-26EL
COPYRIGHT BY
RAND McNALLY & COMPANY
MADE IN U.S.A.

Scale 1:16 000 000; one inch to 250 miles. Polyconic Projectio
Elevations and depressions are given in feet

b

Inset b — Puerto Rico

ATLANTIC OCEAN

Arecibo   San Juan
Aguadilla   Bayamón   CABEZAS DE SAN JUAN   ST. THOMAS (U.S.A.)   TORTOLA (Br.)
PTA. HIGUERO   Utuado   Fajardo   CULEBRA   Charlotte Amalie   ST. JOHN (U.S.A.)
PUERTO RICO   Caguas   Vieques
Mayagüez   (U.S.A.)   Humacao   VIEQUES
Coamo   Cayey
Ponce   Salinas   Guayama

CABO ROJO

CARIBBEAN SEA

Christiansted
SAINT CROIX (U.S.A.)

Scale 1:4 000 000
0 10 20 30 40 Miles
0 10 20 30 40 50 60 Kilometers

©RMcN

c

Inset c — St. Thomas

LITTLE HANS LOLLICK   64°50'
OUTER BRASS   HANS LOLLICK
INNER BRASS   PICARA PT   GRASS CAY
STORMY PT.   THATCH CAY
ST. THOMAS
Crown Mt (U.S.A.) 1558   Charlotte Amalie
(St. Thomas)   Nadir
WATER   St. Thomas Harbor
FLAMINGO PT

18°   20'

Scale 1:500 000

©RMcN

Main Map

W. VIRGINIA   Richmond   Roanoke   Raleigh   Norfolk
VIRGINIA   NORTH CAROLINA   Chesapeake Bay
Mt. Mitchell   Charlotte   CAPE HATTERAS   Pamlico
SOUTH CAROLINA   Columbia   Wilmington   CAPE FEAR
Augusta   Charleston
GEORGIA   Savannah
Tallahassee   Jacksonville
St. Augustine
Ocala
FLORIDA   CAPE CANAVERAL
Tampa   W. Palm Beach
Tampa Bay   MIAMI
CAPE SABLE   Lake Okeechobee
Key West   FLORIDA KEYS

ATLANTIC OCEAN

BERMUDA (Br.)

NORTH AMERICAN BASIN

Straits of Florida
Nassau
GRAND BAHAMA   GREAT ABACO
B A H A M A S
ANDROS   ELEUTHERA   CAT
SAN SALVADOR (WATLING)
LONG

HAVANA   Guanabacoa   Matanzas
Marianao   Cárdenas
del Río   Santa Clara   Sancti Spíritus
Cienfuegos   Ciego de Ávila   Nuevitas
C U B A   Trinidad   Camagüey
ISLA DE LA JUVENTUD   Holguín
Manzanillo   Guantánamo
GRAND CAYMAN (Br.)   SIERRA MAESTRA   PUNTA MAISI
C. CRUZ   Santiago de Cuba   Cap-Haïtien
G R E A T E R   W E S T   Gonaïves
Montego Bay   Mt. Denham 2236   Port Antonio
Spanish Town   ÎLE DE LA GONÂVE
JAMAICA   Kingston
A N T I L L E S   H I S P A N I O L A

ACKLINS
CAICOS (Br.)   TURKS (Br.)
GT. INAGUA

Puerto Plata   Santiago de los Caballeros   SAMANA
Sánchez
HAITI   DOMINICAN REPUBLIC   Pico Duarte 3175   C. ENGAÑO
Port-au-Prince 10 417   Santo Domingo
Mona Passage   PUERTO RICO TRENCH   ▽ 28 374
Mayagüez   San Juan
Ponce   Charlotte Amalie   VIRGIN IS.   ST. THOMAS (U.S.A.)   ANGUILLA (Br.)
PUERTO RICO (U.S.A.)   SAINT CROIX (U.S.A.)   BARBUDA
ST. KITTS AND NEVIS   ANTIGUA AND BARBUDA
MONTSERRAT (Br.)   Pointe-à-Pitre
V. Soufrière 4813   GUADELOUPE (Fr.)
Basse-Terre   DOMINICA
L E E W A R D
MARTINIQUE (Fr.)   Fort-de-France
ST. LUCIA
ST. VINCENT AND THE GRENADINES   BARBADOS
Kingstown   Bridgetown
W I N D W A R D   GRENADA
L E S S E R   A N T I L L E S   TOBAGO

ATLANTIC OCEAN

CARIBBEAN SEA

AMERICA
Bluefields
José   Limón
Cartago   Golfo de los Mosquitos
Colón   PANAMA   Portobelo
Santiago   David   Panamá   Antón
PEN. DE AZUERO   Golfo de Panamá
ISLA DE MALPELO (Colombia)
Buenaventura   Cali   Palmira
Medellín   Manizales   Pereira   Armenia   Ibagué   Girardot   Villavicencio
C O L O M B I A   BOGOTÁ   Tunja
Barrancabermeja   Bucaramanga
Cúcuta   San Cristóbal   Pamplona
Ocaña   Mérida   Valera   Trujillo
Magangué   Montería   Sincelejo   Mompós   Lorica
Cartagena   Soledad   Barranquilla   Ciénaga   Santa Marta
PUNTA DE GALLINAS   PENÍNSULA DE GUAJIRA
Golfo de Venezuela   Maracaibo   Cabimas
Lago de Maracaibo   San Felipe
Coro   PEN. DE PARAGUANA
ARUBA (Neth.)   CURAÇAO (Neth.)   BONAIRE (Neth.)
PUNTA SAN ROMAN   Willemstad
Puerto Cabello   La Guaira   CARACAS   Cumaná
Valencia   Maracay   Puerto la Cruz   Carúpano
Barquisimeto   ISLA LA TORTUGA   ISLA DE MARGARITA
Guanare   Calabozo   El Tigre   Maturín
Puerto de Nutrias   San Fernando de Apure
V E N E Z U E L A   TRINIDAD AND TOBAGO   Port of Spain   TRINIDAD
Cerro Icutú 7800 △   Ciudad Guayana   Morawhanna
Cerro Bolívar   Ciudad Bolívar
Río Orinoco   GUYANA
San Fernando de Atabapo   SERRA PACARAIMA
B R A Z I L

Longitude West of Greenwich

Scale bar (main map)

50 100 200 300 400 500 Miles
100 200 400 600 800 Kilometers

Relief

Meters		Feet
3050		10 000
1525		5000
610		1000
305		1000
152.5		500
0	Sea Level	0
152.5		500
1525		5000
3050		10 000
6100		20 000

Cities and Towns legend

Cities and Towns	
0 to 50,000 ○	500,000 to 1,000,000 ◎
50,000 to 500,000 ⊙	1,000,000 and over

South America

Floodplain of the Amazon River, Brazil

With an area of 6.9 million square miles (17.8 million sq km), triangular-shaped South America is fourth among the continents in size. The Andes, which pass through seven of the continent's 13 mainland countries, are the longest mountain chain in the world. The mighty Amazon River carries a greater volume of water than any other river: 46 million gallons per second flow into the Atlantic Ocean. The Amazon basin contains an estimated one-fifth of the world's fresh water and is home to the world's largest rain forest with its countless plant and animal species. Angel Falls, in a remote Venezuelan forest, is the world's highest waterfall, dropping 3,212 feet (979 m), or almost the height of three Empire State Buildings.

One of South America's other great wonders is manmade. High in the Peruvian Andes lie the ruins of the sacred city of Machu Picchu, built centuries ago by the Incas. The city has an exquisite design and was built with remarkable skill. The Inca population, like most of South America's other native peoples, declined rapidly after the arrival of Europeans in the early 16th century.

South America at a glance

Land area:
6,900,000 square miles (17,800,000 sq km)

Estimated population:
391,890,000

Population density:
57/square mile (22/sq km)

Mean elevation:
1,800 feet (550 m)

Highest point:
Cerro Aconcagua, Argentina,
22,831 feet (6,959 m)

Lowest point:
Laguna del Carbón, Argentina,
344 feet (105 m) below sea level

Longest river:
Amazon-Ucayali, 4,000 mi (6,400 km)

Number of countries
(incl. dependencies): 15

Largest independent country:
Brazil, 3,300,172 square miles
(8,547,404 sq km)

Smallest independent country:
Suriname, 63,037 square miles
(163,265 sq km)

Most populous independent country:
Brazil, 197,550,000

Least populous independent country:
Suriname, 480,000

Most populous metropolitan area:
São Paulo, Brazil, population 18.8 million

Jagged peaks of the Andes rise at the western edge of Argentina's Patagonia region.

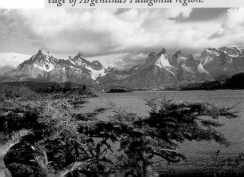

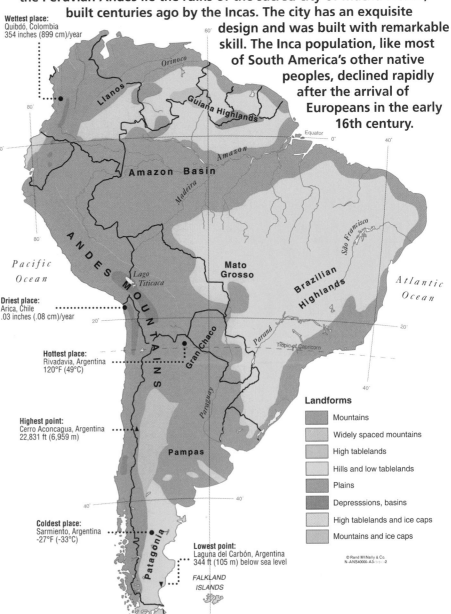

Wettest place:
Quibdó, Colombia
354 inches (899 cm)/year

Driest place:
Arica, Chile
.03 inches (.08 cm)/year

Hottest place:
Rivadavia, Argentina
120°F (49°C)

Highest point:
Cerro Aconcagua, Argentina
22,831 ft (6,959 m)

Coldest place:
Sarmiento, Argentina
-27°F (-33°C)

Lowest point:
Laguna del Carbón, Argentina
344 ft (105 m) below sea level

Landforms

- Mountains
- Widely spaced mountains
- High tablelands
- Hills and low tablelands
- Plains
- Depresssions, basins
- High tablelands and ice caps
- Mountains and ice caps

© Rand McNally & Co.
N-ANS40000-A3-⌐-⌐--2

Map labels: Orinoco, Llanos, Guiana Highlands, Equator, Amazon, Amazon Basin, Madeira, São Francisco, Mato Grosso, Brazilian Highlands, Pacific Ocean, Lago Titicaca, Atlantic Ocean, ANDES MOUNTAINS, Gran Chaco, Paraná, Tropic of Capricorn, Paraguay, Pampas, Patagonia, FALKLAND ISLANDS, TIERRA DEL FUEGO

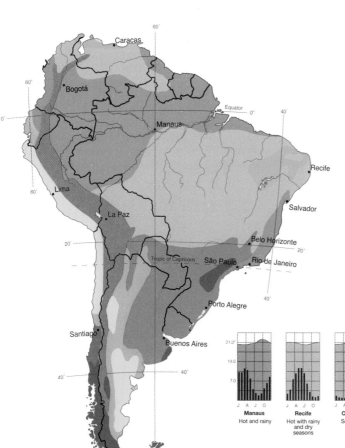

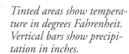

Climate

South America's most predominant climate zones are the vast tropical rain forests and tropical savannas which cover most of the northern half of the continent. In the rain forests, rain falls throughout the year, averaging 60 to 80 inches (152 to 203 cm) annually. Daytime temperatures usually exceed 80° F (27° C). The tropical savanna regions experience the same high temperatures but less rainfall, with a dry season in winter. A temperate climate, with milder temperatures and moderate rainfall, prevails throughout much of southern South America, east of the Andes. Arid to semiarid conditions are found in the far south and at Brazil's eastern tip.

Manaus Hot and rainy	**Recife** Hot with rainy and dry seasons	**Caracas** Semiarid	**Lima** Very dry	**Santiago** Hot, dry summer / mild, rainy winter	**Buenos Aires** Warm, humid summer / mild winter	**Punta Arenas** Mild and rainy	**Extensive uplands** Climate varies with elevation and latitude

Tinted areas show temperature in degrees Fahrenheit. Vertical bars show precipitation in inches.

Population

South America is the fourth most-densely populated continent with 57 people per square mile (22 per sq km). Despite this relatively low figure, the continent is intensely urban because the Andes and the Amazon rain forest render most of it either inaccessible or unsuitable for farming. More than 90% of South America's 392 million people live within 150 miles (240 km) of the coast. São Paulo, Brazil, with a metropolitan population of more than 18 million, is the world's sixth-largest metropolitan area. Most South Americans are mestizo—of mixed European and Indian descent. Spanish is the predominant language, followed by Portuguese. More than 90% of the people are Roman Catholics.

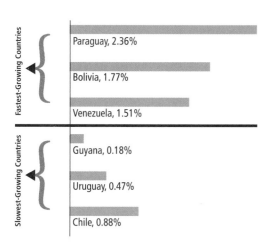

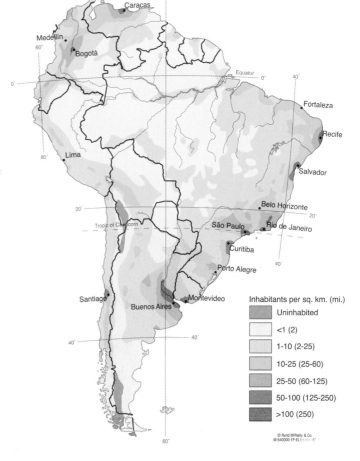

Inhabitants per sq. km. (mi.)

- Uninhabited
- <1 (2)
- 1-10 (2-25)
- 10-25 (25-60)
- 25-50 (60-125)
- 50-100 (125-250)
- >100 (250)

Environments and Land Use

Land suitable for farming is very limited in South America, covering only about 6% of the continent. Small, family-run subsistence farms are common, and typical crops are maize, wheat, and potatoes. Despite the scarcity of arable land, commercial agriculture for export is a major part of the economies of several countries. Ecuador is the world's leading exporter of bananas, while Brazil and Colombia grow almost 40% of the world's coffee beans. Brazil is also a major exporter of sugar. Chile has developed a large trade in produce—such as tomatoes and grapes—that is exported to North America during its winter months (South America's summer months). Production of coca, the basis for illicit drugs, has become a part of the rural economies of Colombia, Bolivia, and Peru.

Cattle ranching is centered on the vast, grassy Pampas region, which extends through northern Argentina, Uruguay, and southern Brazil. Sheep, raised both for meat and wool, are important throughout the Andes and southern Argentina. About 25% of the continent is suitable for grazing.

As South America's population grows, pressure builds to clear more land for farming. Much expansion has taken place in the Amazon basin at the cost of millions of acres of rain forest, which are cleared of trees and drained. Balancing the demands of the population with the need to preserve the rain forest is one of the continent's most pressing issues.

Coffee plantation in the Brazilian highlands

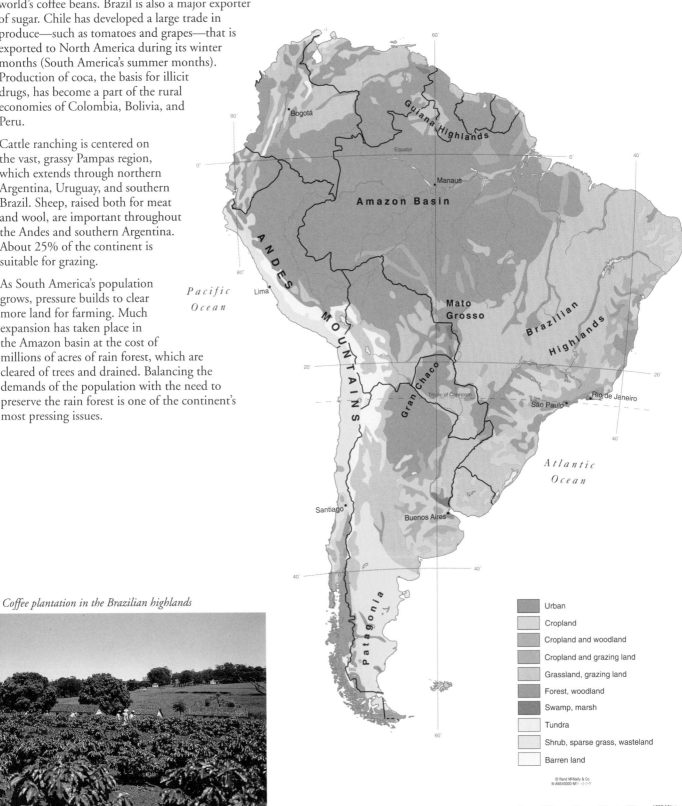

Urban
Cropland
Cropland and woodland
Cropland and grazing land
Grassland, grazing land
Forest, woodland
Swamp, marsh
Tundra
Shrub, sparse grass, wasteland
Barren land

© Rand McNally & Co.
N-ANS40000-M1--2-2-1

Destruction of the Rain Forest

The Amazonian rain forest contains an abundance and diversity of life that is matched by few places in the world. In fact, it has been estimated that the plant and animal species of Amazonia account for nearly one-half of those found on Earth. New plants and animals are constantly being discovered, and scientists have found in Amazonian plants a treasure trove of new substances, some of which are now being used to produce life-saving medicines. It is thought that cures for many more diseases could be found in the plants yet to be studied.

In recent decades, nearly 10% of the rain forest's original 1.58 million square miles (4.09 million sq km) has been cleared (see map below) for farming, cattle ranching, mining, and commercial logging. The most effective way to clear the land is the "slash-and-burn" method, which has been practiced by indigenous peoples on an insignificant scale for centuries. Today, widespread usage of this method is destroying vast areas of the rain forest, and smoke from the fires is polluting the atmosphere and possibly contributing to global warming. The destruction also imperils the Indians living within the forest; their numbers have shrunk by more than half in this century alone.

The plight of the Amazonian rain forest has raised concern among many South Americans as well as people throughout the world. One of the rain forest's greatest champions was a Brazilian named Chico Mendes who on numerous occasions confronted and drove off workers hired by cattle ranchers to clear areas of the forest. Through his activism, Mendes made some strong enemies, one of whom gunned him down outside his home in 1988.

There are those who argue that, in order to grow economically and support its expanding population, South America must make full use of the lands of the Amazon basin. They point out that many developed countries are guilty of similar environmental exploitation at home.

The irony of the destruction of the Amazonian rain forest is that once the land is cleared of its native plants and trees, it is ill-suited for the demands of crops. After just a few years, the soil's fertility is exhausted. The people who cleared the land soon abandon it, leaving a landscape that has been robbed of its biodiversity.

In recent years, Brazil and other countries have strengthened legislation aimed at protecting the rain forest. However, they lack the resources to effectively enforce the laws, and today destruction of the rain forest continues at an alarming rate.

The Juruá River, at left, and a clearwater slough wind through the dense Amazon rain forest near Eirunepé, Brazil.

Extent of Tropical Rain Forest

Original extent of rain forest

Current extent of rain forest

© Rand McNally
M-540000-8A-EL1-1-1- -1

ATLANTIC OCEAN

Tropic of Cancer

HAVANA

CUBA

Yucatán Channel

Bahia de Campeche

PEN DE YUCATÁN

Gulf of Honduras

CARIBBEAN SEA

INDIES

HISPANIOLA

San Juan

PUERTO RICO (U.S.A)

JAMAICA

PUERTO RICO TRENCH

Windward Passage

NORTH AMERICAN BASIN

GUADELOUPE (Fr.)

MARTINIQUE (Fr.)

BARBADOS

CENTRAL

Lago de Nicaragua

AMERICA

Panamá

PUNTA DE GALLINAS

Golfo de Venezuela

TRINIDAD AND TOBAGO

Port of Spain

ISLA DEL COCO (Costa Rica)

ISLA DE MALPELO (Colombia)

Golfo del Darién

Golfo de Panamá

PAN DO

Barranquilla

Cartagena

Maracaibo

La Guaira

Valencia

CARACAS

Mérida

Ciudad Bolívar

Cerro Icutú △7800

VENEZUELA

GUYANA

Georgetown

Paramaribo

SURINAME

FR. GUIANA

Cayenne

ARCHIPIÉLAGO DE COLÓN (GALÁPAGOS ISLANDS) (Ec.)

Medellín

BOGOTÁ

Nevado del Tolima 17 110

COLOMBIA

Boa Vista do Rio Branco

GUIANA HIGHLANDS

Quito

Cotopaxi 19 347

ECUADOR

Guayaquil

Chimborazo 20 702

Guaviare

Negro

Branco

ILHA DE MARAJÓ

Equator

ROCEDOS SÃO PEDRO E SÃO PAULO (Brazil)

Iquitos

Leticia

Japurá

Putumayo

Manaus (Manáos)

Amazon (Amazonas)

Belém (Pará)

São Luís (Maranhão)

Golfo de Guayaquil

Chiclayo

Trujillo

Nevs. Huascarán 22 133

Marañón

Ucayali

(Solimões)

Juruá

Purús

Madeira

Tapajós

Xingú

Tocantins

Rio

Fortaleza (Ceará)

Natal

João Pessoa (Paraíba)

RECIFE (Pernambuco)

Maceió

ARQUIPÉLAGO FERNANDO DE NORONHA (Brazil)

CABO DE SÃO ROQUE

PERU

ANDES

LIMA

Callao

Cusco

Volcán Misti

BRAZIL

CHAPADA DE MATO GROSSO

Cuiabá

Roosevelt

Paraguai

BRAZILIAN HIGHLANDS

SERRA DO PIAUÍ

Salto Paulo Afonso

Salto

Salvador (Bahia)

Arequipa

Mollendo

BOLIVIA

Nev. Illimani 20 741

La Paz

Sucre

Potosí

Diamantina

Brasília

SERRA DO ESPINHAÇO

Belo Horizonte

Pico da Bandeira 9482

Vitória

PACIFIC OCEAN

ISLA DE SAN FÉLIX (Chile)

ISLA DE SAN AMBROSIO (Chile)

Tropic of Capricorn

Antofagasta

Iquique

Lago de Poopó

PERU-CHILE TRENCH

DESERTO DE

Salta

Cerro Azufre 19 947

Copiapó

Coquimbo

Cerro Aconcagua 22 835

GRAN CHACO

PARAGUAY

Asunción

Pilcomayo

Bermejo

Corrientes

Iguassú Falls

Paraná

SÃO PAULO

Santos

RIO DE JANEIRO

CABO FRIO

Florianópolis

ISLAS DE JUAN FERNÁNDEZ (Chile)

Valparaíso

SANTIAGO

Concepción

Valdivia

Puerto Montt

Tucumán

Córdoba

Mendoza

Santa Fe

Rosario

BUENOS AIRES

La Plata

PAMPAS

Salto

URUGUAY

MONTEVIDEO

Río Grande

Porto Alegre

ATLANTIC OCEAN

Colorado

Bahía Blanca

Viedma

Golfo San Matías

Río de la Plata

ARGENTINA

CHILE

ISLA DE CHILOÉ

ARCHIPIÉLAGO DE LOS CHONOS

Monte Valentín 12 314

Chubut

Comodoro Rivadavia

Golfo San Jorge

WELLINGTON

HANOVER

DESOLACIÓN

Río Gallegos

Punta Arenas

Mt. Sarmiento 8100

Estrecho de Magallanes

TIERRA DEL FUEGO

ISLA DE LOS ESTADOS

CABO DE HORNOS (CAPE HORN)

FALKLAND IS. (ISLAS MALVINAS) (Br.)

Stanley

Drake Passage

SOUTH GEORGIA (Br.)

SOUTH SANDWICH ISLANDS

SOUTH ORKNEY IS. (Br.)

SOUTH SHETLAND IS. (Br.)

ANTARCTIC PENINSULA

JOINVILLE

JAMES ROSS

Antarctic Circle

A-540000-26 4-7-16

COPYRIGHT BY RAND McNALLY & COMPANY MADE IN U.S.A.

Longitude West of Greenwich

40,000 SQ MI AREA

0   300   600

Miles

0   200   400   600   800   1000 Miles

0   400   800   1200   1600 Kilometers

Scale 1:40 000 000; one inch to 630 miles. Lambert's Azimuthal, Equal Area Projection
Elevations and depressions are given in feet

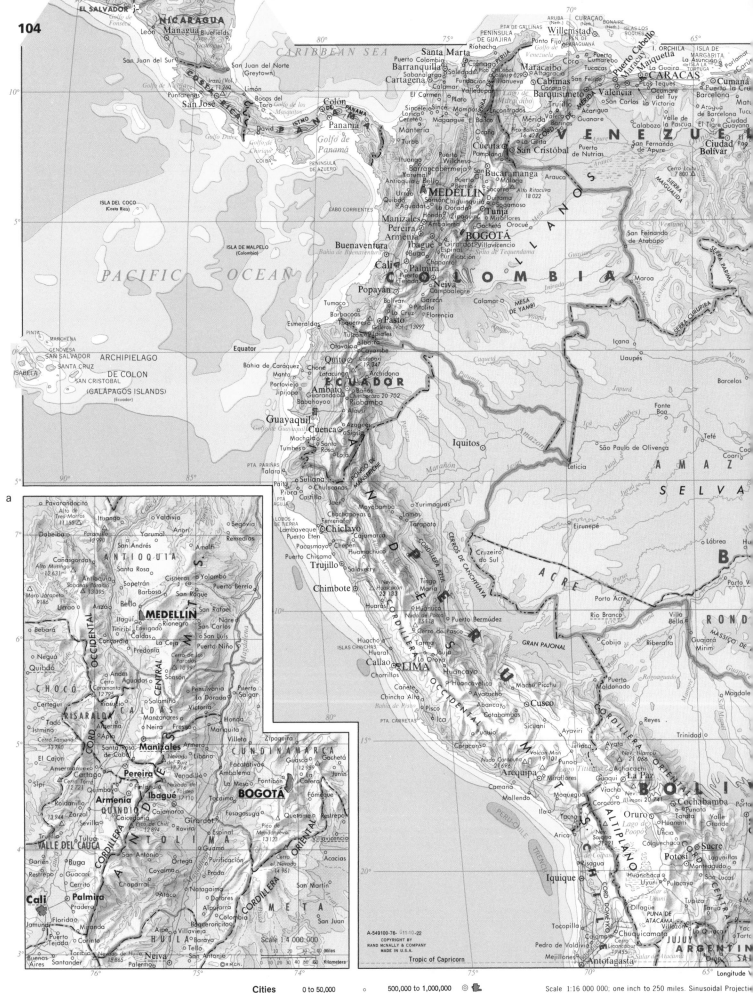

Cities and Towns

0 to 50,000	○
50,000 to 500,000	◉
500,000 to 1,000,000	◎
1,000,000 and over	⬤

Scale 1:16 000 000; one inch to 250 miles. Sinusoidal Projecti
Elevations and depressions are given in feet

b

Inset map (top right)

CARIBBEAN SEA

FALCON
Tocuyo de la Costa
Chichiriviche
CAYO SOMBRERO
Tucacas
Golfo Triste
ISLA DE MARGARITA
Boca del Pozo △ 2303
PUNTA ARENAS
Punta de Piedras
NUEVA ESPARTA
ISLA CUBAGUA
PUNTA DE ARAYA
Maiquetía
Guaira
Naiguatá
La Sabana
ISLA LA TORTUGA
Manicuare
CUMANÁ
Puerto Cabello
Carayaca
Caraballeda
CABO CODERA
SUCRE
Nereri
Morón
CARACAS
DISTRITO FEDERAL
Guatire
Higuerote
Las Vegas
Montalbán
El Cambur
Pico Central 2988 △
Santa Lucía 9072
Río Chico
Puerto La Cruz
Guanta
Miranda
Guacara
Petare
San Francisco
Laguna de la Tacarigua
Puerto Piritu
8000 △
Maracay
Los Teques
MIRANDA
Caucagua
El Hatillo
Barcelona
CARABOBO
Lago de Valencia
Santa Teresa
Ocumare del Tuy
Boca de Uchire
Clarines
Bergantín
Valencia
Cagua
Victoria
Cúa
Araguita
Sabana de Uchire
Píritu
Guarenas
San Sebastián
San Casimiro
Altagracia de Orituco
Soublette
San Miguel
El Pilar
Tinaquillo
Güigue
Villa de Cura
San Juan
San José de Guaribe
San Pablo
Santa Inés
COJEDES
San Juan de los Morros
Parapara
Camatagua
Valle de Guanape
San Antonio
Onoto
San Mateo
GUÁRICO
Dos Caminos
Barbacoas
Memo
GUÁRICO
Aragua de Barcelona
Santa Rosa
Scale 1:4 000 000
0 10 20 30 40 Miles
0 10 20 30 40 50 60 Kilometers
©R.M.C.N.
Libertad de Orituco
Pescado
ANZOÁTEGUI
Anaco

Main map

TOBAGO
Port of Spain
TRINIDAD AND TOBAGO
Trinidad
Boca Grande
Morawhanna
Georgetown
Bartica
Rosignol
New Amsterdam
Wismar
Rockstone
Skeldon
Nieuw Nickerie
Paranam
Totness
Paramaribo
Moengo
Albina
St. Laurent
ILE DU DIABLE (DEVIL'S I.)
Sinnamary
SURINAME
FRENCH GUIANA
Cayenne
CABO ORANGE
GEBERGTE
Saint-Georges
TUMUC-HUMAC MTS.
ACARAÍ MTS.
Vista do Branco
Amapá
AMAPÁ
ATLANTIC OCEAN
Macapá
Mazagão
ILHA DE MARAJÓ
ILHA CAVIANA
Marapanim
Equator
Bragança
Manaus (Manáos)
Faro
Óbidos
Alenquer
Breves
Belém (Pará)
Abaetetuba
São Luís (Maranhão)
Cururupú
Parintins
Santarém
Cametá
Alcântara
Tutóia
Camocim
Itacoatiara
ILHA TUPINAMBARANAS
Altamira
Tucuruí
Rosário
Viana
Itapecurú-Mirim
Parnaíba
Acaraú
FORTALEZA (Ceará)
Borba
Maués
Itaituba
Brasília Legal (Fordlândia)
Monção
Brejo
SERRA DA IBIAPABA
Sobral
Maranguape
PARÁ
São João do Araguaia
Codó
Pedreiras
Caxias
Campo Maior
Ipu
Baturité
Aracati
Areia Branca
SERRA DOS CARAJÁS
Araguatins
Grajaú
Barra do Corda
Teresina
Senador Pompeu
Crateús
Quixadá
Russas
Mossoró
RIO GRANDE DO NORTE
Ceará-Mirim
ARQUIPÉLAGO FERNANDO DE NORONHA (Brazil)
MARANHÃO
Miradoro
Amarante
Iguatu
Icó
Currais Novos
Nova Cruz
Natal
FERNANDO DE NORONHA
Tocantinópolis
Riachão
Loreto
Floriano
Picos
Oeiras
Crato
Juàzeiro do Norte
Flores
Patos
Campina Grande
João Pessoa (Paraíba)
ATOL DAS ROCAS (Brazil)
Carolina
Balsas
PLANALTO DA BORBOREMA
Nazaré da Mata
Granito
Sertânia
Jaboatão
Olinda
PIAUÍ
Santa Filomena
São Raimundo Nonato
Paulistana
Juàzeiro
Cabrobó
Caruaru
RECIFE (Pernambuco)
Miracema do Tocantins
Palmas
Parnaguá
PERNAMBUCO
Garanhuns
Palmares
Pôrto de Pedras
Porto Nacional
SERRA DO RONCADOR
Petrolina
Palmeira dos Índios
TABOLEIRO
TOCANTINS
Natividade
Barra
SERRA DO PIAUÍ
Jeremoabo
Propriá
ALAGOAS
Maceió
Coruripe
SERGIPE
Penedo
SERRA DO ESTRONDO
CHAP. DAS MANGABEIRAS
Senhor do Bonfim
Itabaiana
Aracaju
São Cristóvão
Barreiras
Morro do Chapéu
Jacobina
Serrinha
Inhambupe
Estância
Correntina
BAHIA
Feira de Santana
Alagoinhas
Catu
Santo Amaro
SERRA FORMOSA
Cavalcante
Lençóis
Cachoeiro
Nazaré
SALVADOR (Bahia)
SERRA DO TOMBADOR
CHAPADA DE MATO GROSSO
Carinhanha
Caetité
Mucugê
Valença
SERRA DOS PARECIS
Diamantino
GROSSO
Pilar de Goiás
Januária
Jequié
Vitória da Conquista
Ilhéus
Mato Grosso
Rosário Oeste
SA. DA TAQUARA
MATO
GOIÁS
Formosa
Rio Pardo de Minas
Pedra Azul
Itabuna
Canavieiras
Cáceres
Barão de Melgaço
Pirenópolis
Goiás
D.F.
Brasília
São Francisco
Montes Claros
Grão Mogol
Belmonte
La Gaiba
GROSSO
Anápolis
Luziânia
Silvânia
Araçuaí
Pôrto Seguro
San José
Coxim
Rio Verde
Morrinhos
Bela Vista de Goiás
Paracatu
Pirapora
Minas Novas
Teófilo Otoni
ARQUIPÉLAGO DOS ABROLHOS
El Robaré
Cáceres
Goiânia
Ipameri
Catalão
Araguari
Corinto
Diamantina
Peçanha
Caravelas
Puerto Suárez
Corumbá
Coxim
Ituiutaba
Curvelo
Gov. Valadares
São Mateus
MATO GROSSO
Campo Grande
Paranaíba
Uberlândia
Uberaba
Araxá
Sete Lagoas
Pará de Minas
MINAS GERAIS
BELO HORIZONTE
Colatina
Aracruz
Vitória
Bahía Negra
DO SUL
Itapira
SA. DE CANASTRA
Formiga
Santa Bárbara
Ponte Nova
Espírito Santo
Guarapari
Fuerte Olimpo
Aquidauana
Nioaque
São José do Rio Prêto
Franca
Barretos
Divinópolis
Conselheiro Lafaiete
Piço do Bandeira 9482
Cachoeiro de Itapemirim
Porto Murtinho
Bella Vista
Presidente Epitácio
Tupã
Ribeirão Prêto
Passos
Represa de Furnas
Barbacena
Itaperuna
Mariscal Estigarribia
Pedro Juan Caballero
Ponta Porã
Araçatuba
Cotandira
Pouso Alegre
St. Dumont
Caldas
Ubá
Campos
Puerto Casado
Puerto Pinasco
Concepción
Bella Vista
Assis
SÃO PAULO
São Carlos
Araraquara
Marília
Bauru
Piracicaba
Rio Claro
Itajubá
Varginha
Caxambu
Juiz de Fora
Nova Friburgo
PARAGUAY
Horqueta
PARANÁ
Londrina
Ourinhos
Botucatu
Campinas
Jundiaí
Taubaté
Petrópolis
RIO DE JANEIRO
Niterói
Salto
Tibagi
Sorocaba
Itajaí
Volta Redonda
Mogi das Cruzes
RIO DE JANEIRO
Tropic of Capricorn
Guairá
Porto Mendes
SÃO PAULO
Santos
Ponta Grossa
Jacarèzinho
Itararé
Castro
São Vicente
Belén
Guarapuava
Iguaçu

Relief legend

Relief	
Meters	Feet
3050	10 000
1525	5000
610	2000
305	1000
152.5	500
0 Sea Level	0
152.5	500
1525	5000
3050	10 000
6100	20 000

0 50 100 200 300 400 500 Miles
0 100 200 400 600 800 Kilometers

Relief

Meters		Feet
3050		10 000
1525		5000
610		2000
305		1000
152.5		500
0	Sea Level	0
152.5		500
1525		5000
3050		10 000
6100	Below Sea Level	20 000

Scale 1:16 000 000; one inch to 250 miles. Sinusoidal Projection
Elevations and depressions are given in feet

0 50 100 200 300 400 500 Miles
0 100 200 400 600 800 Kilometers

a BUENOS AIRES
Scale 1:1 000 000
0 5 10 Miles
0 4 8 12 16 Kilometers
©RMCN.

b RIO DE JANEIRO
Scale 1:1 000 000
0 5 10 Miles
0 4 8 12 16 Kilometers
©RMCN.

A-549200-76   COPYRIGHT BY RAND McNALLY & COMPANY MADE IN U.S.A.

Longitude West of Greenwich

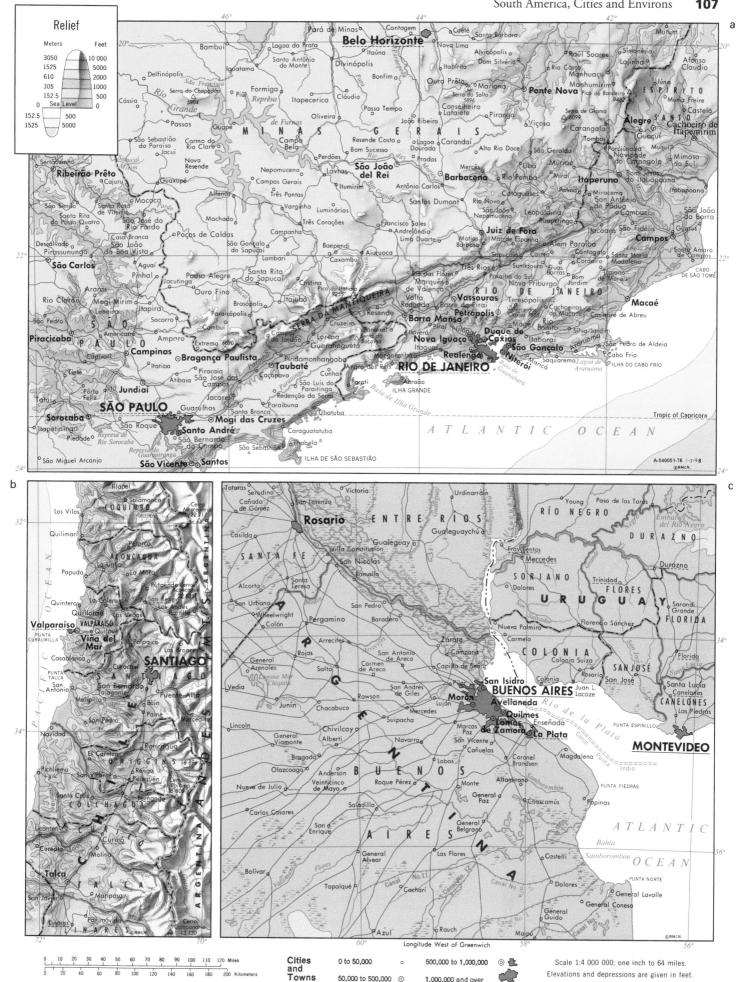

Europe

Europe is smaller than every other continent except Australia. In a sense, Europe is not really a continent at all, since it is part of the same vast landmass as Asia. Geographers sometimes refer to this landmass as a single continent, Eurasia. Europe occupies only about 18% of the land area of Eurasia.

Europe can be described as an enormous peninsula, stretching from the Ural Mountains, Ural River, and Caspian Sea in the east, to the Atlantic Ocean in the west; and from the Arctic Ocean in the north to the Mediterranean Sea, Black Sea, and Caucasus mountains in the south. The British Isles, Iceland, Corsica, Crete, and thousands of smaller islands that lie off the European mainland are usually considered as part of the continent.

A sweep of mountain ranges, including the Pyrenees, Alps and Carpathians, divides the colder, wetter north from the sun-drenched south.

Europe at a glance

Land area:
3,800,000 square miles (9,900,000 sq km)

Estimated population:
728,420,000

Population density:
192/square mile (74/sq km)

Mean elevation:
980 feet (300 m)

Highest point:
Gora El'brus, Russia,
18,510 feet (5,642 m)

Lowest point:
Caspian Sea, Asia-Europe,
92 feet (28 m) below sea level

Longest river:
Volga, 2,194 mi (3,531 km)

**Number of countries
(incl. dependencies):** 50

Largest independent country:
Russia (Europe/Asia),
6,592,849 square miles
(17,075,400 sq km)

Smallest independent country:
Vatican City, 0.2 square miles
(0.4 sq km)

**Most populous
independent country:**
Russia (Europe/Asia),
140,370,000

**Least populous
independent country:**
Vatican City, 800

Most populous metropolitan area:
Moscow, Russia,
population 10.5 million

The Alps tower above a village in the Virgen Tal valley of western Austria.

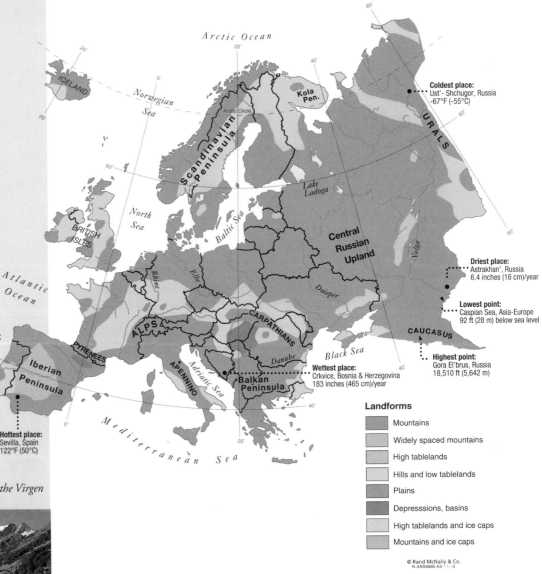

Coldest place:
Ust'- Shchugor, Russia
-67°F (-55°C)

Driest place:
Astrakhan', Russia
6.4 inches (16 cm)/year

Lowest point:
Caspian Sea, Asia-Europe
92 ft (28 m) below sea level

Highest point:
Gora El'brus, Russia
18,510 ft (5,642 m)

Wettest place:
Crkvice, Bosnia & Herzegovina
183 inches (465 cm)/year

Hottest place:
Sevilla, Spain
122°F (50°C)

Landforms

- Mountains
- Widely spaced mountains
- High tablelands
- Hills and low tablelands
- Plains
- Depresssions, basins
- High tablelands and ice caps
- Mountains and ice caps

© Rand McNally & Co.
N-ANS50000-A3- -1--1--2

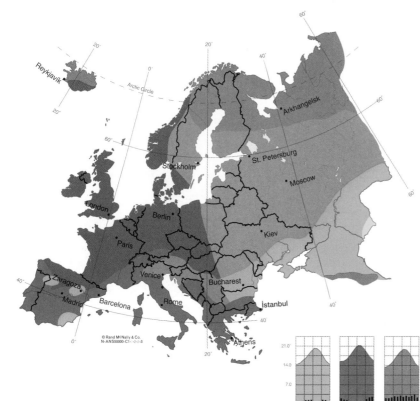

Climate

Warm, moist air masses flowing in from the Atlantic Ocean give much of Europe a mild climate and abundant precipitation. Cities like London, Paris, and Rome all enjoy warmer weather than cities at similar latitudes in North America and Asia. The moderate winds don't reach eastern Europe, where the winters are long and cold and the summers short and cool. The same is true in the northern regions of Scandinavia.

Much of the south enjoys a Mediterranean climate, marked by short, rainy winters and long, dry summers. Indeed, the many beaches and islands found throughout the region are popular with vacationers year-round.

Tinted areas show temperature in degrees Fahrenheit. Vertical bars show precipitation in inches.

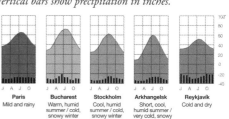

Zaragoza	Athens	Venice	Paris	Bucharest	Stockholm	Arkhangelsk	Reykjavík
Semiarid	Hot, dry summer / mild, rainy winter	Warm, humid summer / mild winter	Mild and rainy	Warm, humid summer / cold, snowy winter	Cool, humid summer / cold, snowy winter	Short, cool, humid summer / very cold, snowy winter	Cold and dry

Extensive uplands
Climate varies with elevation and latitude

Population

Europe is the second most densely populated continent. Only Asia has a greater population density. However, Europe's density varies dramatically from country to country. The Netherlands, for instance, has a density of 1,032 people per square mile (398 per sq km), making it one of the most densely populated countries in the world. In contrast, Norway has only 37 people per square mile (14 per sq km).

A vast array of ethnic groups and cultures can be found in Europe's relatively small area. Throughout the centuries, this diversity has enriched European culture while also leading to many hostilities. Of the 60 languages spoken, the majority are derived from Latin, Germanic or Slavic roots. Most Europeans are Christian, either Protestant or Roman Catholic.

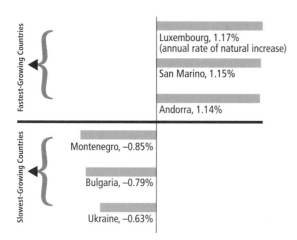

Luxembourg, 1.17% (annual rate of natural increase)
San Marino, 1.15%
Andorra, 1.14%
Montenegro, −0.85%
Bulgaria, −0.79%
Ukraine, −0.63%

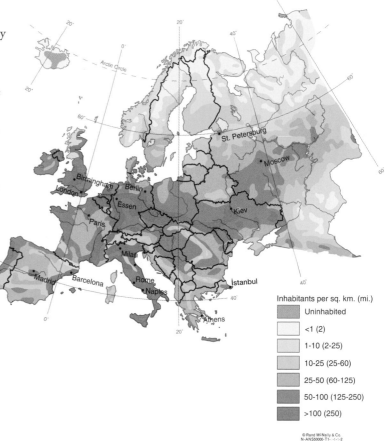

Inhabitants per sq. km. (mi.)
Uninhabited
<1 (2)
1-10 (2-25)
10-25 (25-60)
25-50 (60-125)
50-100 (125-250)
>100 (250)

Environments and Land Use

Given the high population density of Europe, it is not surprising that evidence of human development can be seen in every part of the continent, with the exception of the northern reaches of Scandinavia. In Western Europe, small farms are surrounded by towns, cities, and industrial areas. Only in the east, in areas such as the vast rolling steppes of the Ukraine, can large farms and unbroken natural vistas be found.

The heavily industrialized countries of Western Europe boast rich economies and high standards of living. Switzerland has a per capita Gross Domestic Product (GDP) approaching U.S. $22,000, the highest in the world. The figures are generally much lower in Eastern Europe. One of the continent's poorest countries is the tiny former Communist state of Albania, which has a per capita GDP of only U.S. $998.

Pollution is an unfortunate by-product of the continent's industry. One example is the scenic Rhine River: in the 1980s, large stretches were found to be so polluted that they were devoid of life. These findings sparked a 20-year program to clean up the river. In general, the countries of Eastern Europe suffer from the worst pollution, as economic development has in the past taken precedence over environmental policies.

The vast forests of Scandinavia support a large paper and wood-products economy. Where forests survive in countries farther to the south, they are often used for recre- ation. Along the Mediterranean, the warm and dry lands support olive and fruit orchards. In many of these areas, agriculture is being supplemented and even replaced by tourism.

Over-fishing has depleted the seas and ocean around Europe. The fleets of countries such as Spain and Great Britain must sail far into the North Atlantic to find the ever-dwindling stocks of fish.

Harvesting grapes from vineyards in Burgundy, France

Political Changes Since 1989

Much of Europe lay in economic and physical ruin after World War II ended in 1945. Germany's cities and industrial centers had been ravaged by aerial bombardment and assaults by the Allied armies. Many other countries, such as Russia, Poland, Belgium, and the Netherlands suffered gravely from Nazi invasions and occupation.

After 1945, tensions among the victorious Allies grew, specifically between the western powers—the United States, Great Britain and France—and the Soviet Union. It became clear that the two sides had vastly different visions for post-war Europe. In 1946, former British prime minister Winston Churchill observed that an "Iron Curtain" had gone down across Europe. It was to stay in place for almost 45 years.

Germany and the city of Berlin were divided between the western powers and the Soviet Union. West Germany quickly joined the other countries of Western Europe in building a stable, affluent democratic society. East Germany became part of a bloc of Eastern European countries dominated by the Soviet Union. These included Poland, Czechoslovakia, Hungary, Romania, Albania, and Bulgaria (see map at right). The economies in these countries were tightly controlled and personal freedoms were severely limited by the Communist governments in power. The two blocs faced each other in a tense, generally non-military standoff called "The Cold War," which lasted for four decades. However, in 1985 winds of reform began sweeping through Eastern Europe. In 1989, Hungary relaxed its borders with Austria, setting off a flow of refugees from the east who had been forbidden to travel to the west. Thus began a dizzying period of change: the next two years saw the collapse of the Soviet Union, the reunification of Germany, independence for the former Soviet republics, and freedom from Soviet influence for the former bloc countries. Although much of the old east seems intent on adopting western ideals of democracy and freedom, the process is not without problems. Switching from communism to market economies has meant hardship for millions. It has also led to ethnic tensions that resulted in the peaceful break-up of Czechoslovakia and the violent civil wars in the former Yugoslavia.

East Germany and West Germany reunited in 1990.

In 1991, the Soviet Union broke up into 15 independent states: Russia, Estonia, Latvia, Lithuania, Belarus, Ukraine, Moldova, Georgia, Armenia, Azerbaijan, Kazakhstan, Turkmenistan, Kyrgyzstan, Uzbekistan, and Tajikistan.

In 1991-92, the former Yugoslavia broke up when Slovenia, Croatia, Macedonia, and Bosnia and Herzegovina declared their independence. In 2003, the remaining republics changed the name of the country from Yugoslavia to Serbia and Montenegro. Montenegro declared its independence from Serbia in 2006. In 2008, the province of Kosovo also declared its independence from Serbia.

In 1993, Czechoslovakia split into two separate countries: the Czech Republic and Slovakia.

Political Change Since 1989

© Rand McNally & Co.
N-ANS50000-P4- -:-:-3

- Former Soviet Union
- Former Czechoslovakia
- Former Yugoslavia
- Former East and West Germany
- Former Soviet-bloc countries

Berlin Wall memorial

40,000 SQ MI
AREA

0   100   200
Miles

Scale 1: 16 000 000; one inch to 250 miles. Conic Projection
Elevations and depressions are given in feet

Longitude West of Greenwich   0°   Longitude East of Greenwich

Relief

Meters		Feet
3050		10 000
1525		5000
610		2000
305		1000
152.5		500
0	Sea Level	0
152.5		Below Sea Level 500
1525		5000
3050		10 000

Scale 1: 16 000 000; one inch to 250 miles. Conic Projection

Elevations and depressions are given in feet

Longitude West of Greenwich   Longitude East of Greenwich

0   50   100   200   300   400   500 Miles

0   100   200   400   600   800 Kilometers

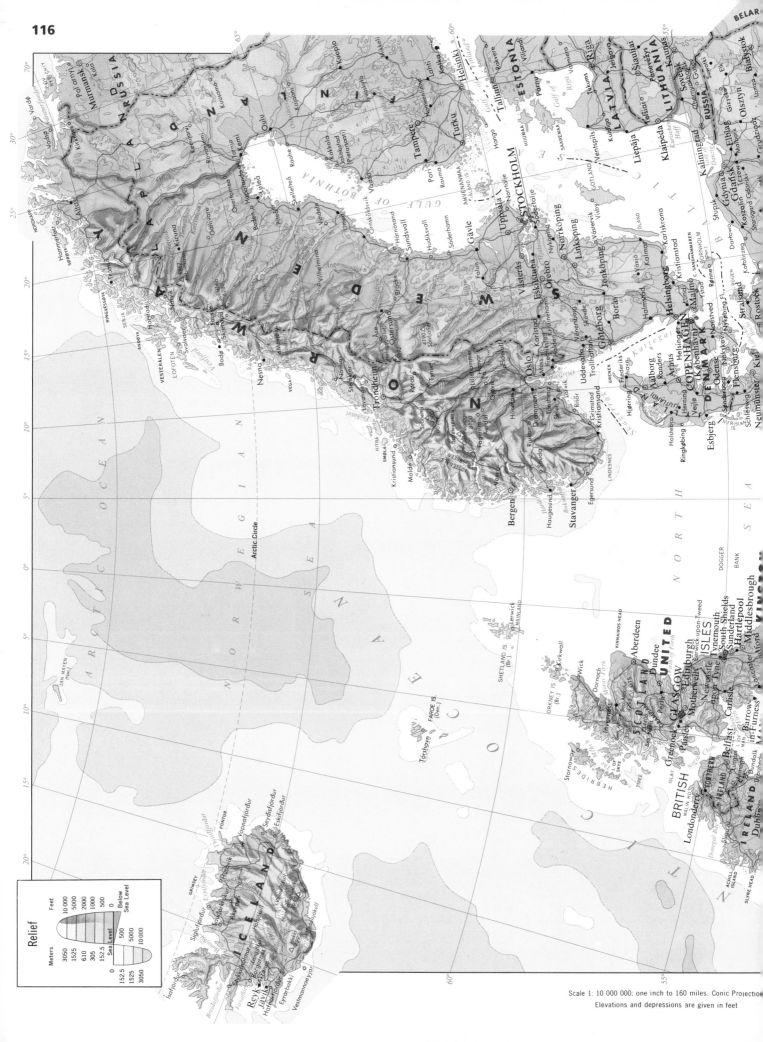

Scale 1:10 000 000; one inch to 160 miles. Conic Projection
Elevations and depressions are given in feet.

ATLANTIC OCEAN

BAY OF BISCAY

FRANCE

SPAIN

PORTUGAL

MOROCCO

ALGERIA

TUNISIA

MEDITERRANEAN SEA

LIGURIAN SEA

TYRRHENIAN SEA

GERMANY

AUSTRIA

SWITZERLAND

SLOVENIA

CORSICA (Fr.)

SARDINIA (It.)

SICILY

MALTA

BALEARS (Sp.)

ILLES

T A R Â B U L U S (TRIPOLITANIA)

GRAND ERG OCCIDENTAL

GRAND ERG ORIENTAL

SAHARAN ATLAS

MOYEN ATLAS

HAUT ATLAS

MONTS DES KSOUR

MONTS DES OULAD NAÎL

CORDILLERA CANTABRICA

PYRENEES

SIERRA MORENA

SIERRA NEVADA

PARIS

FRANKFURT

PRAGUE (Praha)

MANNHEIM

STUTTGART

MUNICH

MADRID

LISBON

BARCELONA

VALÈNCIA

ROME (Roma)

NAPLES (Napoli)

PALERMO

TUNIS

ALGIERS (El Djazaïr)

Tripoli (Tarābulus)

MONACO

VATICAN CITY

SAN MARINO

ANDORRA

LIECHTENSTEIN

Cherbourg · Le Havre · Amiens · St. Quentin · Koblenz · Wiesbaden
Brest · Morlaix · Caen · Rouen · Reims · Metz · Luxembourg · Trier · Mainz · Worms · Darmstadt · Bamberg · Karlovy Vary
Quimper · Lorient · Rennes · St. Brieuc · St. Malo · Alençon · Chartres · Versailles · St. Denis · Châlons-sur-Marne · Verdun · Nancy · Strasbourg · Karlsruhe · Heilbronn · Nürnberg
St. Nazaire · Angers · Le Mans · Orléans · Troyes · Colmar · Freiburg · Ulm · Augsburg
Nantes · Cholet · Tours · Blois · Bourges · Nevers · Dijon · Besançon · Basel · Zürich · Innsbruck
Poitiers · Châtellerault · Châteauroux · Moulins · Mâcon · Bourg-en-Bresse · Genève · Lausanne · Bern · Luzern
La Rochelle · Rochefort · Limoges · Clermont-Ferrand · Vichy · Roanne · Lyon · Chambéry · Grenoble
Bordeaux · Périgueux · Angoulême · Libourne · St. Étienne · Valence
Bayonne · Mont-de-Marsan · Agen · Montauban · Albi · Nîmes · Avignon · Arles · Aix-en-Provence · Nice · Cannes
Pau · Tarbes · Toulouse · Carcassonne · Béziers · Narbonne · Montpellier · Marseille · Toulon · Hyères

Milan · Novara · Turin · Asti · Genoa · Bergamo · Vicenza · Treviso · Trieste · Venice · Padova
Cremona · Verona · Mantova · Pavia · Piacenza · Alessandria · Parma · Modena · Bologna · Ferrara · Ravenna · Rimini · Forlì
La Spezia · Livorno · Pisa · Lucca · Pistoia · Florence · Arezzo · Perugia · Siena · Ancona · Pesaro

A Coruña · Ferrol · Gijón · Oviedo · Santander · Bilbao · San Sebastián · Pamplona · Logroño · Zaragoza
Vigo · Pontevedra · León · Burgos · Soria · Lleida
Porto · Braga · Zamora · Valladolid · Segovia · Guadalajara
Salamanca · Ávila · Barcelona · Tarragona · Sabadell · Manresa · Girona
Coimbra · Cáceres · Toledo · Cuenca · Castelló de la Plana
Badajoz · Mérida · Ciudad Real · Albacete · València · Palma
Sevilla · Córdoba · Jaén · Linares · Alcoi · Alacant
Huelva · Cádiz · Jerez de la Frontera · Granada · Murcia · Cartagena · Almería
Tanger · Ceuta (Sp.) · Málaga · Melilla (Sp.)

Tetouan · Oujda · Fès · Meknès · Rabat · Salé · Kenitra · Larache
Oran (Wahran) · Mostaghanem · Tlemcen · Sidi bel Abbès · Tiaret · Saïda
Mestghanem · Cherchell · Tizi Ouzou · Béjaïa · Jijel · Skikda · Annaba · Constantine
Bizerte · Menzel Bourguiba · Nabeul · Sousse · Kairouan · Sfax · Gabès · Gafsa
Laghouat · Ghardaïa · Ouargla · Touggourt · El Oued · Biskra · Batna
Béchar · Adrar · Timimoun · El Menia

Ghudāmis · Nālūt · Zuwārah · Misrātah · Al Khums

Relief

Meters	Feet
3050	10000
1525	5000
610	2000
305	1000
152.5	500
0 Sea Level	0
	Below
152.5	Sea Level
1525	500
3050	5000
	10000

Longitude West of Greenwich 0° Longitude East of Greenwich

Scale 1:10 000 000; one inch to 160 miles. Bonne's Projection
Elevations and depressions are given in feet

Countries and regions: POLAND, SLOVAKIA, HUNGARY, CROATIA, BOSNIA AND HERZEGOVINA, SERBIA, MONT. (Montenegro), ROMANIA, MOLDOVA, UKRAINE, RUSSIA, GEORGIA, BULGARIA, MACEDONIA, ALBANIA, GREECE, TURKEY, ASIA MINOR, CYPRUS, SYRIA, LEBANON, ISRAEL, JORDAN, SAUDI ARABIA, EGYPT, LIBYA

Seas and water: BLACK SEA, SEA OF AZOV, AEGEAN SEA, IONIAN SEA, ADRIATIC SEA, MEDITERRANEAN SEA, RED SEA, DEAD SEA, Marmara Denizi, Antalya Körfezi, Golfo di Taranto, Khalīj Surt (Gulf of Sidra)

Poland / Slovakia / Hungary / Czech area:
Zabrze, KATOWICE, Rzeszów, Jarosław, Brody, Starokostiantyniv, Kraków, POLAND, Tarnów, L'viv, Ternopil, Khmel'nyts'kyi, Vinnytsia, Smila, BESKID MTS, CARPATHIANS, Ostrava, Žilina, Frankivs'k, Kamianets-Podil's'kyi, Stryi, Ivano-Frankivs'k, Zhmerynka, Haisyn, Uman, Kirovohrad, Znojmo, Banská Bystrica, Košice, Prešov, Uzhhorod, Mukacheve, Khust, Tul'chyn, Mohyliv-Podil's'kyi, Soroka, Balta, Pervomais'k, VIENNA, Bratislava, Nové Zámky, Miskolc, Nyíregyháza, Satu Mare, Baia Mare, Rădăuți, Ananiv, Novoukrainka, Kryvyi Rih, Wiener Neustadt, Győr, BUDAPEST, Székesfehérvár, Debrecen, Hajdúszoboszló, Simleu, Silvaniei, Dej, Piatra-Neamț, Bacău, Huși, Bălți, Orhei, Tighina, Tiraspol, Pápa, Szombathely, Kecskemét, Szolnok, Cluj, Napoca, Aiud, Târgu Mureș, Sfântu Gheorghe, Bârlad, Chișinău, Kherson, Balaton, Nagykanizsa, Szekszárd, Pécs, Szeged, Arad, Békéscsaba, HUNGARY, Alba Iulia, Sibiu, Brașov, Râmnicu Sărat, Galați, Cahul, Bolgrad, Ismayil, Vylkove, Mykolaiv

Romania / Moldova / Ukraine:
MOLDOVA, Iași, ROMANIA, CARPATII MERIDIONALI (TRANSYLVANIAN ALPS), Lugoj, Deva, Hunedoara, Câmpulung, Târgu Jiu, Pitești, Târgoviște, Ploiești, Buzău, Brăila, Tulcea, Sulina, Subotica, Senta, Sombor, Vršac, Timișoara, Drobeta-Turnu Severin, Craiova, Roșiori de Vede, Turnu Măgurele, Tutrakan, Silistra, Călărași, BUCHAREST, Constanța, M. KALIAKRA, Novi Sad, Zrenjanin, Pančevo, Vidin, Nikopol, Svishtov, Razgrad, Dobrich, Varna (Stalin), Odesa, Bilhorod-Dnistrovs'kyy, Chornomors'ke, M. TARKHANKUT, Ievpatoriia

Crimea / Black Sea coast:
KRYMS'KYI PIVOSTRIV (CRIMEAN PEN.), Simferopol', Sevastopol', M. SARYCH, Yalta, Feodosiia, Anapa, Novorossiysk, Kerch, Dzhankoi, Henichres'k, Melitopol', Berdians'k, Yeysk, Tuapse, Sochi, Sukhumi, GEORGIA, Primorsko-Akhtarskaya, Timashevskaya, Temryuk, Krasnodar, Maykop, Labinsk, Armavir, Kropotkin, Stavropol', Tikhoretsk, Rostov-na-Donu, DONETS'K, Novocherkassk, Sal'sk, Taganrog, Mariupol'

Ukraine interior:
Zvenyhorodka, Shpola, Kremenchuk, Pavlohrad, Syni'nykove, Sýnel'nykove, DNIPROPETROVS'K, Zaporizhzhia, Dniprodzerzhyns'k, Novomoskovs'k, Nikopol', Kakhovs'ke Vdskh., Kakhovka

Serbia / Balkans:
SERBIA, Belgrade (Beograd), Kragujevac, Kraljevo, Niš, Pirot, Loznica, Šabac, Bijeljina, Tuzla, Banja Luka, Gradačac, BOSNIA AND HERZEGOVINA, Sarajevo, Mostar, Pljevlja, Novi Pazar, Priština, Prizren, STARA PLANINA (BALKAN MTS), Sofia (Sofiya), Pernik, Kyustendil, Pazardzhik, Plovdiv, Stara Zagora, Sliven, Yambol, Burgas, Pomorie, Gulf of Burgas, Nikopol, Pleven, Veliko Tŭrnovo, Shumen, Ruse, Lom, Vratsa, BULGARIA, Khaskovo, Kŭrdzhali, RHODOPE MTS, Edirne, Kırklareli, Tekirdağ

Montenegro / Albania:
MONTENEGRO, Podgorica, Ulcinj, Tiranë, Durrës, Elbasan, Korçë, Vlorë (Valona), Gjirokastër, ALBANIA, MACEDONIA, Skopje, Tetovo, Bitola, Prilep, PINDOS DROS, Dubrovnik, Sveti Palagruža (Cro.), LASTOVO, MLJET, Šibenik, Split, Trogir, BRAC, HVAR, KORČULA, VIS

Italy (left edge):
Monte Sant'Angelo, Barletta, Molfetta, Bari, Altamura, Potenza, Taranto, Brindisi, Lecce, Rossano, Nicastro, Catanzaro, Reggio di Calabria, C. S. MARIA DI LEUCA, Golfo di Taranto, Siracusa, Strait of Otranto

Greece:
GREECE, Thessaloníki, Kavála, Sérres, Édessa, Flórina, Kastoriá, Kozáni, Lárisa, Vólos, Tríkala, Ioánnina, Árta, Lamía, Levádia, Thíva (Thebes), Khalkída, ATHENS (Athína), Peiraiás, Kórinthos, Trípoli, Spárti, Kalamáta, Kyparissía, Pýrgos, Pátra, Agrínio, Mesolóngio, Zákynthos, AKRA TAÍNARO, ANTIKYTHIRA, KÝTHIRA, KRETE (CRETE), Chaniá, Iráklio, GAVDOS, KÁSOS, KÁRPATHOS, ÁKRA MALÉAS, Ródos (RODOS), SÝMI, ASTYPALAIA, AMORGÓS, NÁXOS, PÁROS, MÍLOS, SÉRIFOS, ÁNDROS, TÍNOS, SÁMOS, KÝKLADES, SKÝROS, ÉVVOIA, ÍOS, Komotiní, Xánthi, Dráma, Alexandroúpoli, SAMOTHRÁKI, THÁSOS, LIMNOS, AGIOS EFSTRATIOS, LÉSVOS, Mytilíni, CHÍOS, KÉRKYRA (Kérkyra), LEFKÁDA, KEFALLINÍA, IONIAN ISLANDS, ZÁKYNTHOS

Turkey:
İSTANBUL, İzmit, Adapazarı, Bolu, Bursa, Bilecik, Beypazarı, Eskişehir, Gemlik, Bandırma, Çanakkale, Balıkesir, Kütahya, Afyon, Bolvadin, Ayvalık, Bergama, Akhisar, Manisa, İzmir, Ödemiş, Uşak, Tire, Aydın, Denizli, Söke, Milas, Muğla, Burdur, Isparta, Konya, Antalya (Adalia), Alanya, Silifke, İçel, Mersin, Tarsus, Adana, Osmaniye, İskenderun, Antakya, Gaziantep, Kilis, Birecik, Şanlıurfa, Kahramanmaraş, Malatya, Elâzığ, Keban Gölü, Sivas, Erzincan, Tokat, Amasya, Çorum, Yozgat, Kırşehir, Ankara (Angora), Nevşehir, Aksaray, Niğde, Ulukışla, Ereğli, Karaman, TOROS DAĞLARI (TAURUS MTS), Zonguldak, Ereğli, Bartın, Kastamonu, Tosya, İskilip, Çankırı, İnebolu, Sinop, Samsun, Ünye, Ordu, Giresun, Trabzon, Rize, Bafra, Çarşamba, Merzifon, Sungurlu, Kayseri, Pınarbaşı, Elbistan, Divriği, Sebinkarahisar, KEREMPE BR, INCE BR, Cide, İğneada, İSTANBUL BOĞAZI (BOSPORUS), İSTANBUL BOĞAZI, ÇANAKKALE BOĞAZI (DARDANELLES), Mustafakemalpaşa, Bilecik

Cyprus / Levant:
CYPRUS, Nicosia, Famagusta, Larnaka, Limassol, The Turkish Republic of Northern Cyprus unilaterally declared its independence on Nov. 15, 1983., Al Lādhiqīyah (Latakia), Ţarţūs, Ḩamāh, Homs, Tarābulus (Tripoli), Beirut, LEBANON, Şaydā (Sidon), Şūr (Tyre), Acre, Haifa, Nazareth, Nablus, Tel Aviv-Yafo, ISRAEL, Jerusalem, Bethlehem, Hebron, Gaza, Beersheba, Amman, JORDAN, Damascus (Dimashq), As Suwaydā, Irbid, Az Zarqā', Ma'ān, Al 'Aqabah, SAUDI ARABIA, Areas occupied by Israel since 1967.

Egypt / Libya:
Shaḩḩāt, Darnah, Tulmaythah, Ţūkrah, Sulunṭah, AL JABAL AL AKHDAR, Tubruq (Tobruk), Banghāzī, Ajdābiyah, Marsā Maṭrūḩ, Sīdī Barrāni, As Sallūm, RA'S AL KANĀIS, Al 'Amirīyah, Alexandria (Al Iskandarīyah), Rashīd, Dumyāţ, Port Said (Būr Sa'īd), Al 'Arīsh, Al Maḩallah al Kubrá, Damanhūr, Ţanţā, Al Manşūrah, Al Ismā'īlīyah, Shibīn al Kawm, Zaqāzīq, Al Hammām, Al 'Alamayn, CAIRO (Al Qāhirah), Suez (As Suways), Būr Tawfīq, Ḩulwān, Al Jīzah, Al Fayyūm, SINAI PEN., Jabal Kātrīnā 8668, Al Wāsiţah, Bani Suwayf, Aţ Fashn, Banī Mazār, Al Minyā, Mallawī, MUNKHAFAD AL QAŢŢĀRAH -436, EGYPT, LIBYA, BARQAH (CYRENAICA), LIBYAN PLATEAU, LIBYAN DESERT, Surt, An Nawfalīyah, Qaşr al Burayqah, Al Uqaylah, Wādī al Fārīgh, Maṣr al Burayqah, Marādah, Jālū (Oasis), Awjilah (Oasis), Jaghbūb, Sūluq, Al Bāwīṭī, Gulf of Suez, Gulf of Aqaba, RED SEA

Note A: Kosovo declared its independence from Serbia on February 17, 2008.

Scale:
0 50 100 150 200 250 300 Miles
0 100 200 300 400 500 Kilometers

Africa

Africa, the second-largest continent, comprises about one-fifth of the world's land area. From the Equator, Africa extends roughly the same distance to the north as it does to the south.

The Drakensberg Mountains in southern South Africa

A high plateau covers much of the continent. The edges of the plateau are marked by steep slopes, called escarpments, where the land angles sharply downward onto narrow coastal plains or into the sea. Many of the continent's great rivers plunge over these escarpments in falls or rapids, and therefore cannot be used as transportation routes from the coast into the continent's interior.

Among Africa's most significant mountain systems are the Atlas range in the far north and the Drakensberg range in the far south. A long string of mountain ranges and highlands running north-south through eastern Africa marks the course of the Rift Valley.

Africa at a glance

Land area:
11,700,000 square miles (30,300,000 sq km)

Estimated population:
985,490,000

Population density:
84/ square mile (33/sq km)

Mean elevation:
1,900 feet (580 m)

Highest point:
Kilimanjaro, Tanzania, 19,340 feet (5,895 m)

Lowest point:
Lac 'Assal, Djibouti, 515 feet (157 m) below sea level

Longest river:
Nile, 4,145 mi (6,671 km)

Number of countries (incl. dependencies): 59

Largest independent country:
Sudan, 967,500 square miles (2,505,813 sq km)

Smallest independent country:
Seychelles, 176 square miles (455 sq km)

Most populous independent country:
Nigeria, 147,735,000

Least populous independent country:
Seychelles, 87,000

Most populous metropolitan area:
Cairo, Egypt, population 11.9 million

Sand dunes in the Sahara

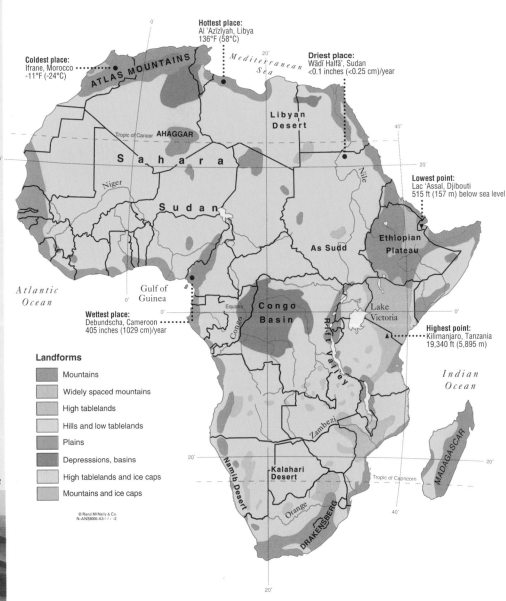

Coldest place:
Ifrane, Morocco
-11°F (-24°C)

Hottest place:
Al 'Azīzīyah, Libya
136°F (58°C)

Driest place:
Wādī Halfā', Sudan
<0.1 inches (<0.25 cm)/year

Lowest point:
Lac 'Assal, Djibouti
515 ft (157 m) below sea level

Wettest place:
Debundscha, Cameroon
405 inches (1029 cm)/year

Highest point:
Kilimanjaro, Tanzania
19,340 ft (5,895 m)

ATLAS MOUNTAINS
Mediterranean Sea
Libyan Desert
Tropic of Cancer AHAGGAR
S a h a r a
Niger
S u d a n
Nile
As Sudd
Ethiopian Plateau
Atlantic Ocean
Gulf of Guinea
Equator
Congo Basin
Congo
Lake Victoria
Rift Valley
Indian Ocean
Zambezi
Namib Desert
Kalahari Desert
Orange
DRAKENSBERG
MADAGASCAR
Tropic of Capricorn

Landforms
- Mountains
- Widely spaced mountains
- High tablelands
- Hills and low tablelands
- Plains
- Depresssions, basins
- High tablelands and ice caps
- Mountains and ice caps

© Rand McNally & Co.
N-ANS8000-A3-   -2

Climate

Africa's most prominent climatic region is the vast Sahara desert which spreads over much of the northern half of the continent. The Sahara experiences scorching daytime temperatures, minimal rainfall, and hot, dry, dust-laden winds that blow nearly continuously. South of the Sahara, the climate becomes increasingly humid, moving through zones of semiarid steppe and tropical savanna to the tropical rain forest that stretches across equatorial Africa from the Atlantic Ocean to the Rift Valley.

The climate patterns of northern Africa are repeated in reverse south of the Equator. The rain forest gives way to zones of decreasing humidity, and desert regions cover western South Africa and Namibia. Africa's mildest, most temperate climates are found along its Mediterranean coast, at its southwestern tip, and in eastern South Africa.

Tinted areas show temperature in degrees Fahrenheit.
Vertical bars show precipitation in inches.

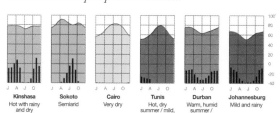

Population

About one-seventh of the world's people live in Africa. It is the second most populous continent. The population is almost evenly divided between the sub-Saharan countries and those bordering the Mediterranean. Large tracts of the Sahara are uninhabited. Despite recurring famines, disease, and warfare, the population is rapidly increasing.

The largest concentrations of people are generally found in regions in which one or more of the following conditions exist: moderate temperatures, ample water supply, and arable land. These regions include Egypt's fertile Nile Valley, the northern coast of the Gulf of Guinea, the highlands of East Africa, and the coastal regions of Morocco, Algeria, and Tunisia, north of the Atlas Mountains.

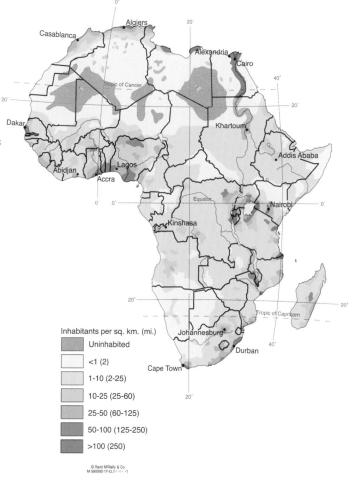

Inhabitants per sq. km. (mi.)

- Uninhabited
- <1 (2)
- 1-10 (2-25)
- 10-25 (25-60)
- 25-50 (60-125)
- 50-100 (125-250)
- >100 (250)

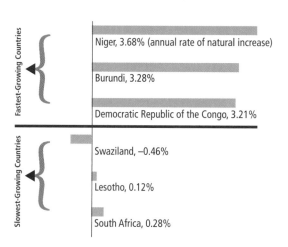

Fastest-Growing Countries

- Niger, 3.68% (annual rate of natural increase)
- Burundi, 3.28%
- Democratic Republic of the Congo, 3.21%

Slowest-Growing Countries

- Swaziland, −0.46%
- Lesotho, 0.12%
- South Africa, 0.28%

Environments and Land Use

Deserts account for one-third of Africa's land area, and they claim new land every year. Drought, over-farming, and over-grazing can quickly turn marginal land, such as that of the Sahel region (also known as the Sudan), into barren wasteland. The huge Sahara desert has itself only existed a short time, in geological terms: cave paintings and other archeological evidence indicate that green pastureland covered the area just a few thousand years ago.

Most Africans are subsistence farmers, growing sorghum, corn, millet, sweet potatoes, and other starchy foods. Commercial farms, most of which date from the colonial period, can be found throughout central and southern Africa, producing cash crops such as coffee, bananas, tobacco, and cacao. One-quarter of the continent's land is suitable for grazing, but disease and drought have made raising animals difficult. Although three out of four Africans work in agriculture, Africa is the only continent that is not self-sufficient for food.

The great rain forests that cover much of equatorial Africa produce mahogany, ebony, and other valuable hardwoods. However, only limited areas of the forests are suitable for logging, and the lack of developed road networks makes it difficult and costly to transport the wood.

Vast mineral reserves are spread throughout the continent. Most are unexploited, but notable exceptions include the diamond mines of South Africa and Namibia, the copper mines of Zambia and Democratic Republic of the Congo, and the oil fields of Nigeria, Libya, and Algeria.

The great concentrations of wildlife for which Africa is famous can still be found in places such as Tanzania's Serengeti Plain and Botswana's Kalahari Desert. In many other parts of the continent, however, wildlife is quickly disappearing as humans encroach on habitat and poachers decimate entire species.

Shepherd with goats in the Sahel (Sudan)

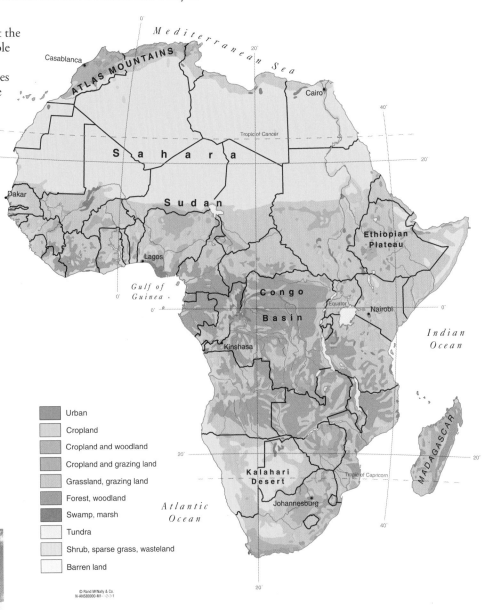

Urban
Cropland
Cropland and woodland
Cropland and grazing land
Grassland, grazing land
Forest, woodland
Swamp, marsh
Tundra
Shrub, sparse grass, wasteland
Barren land

© Rand McNally & Co.
N-ANS80000-M1- -2-/-1

0 200 400 600 800 1000 Miles
0 300 600 900 1200 1500 Kilometers

Field of sorghum in Zimbabwe

Africa: from Colonial Rule to Independence

The origins of Europe's colonization of Africa can be traced back to the 1500s, when a lucrative slave trade developed to supply European settlers in the New World with laborers. Africa became the primary source for slaves: between the mid-1500s and the mid-1800s, 11 million Africans were captured and sold into slavery.

When the slave trade was banned across Europe in the early 1800s, commercial trade with Africa continued. In the second half of the century, competition for Africa's minerals and other raw materials intensified, and between 1880 and 1914, France, Britain, Italy, Portugal, Belgium, Spain, and Germany annexed large areas of Africa. Colonial rule was often characterized by racial prejudice and segregation.

In the late 19th and early 20th centuries, Egypt, Ethiopia, and South Africa began to break free from colonial influence. For most of Africa, however, colonial rule persisted through the mid-1900s, although it faced growing bitterness and nationalist sentiment. As the colonial powers struggled through two world wars, and as their international dominance declined, it became increasingly difficult for them to maintain their empires.

In 1951, Libya gained its independence, following a UN resolution that ended British and French control. Sudan peacefully won independence from Britain and Egypt in 1956. A year later, Britain granted independence to the Gold Coast, which became the new country of Ghana. Guinea separated from France in 1958, followed by all of the other French colonies in 1960. Anti-colonial movements gathered strength across Africa, and by the end of the 1970s, a total of 43 countries had become independent.

The end of colonial rule, however, has not brought peace and prosperity. Many of the newly freed countries were ill-prepared for independence. Their economies were oriented to fit the needs of the now-departed colonists, few transportation networks existed, and dictators and rival despots fought for power in civil wars.

Further, most Africans identify themselves primarily with the tribe to which they belong. The political delineations established by the European powers have little meaning and often conflict with traditional tribal boundaries. In some cases, enemy tribes found themselves pushed together in a single country; in others, single tribes were divided among several countries. These conditions have already brought much warfare and hardship.

Still, Africa is a land of promise and opportunity. The rich diversity of its people and abundance of its resources should inevitably enable the continent to realize its potential.

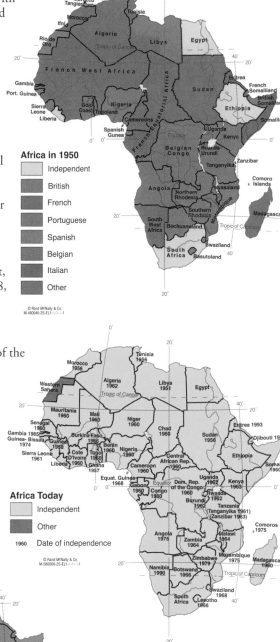

Africa in 1950

- Independent
- British
- French
- Portuguese
- Spanish
- Belgian
- Italian
- Other

© Rand McNally & Co.
M-480045-2S-EL1-¦-¦-¦-1

Africa Today

- Independent
- Other
- 1960   Date of independence

© Rand McNally & Co.
M-580000-2S-EL1-¦-¦-¦-1

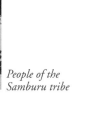

People of the Samburu tribe

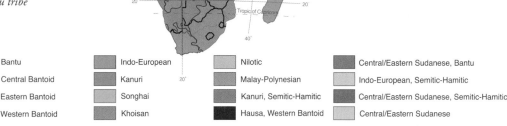

Ethno-linguistic Groups

Semitic-Hamitic	Bantu	Indo-European	Nilotic	Central/Eastern Sudanese, Bantu
Mande	Central Bantoid	Kanuri	Malay-Polynesian	Indo-European, Semitic-Hamitic
Guinean	Eastern Bantoid	Songhai	Kanuri, Semitic-Hamitic	Central/Eastern Sudanese, Semitic-Hamitic
Hausa	Western Bantoid	Khoisan	Hausa, Western Bantoid	Central/Eastern Sudanese

© Rand McNally & Co.
M-580000-1D-EL1-¦-¦-¦-1

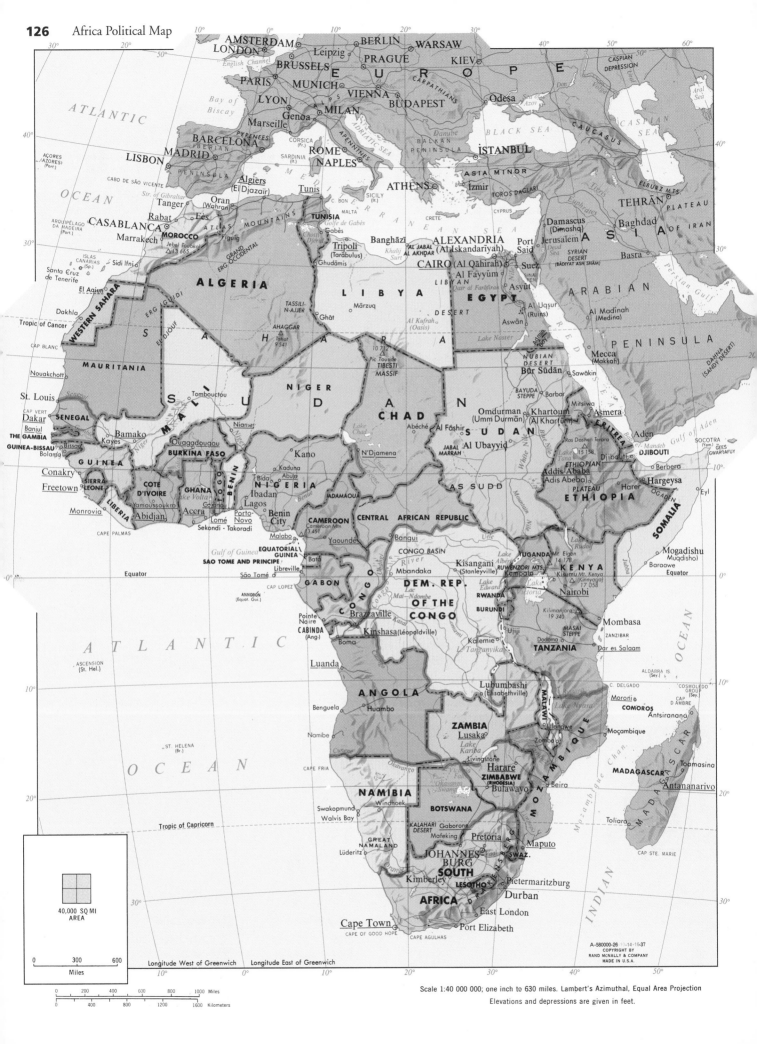

40,000 SQ MI AREA

0 300 600
Miles

0 200 400 600 800 1000 Miles
0 400 800 1200 1600 Kilometers

Scale 1:40 000 000; one inch to 630 miles. Lambert's Azimuthal, Equal Area Projection
Elevations and depressions are given in feet.

A-580000-26 10-14-10-37
COPYRIGHT BY
RAND MCNALLY & COMPANY
MADE IN U.S.A.

Longitude West of Greenwich   Longitude East of Greenwich

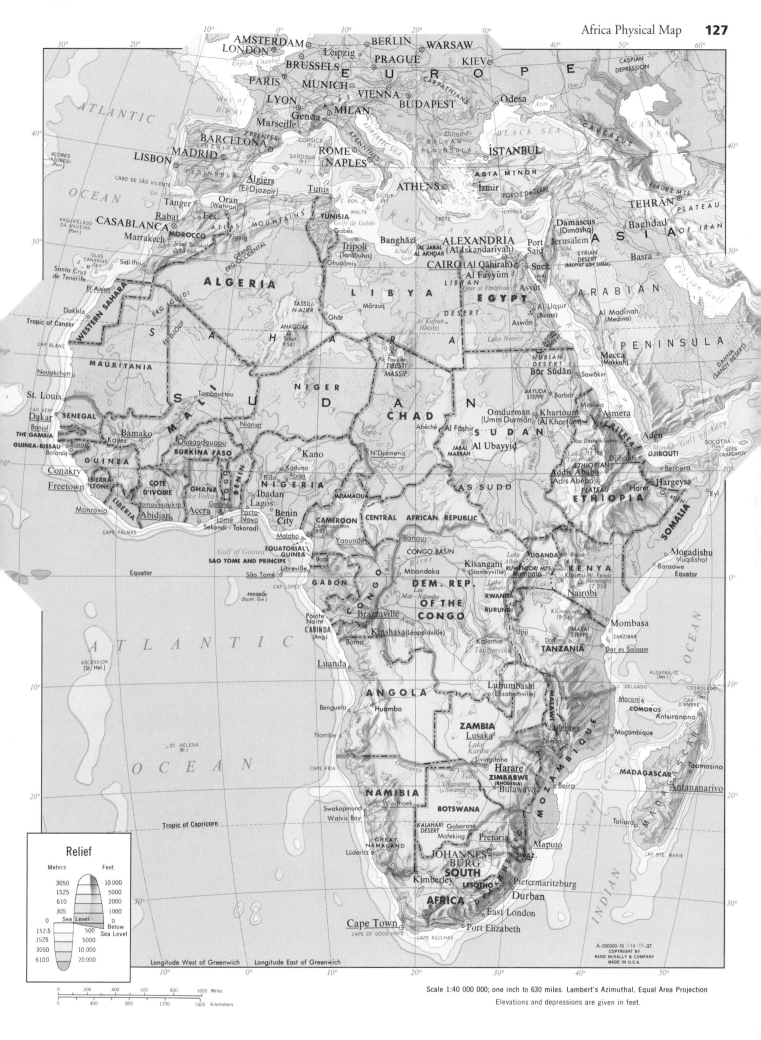

Scale 1:40 000 000; one inch to 630 miles. Lambert's Azimuthal, Equal Area Projection
Elevations and depressions are given in feet.

Relief

Meters	Feet
3050	10 000
1525	5000
610	2000
305	1000
0 Sea Level	0
	Below Sea Level
152.5	500
1525	5000
3050	10 000
6100	20 000

Longitude West of Greenwich   Longitude East of Greenwich

0   200   400   600   800   1000 Miles
0   400   800   1200   1600 Kilometers

A-580000-76 B 14 -16 -37
COPYRIGHT BY
RAND McNALLY & COMPANY
MADE IN U.S.A.

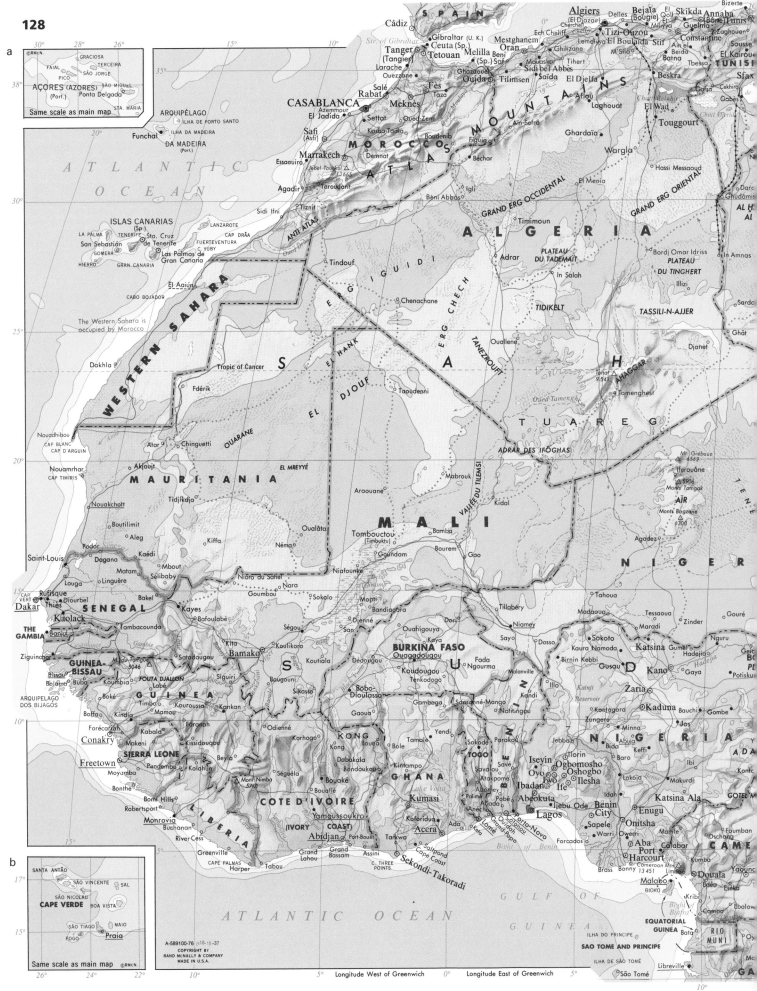

128

Scale 1:16 000 000; one inch to 250 miles. Sinusoidal Projection
Elevations and depressions are given in feet

a

ARQUIPÉLAGO
GRACIOSA
TERCEIRA
SÃO JORGE
FAIAL
PICO
AÇORES (AZORES)
(Port.)
Ponta Delgada
SÃO MIGUEL
STA. MARIA

Same scale as main map

b

SANTA ANTÃO
SÃO VICENTE
SAL
SÃO NICOLAU
BOA VISTA
CAPE VERDE
SÃO TIAGO
MAIO
FOGO
Praia

Same scale as main map

SPAIN
Cádiz
Gibraltar (U.K.)
Ceuta (Sp.)
Tanger (Tangier)
Tetouan
Larache
Ouezzane
CASABLANCA
El Jadida
Rabat
Salé
Meknès
Fès
Taza
Safi (Asfi)
Kasba-Tadla
Settat
Oued-Zem
Boudenib
Demnat
MOROCCO
Marrakech
Essaouira
Jebel Toubkal 13665
Agadir
Taroudant
Tiznit
Sidi Ifni
ANTI ATLAS
ATLAS MOUNTAINS
Figuig
Béchar
Igli
Béni Abbès
Ouarzazate
GRAND ERG OCCIDENTAL

Algiers (El Djazair)
Dellys
Bejaïa (Bougie)
El Qoll
Skikda
Annaba
Bône
Bizerte
Tunis
Blida
Tizi-Ouzou
Constantine
Sétif
TUNISIA
Sousse
Sfax
Gabès

ALGERIA
Ghardaïa
Laghouat
El Djelfa
El Wad
Touggourt
Wargla
Hassi Messaoud
Ghudâmis
AL HAMRA
El Menia
In Amnas
In Salah
Bordj Omar Idriss
PLATEAU DU TINGHERT
Illizi
PLATEAU DU TADEMAÏT
TIDIKELT
TASSILI-N-AJJER
Ghât
Djanet
Sarda
Tamanrasset
Tahat 9541
AHAGGAR
S A H A R A

ISLAS CANARIAS (Sp.)
LA PALMA
TENERIFE
Sta. Cruz de Tenerife
GOMERA
HIERRO
GRAN CANARIA
Las Palmas de Gran Canaria
San Sebastián
LANZAROTE
FUERTEVENTURA
CAP DRÂA
C. YUBY

ARCHIPÉLAGO DE PORTO SANTO
ILHA DA MADEIRA (Port.)
Funchal
DA MADEIRA

ATLANTIC OCEAN

WESTERN SAHARA
El Aaiún
CABO BOJADOR
The Western Sahara is occupied by Morocco
Dakhla
Tropic of Cancer
Nouâdhibou
CAP BLANC
CAP D'ARGUIN
Nouamrhar
CAP TIMIRIS

Tindouf
ERG IGUIDI
ERG CHECH
EL HANK
EL DJOUF
Taoudenni
Chenachane
Ouallene
TANEZROUFT
TUAREG
ADRAR DES IFOGHAS
Mr Gréboun 4562
Iférouane
5906
Monts Tamgak
AÏR
Monts Bagzane 6300
Agadez
NIGER
TÉNÉ

MAURITANIA
Fdérik
Atar
Chinguetti
Akjoujt
OUARANE
EL MREYYÉ
Tidjîkdja
Nouakchott
Boutilimit
Aleg
Kiffa
Néma
Oualâta
Mabrouk
Araouane
Kidal
VALLÉE DU TILEMSI
VALLÉE DU TILEMSI

MALI
Tombouctou (Timbuktu)
Bamba
Goundam
Bourem
Gao
Niafounké
Saint-Louis
Podor
Dagana
Louga
Matam
Sélibaby
Mbout
Kaédi
Nioro du Sahel
Nara
Sokolo
Goumbou
Kayes
Bafoulabé
Kita
Satadougou
SENEGAL
Dakar
Rufisque
Thiès
Diourbel
Kaolack
THE GAMBIA
Banjul
Ziguinchor
GUINEA-BISSAU
Bissau
Bolama
Buba
ARQUIPÉLAGO DOS BIJAGÓS
Boké
Boffa
Kindia
Forécariah
Conakry
SIERRA LEONE
Makeni
Freetown
Moyamba
Bonthe
Bomi Hills
Robertsport
Monrovia
Buchanan
LIBERIA
River Cess
Greenville
CAPE PALMAS
Harper
Tabou

Bakel
Ségou
Bamako
Koulikoro
Koutiala
Sikasso
Bougouni
Bobo-Dioulasso
San
Djenné
Mopti
Bandiagara
Dori
Ouahigouya
Kaya
BURKINA FASO
Ouagadougou
Koudougou
Tenkodogo
Dédougou
Gaoua
Gambaga
KONG
Kong
Bouna
Bole
Dabakala
Bondoukou
Séguéla
Korhogo
Odienné
Beyla
Kissidougou
Kabala
Kolahun
Pandembu
Kailahun
Mont Nimba 5761
Bouaké
Bouaflé
COTE D'IVOIRE (IVORY COAST)
Yamoussoukro
Abidjan
Grand Lahou
Grand Bassam
Assini
THREE POINTS
Port-Bouët

Kaya
Tillabéry
Niamey
Say
Dosso
Dori
Fada Ngourma
Malanville
Kandi
Gambaga
Natitingou
Sansanné-Mango
TOGO
Sokodé
Yendi
Tamale
Kintampo
GHANA
Kumasi
Koforidua
Accra
Tarkwa
Sekondi-Takoradi
Cape Coast
Saltpond
Keta
BENIN
Savalou
Abomey
Palimé
Atakpamé
Savé
Pobè
Anécho
Grand-Popo
Lomé
Cotonou
Porto-Novo
Ada
Ouidah

Tahoua
Madaoua
Tessaoua
Zinder
Gouré
Maradi
Sokoto
Kaura Namoda
Birnin Kebbi
Gusau
Illo
Kontagora
Zungeru
Minna
NIGERIA
Abuja
Baro
Lokoja
Ibi
Makurdi
Keffi
Jos
Kaduna
Bauchi
Gombe
Zaria
Kano
Gaya
Hadejia
Katsina
Gumel
Nguru
Geidam
Potiskum
Lagos
Ikeja
Ibadan
Abeokuta
Ijebu Ode
Benin City
Ife
Ilesha
Oshogbo
Ogbomosho
Oyo
Iwo
Iseyin
Ilorin
Onitsha
Sapele
Warri
Forcados
Aba
Port Harcourt
Owerri
Enugu
Calabar
Katsina Ala
Foumban
Dschang
CAMEROON
Mamfe
Kumba
Douala
Bonny
Brass
Cameroon Mtn 13451
Malabo
BIOKO
Kribi
Yaoundé
EQUATORIAL GUINEA
RIO MUNI
Bata
Ebolowa
Eséka
Edéa
Campo
Libreville
GABON
ILHA DO PRINCIPE
SAO TOME AND PRINCIPE
ILHA DE SÃO TOMÉ
São Tomé
GULF OF GUINEA
ATLANTIC OCEAN
Bight of Benin
Bight of Biafra

GUINEA
Timbo
Labé
Mamou
Kindia
Faranah
Dabola
Kouroussa
Kankan
Siguiri
FOUTA DJALLON
Mt. du Tangué 5046
Mont Nimba
Moyamba

Longitude West of Greenwich
Longitude East of Greenwich

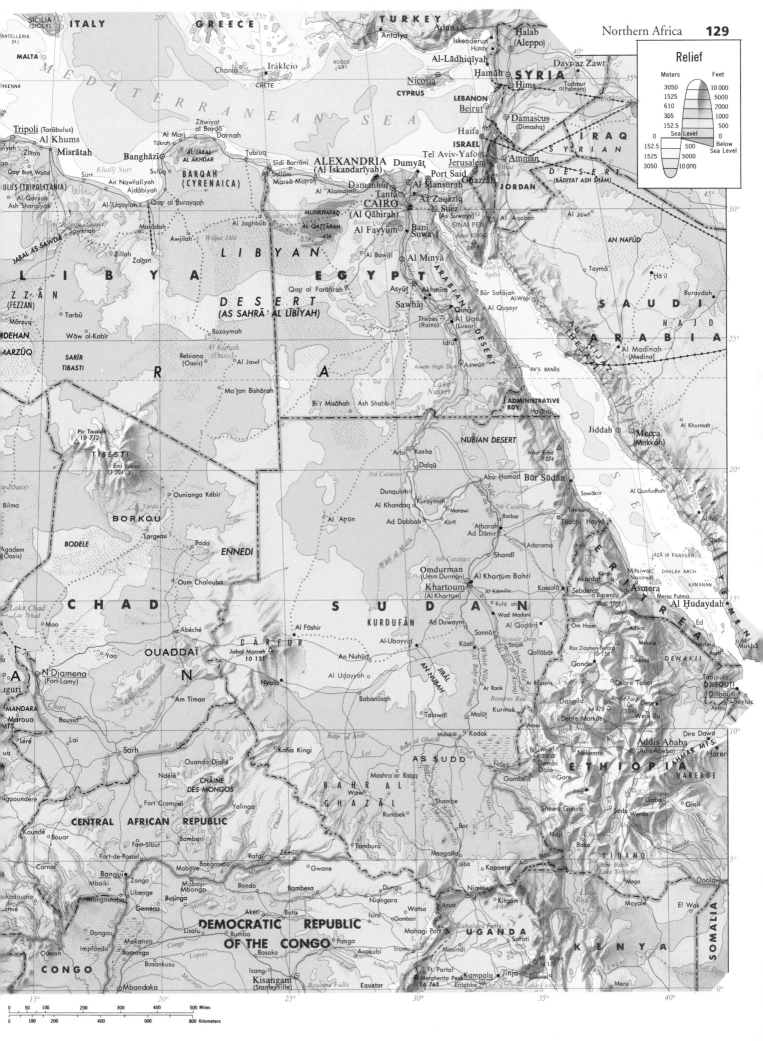

ATLANTIC OCEAN

GABON

Libreville
Kango
Ndjolé
Lambaréné
Moanda
Franceville
Lastoursville
Tchibanga
Mbigou
Sibiti
Mayumba
Sette Cama
Port Gentil
Equator
Ogooué

Owando
Irébou
Mbandaka
Bikoro
Boende
Lukolela
Mondombe
Itoko
Ubundu
Inongo
Monkoto
Bolobo
Mushie
Lukenie
Bandundu
Kole
Kindu
Brazzaville
Kinshasa (Léopoldville)
Pointe-Noire
Landana
Tshela
Boma
Matadi
Mbanza-Ngungu
Kikwit
Lusambo
Kongolo
Kabambare
Uvira

DEMOCRATIC REPUBLIC OF THE CONGO (ZAIRE)

CABINDA (Angola)
Cabinda
Nóqui
Soyo
M'banza Congo
Bembe
N'zeto
Ambriz
Luanda
Caxito
Golungo Alto
Kalandula
Malanje
Catete
Dondo
Porto Amboim
Sumbe
Waku Kungo

Lukala
Kasai
Tshikapa
Ilebo
Bena Dibele
Lusambo
Kananga (Luluabourg)
Kabinda
Kabalo
Kamina
KATANGA
Kongolo
Kalemie
Moba
Karema
Kabongo
Mutombo Mukulu
Bukama
Kasenga
Kasama
Mporokoso

TANZA
Rwanda
Kigali
Burundi
Gitega
Bujumbura
Kigoma
Tabora
Kilimatinde
Dodo
Kasongo
Ankoro

ANGOLA
Lobito
Benguela
Chinguar
Kuito
Huambo
Caconda
Dongo
Cuchi
Lubango
Cassinga
SERRA DA CHELA
Namibe
Tombua
PENÍNSULA DOS TIGRES
Cahama
Humbe
Xangongo
Cangumbe
Luena
Munhango
Mongu
BAROTSELAND
Dima

ZAMBIA
Kolwezi
Tenke
Kambove
Likasi
Lubumbashi (Elisabethville)
Chingola
Ndola
Sakania
Kasempa
Mansa
Serenje
Mchinji
Lusaka
Kafue
Mazabuka
Pemba
Kalomo
Livingstone
Zumbo
Cabora Bassa Res.
Chipata
Tete
MALAWI
Litongwe
Lilongwe

CAPRIVI STRIP
Victoria Falls
Hwange
ZIMBABWE
Kadoma
Chegutu
Kwekwe
Gweru
Shurugwi
Chivhu (Enkeldoorn)
Harare (Salisbury)
Chitungwiza
Chinhoyi
Shamva
Marondera
Mutare (Umtali)
Vila de Manica
Dondo
Beira
(RHODESIA)
Masvingo
Bulawayo
Zvishavane
Tuli
Messina

MOZAMBIQUE
Nova Mambone
Vilanculos
ILHA DO BAZARUTO
Inharrime
Inhambane
Massinga

OWAMBO
Namutoni
Tsumeb
Etoshapan
Otavi
Grootfontein
Otjiwarongo
NAMIBIA
Brandberg 8550
Omaruru
Karibib
Usakos
Okahandja
DAMARALAND
Windhoek
Swakopmund
Walvis Bay
Rehoboth
Gobabis
CAPE FRIA
Ruacana Falls

BOTSWANA
Maun
Ntwetwe Pan
Nwetwe Pan
Okavango Swamp
Ngami
Lake Xau
Ghanzi
Francistown
Old Tate
Serowe
Palapye
KALAHARI DESERT
Mochudi
Molepolole
Gaborone
Lobatse
Mmabatho
Tshabong

Louis Trichardt
Thohoyandou
TRANSFRONTIER
Pietersburg
Potgietersrus
Nylstroom
Pretoria
Krugersdorp
JOHANNESBURG
Benoni
Germiston
Komatipoort
Barberton
Carolina
Lydenburg
Maputo (Lourenço Marques)
SWAZILAND
Lobamba
Mbabane
Manzini
Xai-Xai
Magude

GREAT NAMALAND
Gibeon
Bethanien
Keetmanshoop
Aroab
Maltahöhe
Lüderitz

SOUTH AFRICA
Mafeking
Vryburg
Potchefstroom
Kroonstad
Welkom
Kuruman
Taung
Upington
Warmbad
Oranjemund
Port Nolloth
BUSHMANLAND
Springbok
Kimberley
Bloemfontein
Hopetown
Prieska
Britstown
De Aar
Victoria West
Middelburg
Carnarvon
Calvinia
Sutherland
Beaufort West
Graaff Reinet
Willowmore
Oudtshoorn
GREAT KARROO
LITTLE KARROO
Mosselbaai
Humansdorp
Port Elizabeth
Uitenhage
Cradock
Bisho
East London
Port Alfred (Kowie)
Port St. Johns
Umtata
Maclear
Scottburgh
Port Shepstone
Harding
KWAZULU
Ladysmith
Nongoma
Ubombo
Vryheid
Wakkerstroom
Piet Retief
Bethlehem
Wepener
LESOTHO
Maseru
Mt. aux Sources 10 822
Cathkin Pk. 10 438
DRAKENSBERG
Pietermaritzburg
Durban
Welkom
Virginia
Vryheid

Malmesbury
Worcester
Paarl
Bredasdorp
Cape Town
CAPE OF GOOD HOPE
CAPE AGULHAS
Saldanha
St. Helenabaai
Hopetown
Springfontein
Aliwal North
Oranje

Tropic of Capricorn

A-589200-76
COPYRIGHT BY
RAND McNALLY & COMPANY
MADE IN U.S.A.

0° Equator
5°
10°
15° Tropic of Capricorn
20°
25°
30°

10° 15° 20° 25° 30° 35°
Longitude East of Greenwich

---

a

CAPE TOWN
ROBBENEILAND
Bloubergstrand
Milnerton
Durbanville
Kanonkop 1502
Parow
Bellville
MOUILLE PT.
Table Bay
Goodwood
Camps Bay
Table Mt. 3567
Pinelands
Nuweland
Wynberg
Ottery
Kuilsrivier
CAPE FLATS
Houtbaai
Muizenberg
Grootkop 3048
Chapman's Bay
Vishoek
SEAL ISLAND
Valsbaai (False Bay)
Kommetjie
Simonstad
Grootkop 1286
Swartkop 2229
SMITSWINKEL VLAKTE
ATLANTIC OCEAN
KAAPPUNT
CAPE OF GOOD HOPE

Scale 1:1 000 000
0   5   10 Miles
0 4 8 16 Kilometers
®RMcN.

---

0 50 100 200 300 400 500 Miles
0 100 200 400 600 800 Kilome

18°30'
15°
20°

b

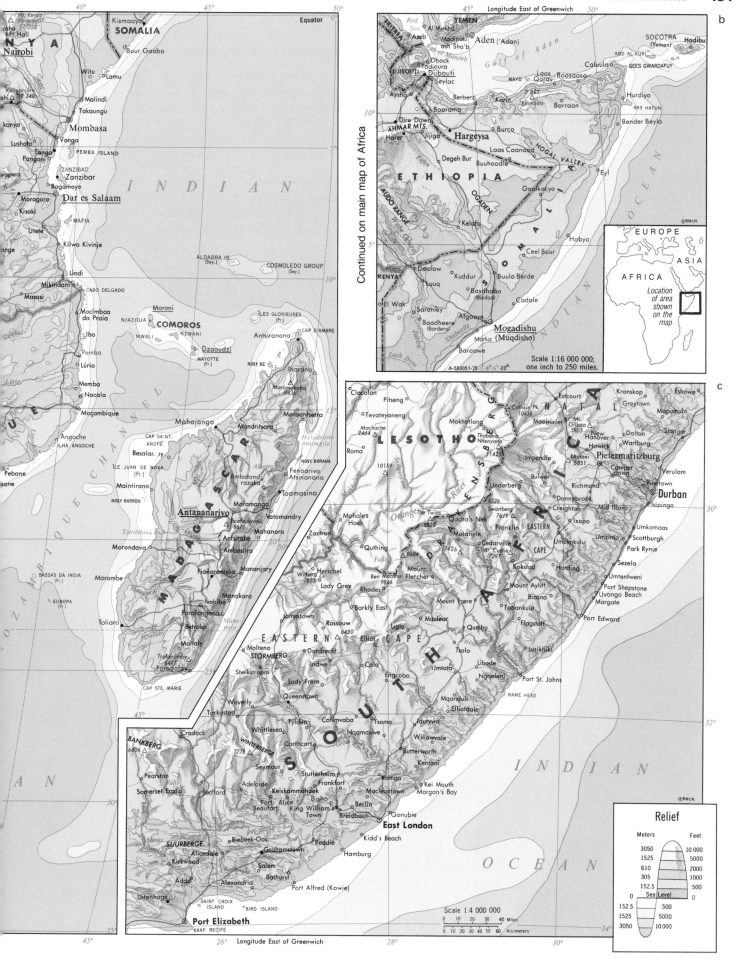

Continued on main map of Africa

Longitude East of Greenwich

YEMEN
Al Mukha
Madinat
ash Sha'b   Aden ('Adan)
SOCOTRA
(Yemen)   Hadibu
Red
Sea
'ABD AL-KURI
ERITREA
Aseb
Bab el-Mandeb
Gulf of Aden
GEES GWARDAFUY
DJIBOUTI
Djibouti
Tadjoura
Obock
Seylac
Laas
Qoray   Boosaaso
Calula
Aysha
MAYD Is.
Berbera
Karin
Hurdiyo
AHMAR MTS.   Jijiga   Hargeysa
Borama
Booraan   Shimbiris
Dire Dawa
7 897
Harer
Laas Caanood   NOGAL VALLEY   RAS HAFUN
Burco
ETHIOPIA
Degeh Bur
Buuhoodle   Eyl
Gaalkacyo

AUDO RANGE
Kelafo
OGADEN
SOMALIA
Ceel Buur
Hobyo

Doolow
KENYA   Xuddur   Buulo Berde
Luuq
Baydhabo
(Baidoa)   Cadale
El Wak   Saraanley
Afgooye
Baadheere
(Bardera)   **Mogadishu**
(Muqdisho)
Lach Dera   Marka
Juba   Baraawe
Shabeelle

EUROPE
ASIA
AFRICA
Location
of area
shown on the
map

Scale 1:16 000 000;
one inch to 250 miles.
A-580051-76

c

KENYA
Mt. Kenya
(Kirinyaga)
17,058
Fr. Hall
Nairobi   **SOMALIA**   Equator
Kismaayo
Buur Gaabo
Witu
Lamu
Kilimanjaro
19 340   Malindi
Takaungu
Mombasa
Vanga
PEMBA ISLAND
Lushoto   Tanga
Pangani
ZANZIBAR
Zanzibar
Bagamoyo
Dar es Salaam
Morogoro
Kisaki
MAFIA
Utete
Kilwa Kivinje
Lindi
Mikindani
Masasi
Mocímboa
da Praia   CABO DELGADO
Ibo
Pemba
Lúrio
Memba
Nacala
Moçambique
MOZAMBIQUE CHANNEL
Angoche
ILHA ANGOCHE
Pebane

INDIAN

ALDABRA IS.
(Sey.)
COSMOLEDO GROUP
(Sey.)

Moroni
COMOROS
NJAZIDJA
MWALI   NZWANI
Dzaoudzi
MAYOTTE
(Fr.)
ÎLES GLORIEUSES
(Fr.)
Antsiranana   CAP D'AMBRE
NOSY BE
Iharana
Maromokotra
2436

Mahajanga
Mandritsara
Maroantsetra
Helodrano
Antongila
NOSY BORAHA
CAP SAINT-
ANDRÉ
Besalampy
Fenoarivo
Atsinanana
Alaotra
ÎLE JUAN DE NOVA
(Fr.)
Ambatond
razaka
Toamasina
Maintirano
NOSY BARREN
Moramanga
Antananarivo
Tsiafajavona
8671   Vatomandry
Antsirabe
Mahanoro
Morondava
Ambositra
Mananjary
BASSAS DA INDIA
(Fr.)
Fianarantsoa
MADAGASCAR
Manakara
EUROPA
(Fr.)
Morombe
Ivohibe
Parafangana
Betroka
Mahaly
Toliara
Tsaratanana
4447
Faradofay
CAP STE. MARIE

INDIAN

Clocolan
Pitseng
DRAKENSBERG
Estcourt   **NATAL**
Kranskop
Eshowe
Teyateyaneng
Cathkin Pk.
10438
Mooirivier
Mt. Gilboa
5803   Greytown
Mapumulo
Machache
9464   Mokhotlong
Thabana
Nlenyana
11425   **LESOTHO**   Impendle
New
Hanover
Howick
Wartburg   Dalton
Stanger
Roma
Ntshoni
5851   **Pietermaritzburg**
Camper
down
Bulwer
10159
Underberg
Richmond
Donnybrook
Pinetown
Verulam
Mohale's
Hoek   The Twins
8326   Creighton
Mid Illovo   Isipingo
Durban
Zastron
Orange   Qacha's Nek
Matatiele
Swartberg
7619
Franklin
Ixopo
Umkomaas
Quthing
9684   Cedarville
Mt. Currie
7297   **EASTERN**
Umzimkulu
Umzinto
Scottburgh
Herschel
7426
Kokstad   **CAPE**   Harding
Park Rynie
Witberg
2853   Lady Grey
Ben Macdhui
9846   Fletcher   Mount Ayliff
Sezela
Rhodes   Tabankulu   Bizana
Umtentweni
Barkly East   Mount Frere
Port Shepstone
Jamestown   Maclear   Qumbu
Lusikisiki
Uvongo Beach
Margate
Rossouw
8430   Elliot   Tsolo
Libode
Port Edward
Molteno   Dordrecht   Cala
Ngqeleni   Port St. Johns
SOUTH   Umtata
STORMBERG   Indwe
RAME HEAD
Sterkstroom
Engcobo
Mqanduli
Elliotdale
Waverly   Lady Frere
Tarkastad   Queenstown
Tsomo   **AFRICA**
Coffimvaba   Idutywa   Willowvale
Cradock   Tylden
Ngamakwe
BANKBERG
6106   Whittlesea   Cathcart   Butterworth
WINTERBERG   Kentani
7778   Seymour
Stutterheim   Komga
Kei Mouth
Pearston   Adelaide   Frankfort
Macleantown   Morgan's Bay
Somerset East
Bedford   Keiskammahoek   Bisho   Berlin
Fort Alice   King William's   Breidbach
Beaufort   Town   Gonubie
SUURBERGE   **East London**
Riebeek-Oos   Peddie   Kidd's Beach
Alicedale
Grahamstown   Hamburg
Kirkwood   Salem
Addo   Bathurst
Alexandria   Port Alfred (Kowie)
Uitenhage
SAINT CROIX
ISLAND   BIRD ISLAND
Port Elizabeth
KAAP RECIFE

INDIAN

OCEAN

Scale 1:4 000 000
Miles
0 10 20 30 40
0 10 20 30 40 50 60 Kilometers

26°   Longitude East of Greenwich   28°   30°

Relief		
Meters		Feet
3050		10 000
1525		5000
610		2000
305		1000
152.5		500
0	Sea Level	0
152.5		500
1525		5000
3050		10 000

Asia

Covering nearly one-third of the Earth's land surface, Asia is by far the largest of the seven continents. It is a land of extremes and dramatic physical contrasts, containing nearly every type of landform, and many of them on a vast scale. It boasts the world's lowest point (the Dead Sea), its highest point (Mt. Everest), its highest and largest plateau (the Plateau of Tibet), and its largest inland body of water (the Caspian Sea).

Wide belts of mountain systems cover much of Asia. The Himalayas, which form a great 1,500-mile (2,400-km) arc south of Tibet, are the highest mountains in the world: more than 90 Himalayan peaks rise above 24,000 feet (7,320 m).

The beginnings of civilization can be traced to three distinct areas of Asia: Mesopotamia, around 4000 B.C.; the Indus River valley, around 3000 B.C.; and China, around 2000 B.C. Eight of the world's major religions—Buddhism, Christianity, Confucianism, Hinduism, Islam, Judaism, Shinto, and Taoism—originated in Asia.

Asia at a glance

Land area:
17,300,000 square miles (44,900,000 sq km)

Estimated population: 4,078,790,000

Population density:
236/square mile (91/sq km)

Mean elevation: 3,000 feet (910 m)

Highest point: Mt. Everest, China (Tibet)-Nepal, 29,028 feet (8,848 m)

Lowest point:
Dead Sea, Israel-Jordan, 1,339 feet (408 m) below sea level

Longest river:
Yangtze (Chang), 3,900 mi (6,300 km)

Number of countries (incl. dependencies): 51

Largest independent country:
Russia (Europe/Asia), 6,592,849 square miles (17,075,400 sq km)

Smallest independent country: Maldives, 115 square miles (298 sq km)

Most populous independent country:
China, 1,341,820,000

Least populous independent country:
Maldives, 395,000

Most populous metropolitan area:
Tokyo, Japan, population 35.7 million

Annapurna, one of the highest mountains in the Himalayas

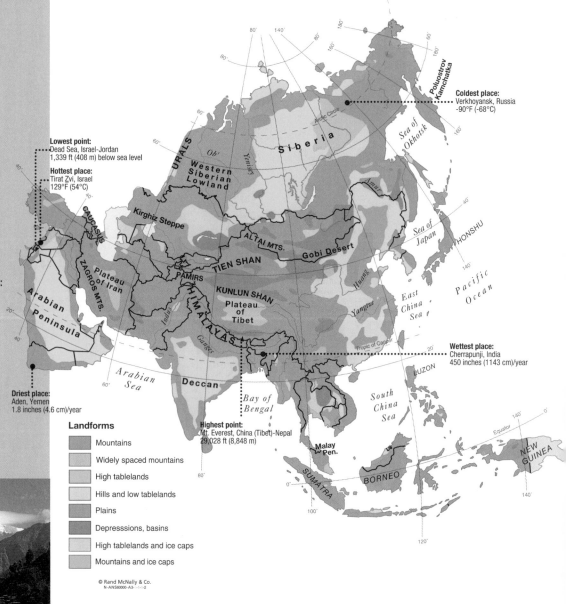

Coldest place:
Verkhoyansk, Russia
-90°F (-68°C)

Lowest point:
Dead Sea, Israel-Jordan
1,339 ft (408 m) below sea level

Hottest place:
Tirat Zvi, Israel
129°F (54°C)

Wettest place:
Cherrapunji, India
450 inches (1143 cm)/year

Driest place:
Aden, Yemen
1.8 inches (4.6 cm)/year

Highest point:
Mt. Everest, China (Tibet)-Nepal
29,028 ft (8,848 m)

Poluostrov Kamchatka · Siberia · Sea of Okhotsk · Arctic Circle · Ob' · Western Siberian Lowland · Yenisey · Amur · HONSHU · Sea of Japan · Kirghiz Steppe · ALTAI MTS. · Gobi Desert · Huang · Pacific Ocean · CAUCASUS · TIEN SHAN · PAMIRS · KUNLUN SHAN · Yangtze · East China Sea · Plateau of Iran · ZAGROS MTS. · Plateau of Tibet · HIMALAYAS · Indus · Arabian Peninsula · Ganges · Arabian Sea · Deccan · Bay of Bengal · Tropic of Cancer · LUZON · South China Sea · Malay Pen. · SUMATRA · BORNEO · NEW GUINEA · Equator

Landforms

- Mountains
- Widely spaced mountains
- High tablelands
- Hills and low tablelands
- Plains
- Depressions, basins
- High tablelands and ice caps
- Mountains and ice caps

© Rand McNally & Co.
N-ANS0000-A3- - - - -2

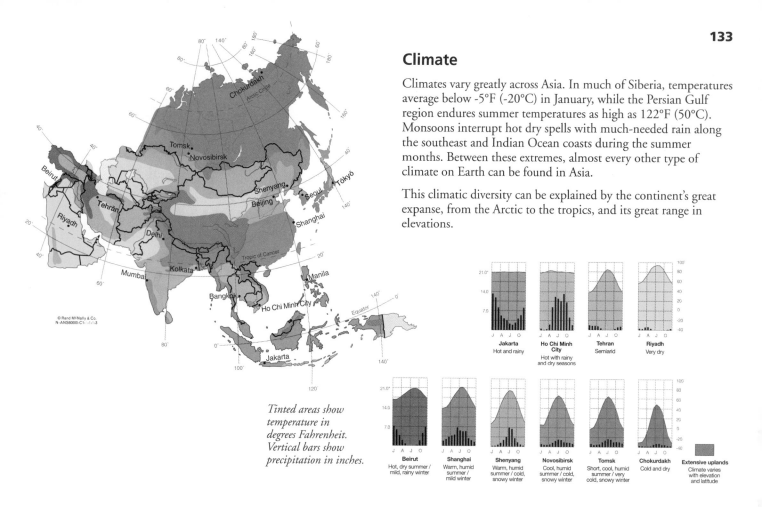

Climate

Climates vary greatly across Asia. In much of Siberia, temperatures average below -5°F (-20°C) in January, while the Persian Gulf region endures summer temperatures as high as 122°F (50°C). Monsoons interrupt hot dry spells with much-needed rain along the southeast and Indian Ocean coasts during the summer months. Between these extremes, almost every other type of climate on Earth can be found in Asia.

This climatic diversity can be explained by the continent's great expanse, from the Arctic to the tropics, and its great range in elevations.

Tinted areas show temperature in degrees Fahrenheit. Vertical bars show precipitation in inches.

Jakarta — Hot and rainy

Ho Chi Minh City — Hot with rainy and dry seasons

Tehran — Semiarid

Riyadh — Very dry

Beirut — Hot, dry summer / mild, rainy winter

Shanghai — Warm, humid summer / mild winter

Shenyang — Warm, humid summer / cold, snowy winter

Novosibirsk — Cool, humid summer / cold, snowy winter

Tomsk — Short, cool, humid summer / very cold, snowy winter

Chokurdakh — Cold and dry

Extensive uplands — Climate varies with elevation and latitude

Population

With more than 4 billion people, Asia is nearly five times as populous as any other continent and is home to more than two out of every three people in the world. If its current annual growth rate continues, Asia's population will exceed 5 billion by the year 2030. The continent contains the two most populous countries in the world, China and India, as well as the most populous metropolitan area, Tōkyō-Yokohama, Japan.

Great concentrations of people are found in India, eastern China, Japan, Vietnam, and on the Indonesian island of Java. In contrast, vast stretches of northern Siberia, Mongolia, western China, and the Arabian Peninsula are only sparsely populated. Numerous desert regions, including Arabia's Rub' al Khālī and China's Takla Makān, are uninhabited.

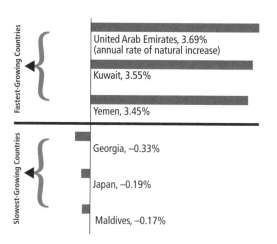

Fastest-Growing Countries

United Arab Emirates, 3.69% (annual rate of natural increase)

Kuwait, 3.55%

Yemen, 3.45%

Slowest-Growing Countries

Georgia, −0.33%

Japan, −0.19%

Maldives, −0.17%

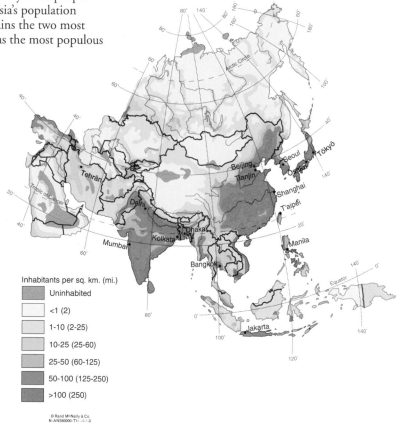

Inhabitants per sq. km. (mi.)

- Uninhabited
- <1 (2)
- 1-10 (2-25)
- 10-25 (25-60)
- 25-50 (60-125)
- 50-100 (125-250)
- >100 (250)

© Rand McNally & Co.
N-ANS60000-T1- -2-1-3

Environments and Land Use

Despite rapid industrialization in Japan, Korea, and Singapore, feeding the enormous and fast-growing population remains Asia's primary economic focus. In China, India, and Indonesia, two-thirds of the work force is engaged in farming. Where arable land exists, it is generally cultivated intensively. Rice is the most commonly grown crop: the continent produces more than 90% of the world's total. Other important crops include wheat, sorghum, millet, maize, and barley.

Asia's major agricultural regions are found in the fertile alluvial valleys, floodplains, and deltas of some of its greatest rivers, such as the Ganges and Brahmaputra in northern India, the Indus in Pakistan, the Huang (Yellow) and Yangtze in eastern China, the Irawaddy in Myanmar (Burma), the Mekong in Cambodia and Vietnam, and the Tigris and Euphrates in Iraq.

Tundra vegetation prevails across the arctic and subarctic regions of Siberia. Farther south, much of the land is densely forested. Deforestation, however, is rampant across the continent. In the colder central and northern areas, whole forests have been cut down to provide wood for heat and cooking. The tropical rain forests of the Indochina Peninsula, Malaysia, Indonesia, and the Philippines are rapidly being destroyed for their valuable hardwood, especially teak.

A wide sweep of semiarid grasslands across Central Asia covers one-quarter of the continent. These immense grazing lands are used by the people of many countries—notably Kazakhstan and Mongolia—for livestock that include almost one-third of the world's cattle, nearly three-fifths of its goats, and half of its pigs. In recent decades, the tremendous petroleum reserves located in the arid west, around the Persian Gulf, have been both a source of wealth and a cause of turmoil. The continent also has less exploited, but sizable reserves of natural gas in Siberia and coal in China.

Harvesting rice from terraced paddies in China's Yunnan province

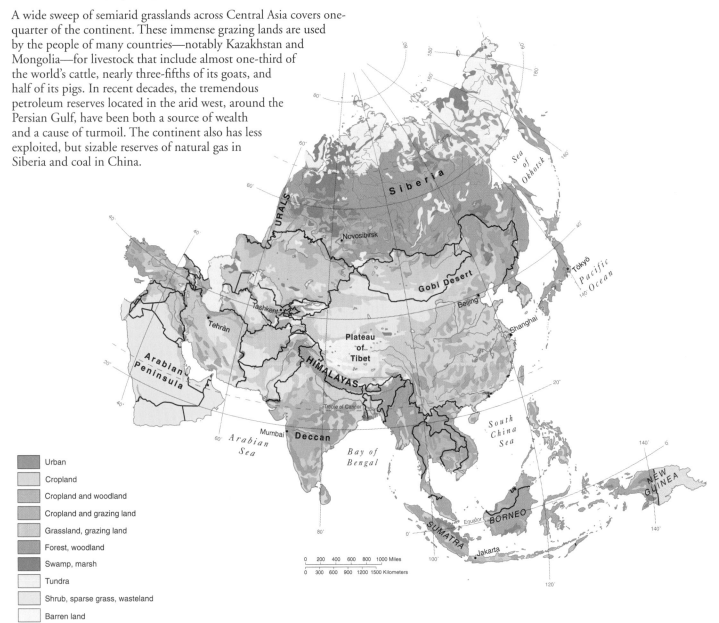

Urban

Cropland

Cropland and woodland

Cropland and grazing land

Grassland, grazing land

Forest, woodland

Swamp, marsh

Tundra

Shrub, sparse grass, wasteland

Barren land

© Rand McNally & Co.
N-ANS60000-M1- -2-7-3

Asia and the Ring of Fire

"Ring of Fire" is the dramatic name given to the volcanoes that nearly encircle the Pacific Ocean. Its existence is explained by plate tectonic theory. According to the theory, Earth's thin crust is broken into sections or plates that move relative to each other. (See Plate Tectonics, pages 12 and 13.)

The giant Pacific plate submerges beneath other plates and plunges into Earth's hot interior, creating deep ocean trenches and causing magma to rise to the surface and erupt as volcanoes. The moving plates also trigger thousands of earthquakes that rumble along the Ring of Fire every year.

The Asian section of the Ring of Fire starts in the north on Russia's Kamchatka Peninsula; swings down through the Kuril Islands; and includes Japan, Taiwan, the Philippines, and Indonesia.

The Kamchatka Peninsula, about the size of California, has more than 100 volcanoes. About 20 of these are active. Klyuchevskaya, the largest active volcano in Kamchatka, and in Eurasia, spews about 60 million tons of basalt a year.

Japan is one of the most earthquake-prone regions in the world. Four plates come together at Japan, and their movement against each other creates constant strain on the earth's crust. In 1995, an earthquake at Kōbe resulted in 5,500 fatalities. Japan's most deadly quake was in 1923, when more than 140,000 lives were lost.

The largest volcanic eruption in recorded history occurred in Indonesia. In 1815, Mt. Tambora shot a column of ash 28 miles into the air. The fallout ruined crops, causing widespread famine. 82,000 people died as a result of Tambora's eruption, most of them from starvation. Gases from Tambora circled the globe and lowered world temperatures by as much as 5°. In 1816, the "year without summer", killing frosts during summer months destroyed crops in Europe and North America.

Mt. Pinatubo, Philippines

The 1991 eruption of Mt. Pinatubo in the Philippines was the second largest volcanic eruption of the 20th century, and approximately ten times as large as the 1980 eruption of Mt. St. Helens in the U.S. state of Washington. Pinatubo blew an ash column about 21 miles into the sky. Although Pinatubo is near a heavily populated area not far from Manilla, authorities were able to warn and evacuate residents in advance, preventing what could have been a major disaster.

The most recent major event within the Ring of Fire occurred on December 26, 2004. A massive earthquake shook the floor of the Indian Ocean near the Indonesian city of Banda Aceh. Measuring 9.0 in magnitude, the earthquake generated tsunamis—huge ocean waves—that struck Indonesia, Thailand, Sri Lanka, India, Madagascar, and continental Africa. The final death toll from the tsunamis and earthquake was 280,000.

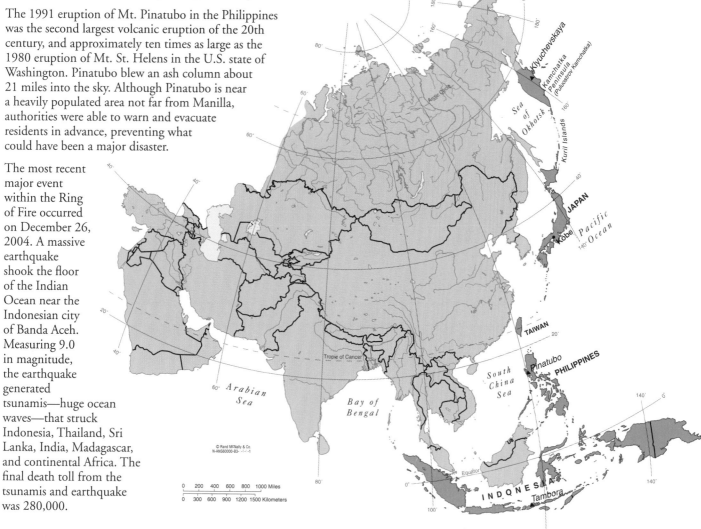

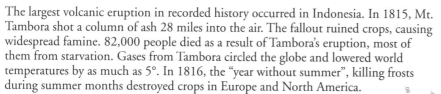

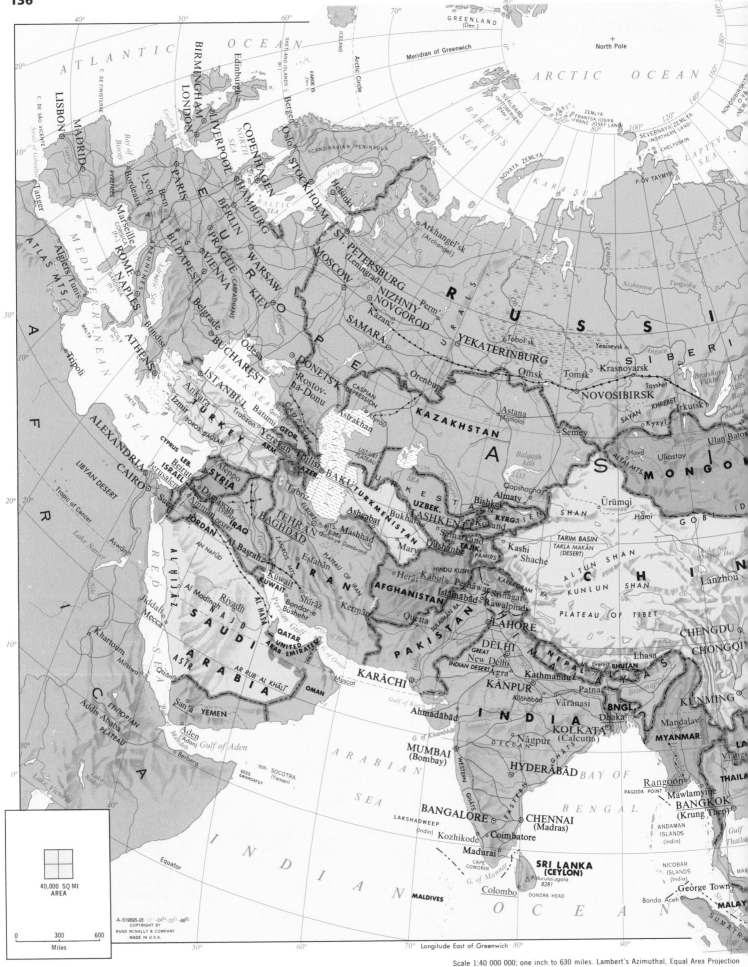

40,000 SQ MI
AREA

0   300   600
Miles

A-519695-26
COPYRIGHT BY
RAND MCNALLY & COMPANY
MADE IN U.S.A.

Longitude East of Greenwich

Scale 1:40 000 000; one inch to 630 miles. Lambert's Azimuthal, Equal Area Projection
Elevations and depressions are given in feet

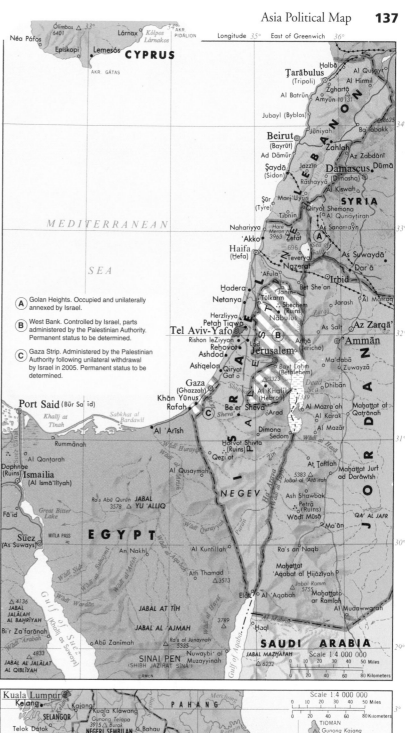

Relief

Meters		Feet
3050		10 000
1525		5000
610		2000
305		1000
0	Sea Level	0
		Below
152.5		500 Sea Level
1525		5000
3050		10 000
6100		20 000

A-519695-76
COPYRIGHT BY
RAND McNALLY & COMPANY
MADE IN U.S.A.

Scale 1:40 000 000; one inch to 630 miles. Lambert's Azimuthal, Equal Area Projection
Elevations and depressions are given in feet

Continued on pages 229

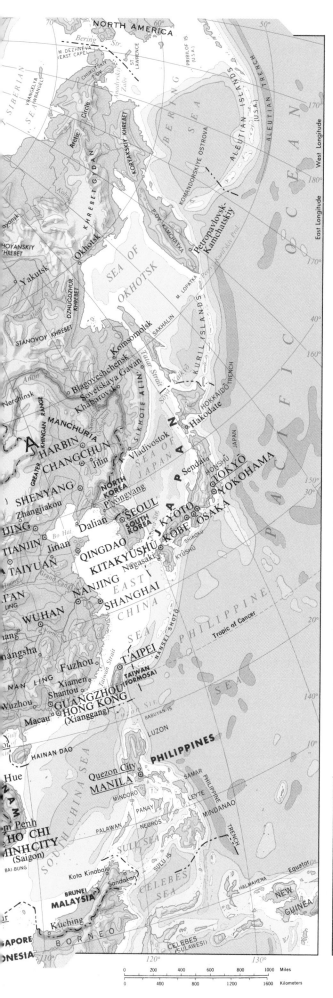

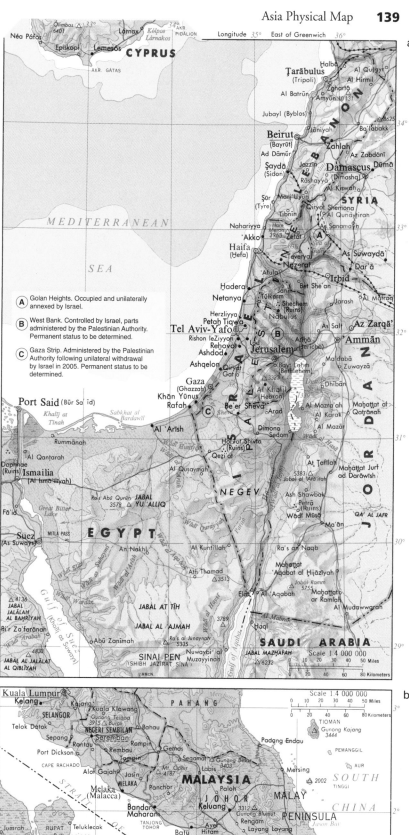

Cities and Towns

0 to 50,000	○	500,000 to 1,000,000	◉
50,000 to 500,000	⊙	1,000,000 and over	

Scale 1:16 000 000; one inch to 250 miles Conic Projection
Elevations and depressions are given in feet.

85° Longitude East of Greenwich 90°

Relief

Meters	Feet
3050	10 000
1525	5000
610	2000
305	1000
152.5	500
Sea Level	0
152.5	500
1525	5000
3050	10 000

Relief

Meters		Feet
3050		10 000
1525		5000
610		2000
305		1000
152.5		500
0	Sea Level	
152.5		500
1525		5000
3050		10 000

Below Sea Level

A-569400-76 11-24-21-43
COPYRIGHT BY
RAND-McNALLY & COMPANY
MADE IN U.S.A.

Scale 1:16 000 000; one inch to 250 miles. Polyconic Projection
Elevations and depressions are given in feet

Longitude East of Greenwich

a

STAN
Balqash köli
+1112
yzylorda
MOYYNQUM
Türkistan
Zhambyl
Bishkek
Shymkent
Arys
ASHKENT
KYRGYZSTAN
Namangan Dzhalal-Abad
Kokand   Andizhan
Khudzhand   Fergana   Osh
Dzhizak
Karshi   TAJIKISTAN
Dushanbe   PAMIRS
Kurgan-Tyube   Garm   pik Ismail Samani   Muztagata   24 757
ermez   Khorog   Murgab
alkha   Mazâr-e Sharif   Feyzâbâd
KUSH   A
HINDU   C   K2
Koh-e Folâdi   Gilgit   Qogir Feng   28 250
14 847   Chitral   KARAKORAM   C   KARAKORAM PASS
Kâbul   KHYBER PASS   JAMMU AND KASHMIR
Ghazni   Peshâwar   Islâmâbâd   Srinagar   B
Râwalpindi   C
Jhelum   Jammu
Dera Ismâil   Sialkot   Amritsar   C
Khân   Gujrânwâla   Jullundur   G
Faisalâbâd   LAHORE   Ludhiâna   Simla
PAKISTAN   PUNJAB   Firozpur   Chandigarh   Dehra Dūn
Multân   Patiâla   Ambâla   UTTARANCHAL
Dera Ghazi   Bhatinda   Sahâranpur   HARYANA Meerut Morâdâbâd
Khân   Bahâwalpur   DELHI   Rampur   Bareilly
Quetta   Bikaner   New Delhi   UTTAR   Shâhjahânpur
Shikârpur   GREAT INDIAN DESERT   Alwar   Agra   Lucknow   Faizâbâd   Gorakhpur
Sukkur   Mathura   PRADESH   KĀNPUR
Mohenjo-Daro   Ajmer   Bhâratpur   Allâhâbâd   Vârânasi
(Ruins)   Jaipur   Gwalior   (Benares)
RĀJASTHĀN   Tonk   Jhânsi   Banda   Mirzâpur   Sasarâm
Jodhpur   Sheopur   JHARKHAND
Shivpuri   Rewa
Hyderâbâd   Udaipur   Kota   Sâgar   Son   Giridih
ACHI   Abu Road   Jhâlawar   Bhopâl   Jabalpur   Rânchi
Pâlanpur   I   Murwara   CHHATTISGARH
Bhuj   Ujjain   VINDHYA RA   JAMSHEDPUR   Burdwân
Māndvi   GUJARAT   AHMADĀBĀD   MADHYA   Bilâspur   Raurkela   Howrah
Rājkot   Indore   PRADESH   Raigarh   KOLKATA
Jâmnagar   Baroda   Burhânpur   Nâgpur   Sambalpur   (Calcutta)
Porbandar   Bhâunagar   Dhule   Akola   Raipur   Jâjpur
Verâval   Diu   Surat   Amrâvati   Wardha
Dāman   Aurangâbâd   Chandrapur   Cuttack
Nâsik   DECCAN   Bhubaneswar
MUMBAI   Ahmadnagar   Puri
(Bombay)   MAHĀRĀSHTRA   Nizâmâbâd
Pune   Warangal   Vishâkhapatnam
Sholâpur   HYDERĀBĀD   Vizianagaram
Kolhâpur   Sāngli   Gulbarga   Râjahmundry
Belgaum   Râichur   Vijayawâda   Kâkinâda
Panaji   Kurnool   Guntûr   Eluru   Machilîpatnam
(Panjim)   Hubli   Bellary
Cuddapah   Nellore
Mangalore   Kolâr   CHENNAI (Madras)
BANGALORE   Vellore   Kânchipuram
Mysore   Salem   Pondicherry
Cuddalore
LAKSHADWEEP   Mahe
(LACCADIVE IS.)   Kozhikode   Kumbakonam
(India)   Coimbatore   Nâgappattinam
Ernâkulam   Tiruchchirâppalli
Madurai

Scale 1:4 000 000

PAKISTAN
AFGHANISTAN   Dargai
Jalâlâbâd   Chârsadda
KHYBER PASS
MORGA RA   Peshâwar

Scale 1:4 000 000
0 10 20 30 40 Miles
0 20 40 60 Kilometers

b

AFGHANISTAN   JAMMU AND KASHMIR   CHINA
HIMACHAL PRADESH   XIZANG (TIBET)   30°
PUNJAB   UTTARANCHAL
PAKISTAN   HARYANA   NEPAL   SIKKIM   ARUNACHAL PRADESH
RĀJASTHĀN   UTTAR PRADESH   BHUTAN   ASSAM   NĀGALAND
Tropic of Cancer   BIHAR   BANGLADESH   MEGHALAYA   MIZORAM
GUJARAT   MADHYA PRADESH   JHARKHAND   WEST BENGAL   20°
7   MAHĀRĀSHTRA   CHHATTISGARH   ORISSA   MYANMAR
5   ARABIAN SEA   KARNATAKA   ANDHRA PRADESH   BAY OF BENGAL
7   6
6   6   6
KERALA   10°
SRI LANKA (CEYLON)
INDIA · POLITICAL

Scale 1:40 000 000

1-TRIPURA
2-MANIPUR
3-LAKSHADWEEP
4-DELHI
5-DĀDRA AND NAGAR HAVELI
6-PONDICHERRY
7-GOA, DAMĀN, AND DIU

XIZANG (TIBET)   Lhasa
GANGDISE SHAN   Gyangze
Mt. Everest   29 028
Dhaulâgiri   Kânchenjunga   28 208
NEPAL   Kathmandu   SIKKIM   ASSAM   ARUNACHAL PRADESH
Lalitpur   Gangtok   Thimphu   BHUTAN   Punakha   Sadiya   D
Darjeeling   Cooch Behar   Sibsâgar   DIPHU PASS
Pûnakha   Gauhâti   Jorhât
MEGHALAYA   NĀGALAND
Shillong   KHASI HILLS   Kohima
Rangpur   Mymensingh   Silchar   Imphâl   Mogaung
BANGLADESH   MANIPUR   Myitkyina
Râjshâhi   Sirâjganj   Bhamo
Dhaka   Comilla
Noâkhâli   MIZORAM   Shwebo   Mandalay
Khulna   Chittagong   Monywa   MYANMAR
Mt. Victoria   10 018   Myingyan   BURMA
PEGU   Yenangyaung   Pyinmana
ARAKAN YOMA   Magwe   Yamethin
Sittwe   Pyo   Myanaung
Sandoway   Henzada   Pathein
BAY OF BENGAL   Rangoon (Yangon)
PAGODA PT.   Mouths of the Irrawaddy

c

Tiruchchirâppalli   Nâgappattinam
Ernâkulam   Thanjâvûr   TAMIL NADU
KERALA   Madurai   Jaffna
Alleppey   Tuticorin   Trincomalee
Quilon   Tirunelveli   Anurâdhapura
Thiruvananthapuram   Puttalam
CAPE COMORIN   SRI LANKA (CEYLON)   Kandy
Colombo   Pidurutalagala 8281
INDIAN OCEAN   Galle   DONDRA HEAD   Matara

Same scale as main map

Area occupied by Pakistan and claimed by India;
Area claimed and occupied by India; status disputed by Pakistan;
Area occupied by China and claimed by India;
Area occupied by India and claimed by China.

0 50 100 200 300 400 500 Miles
0 100 200 400 600 800 Kilometers

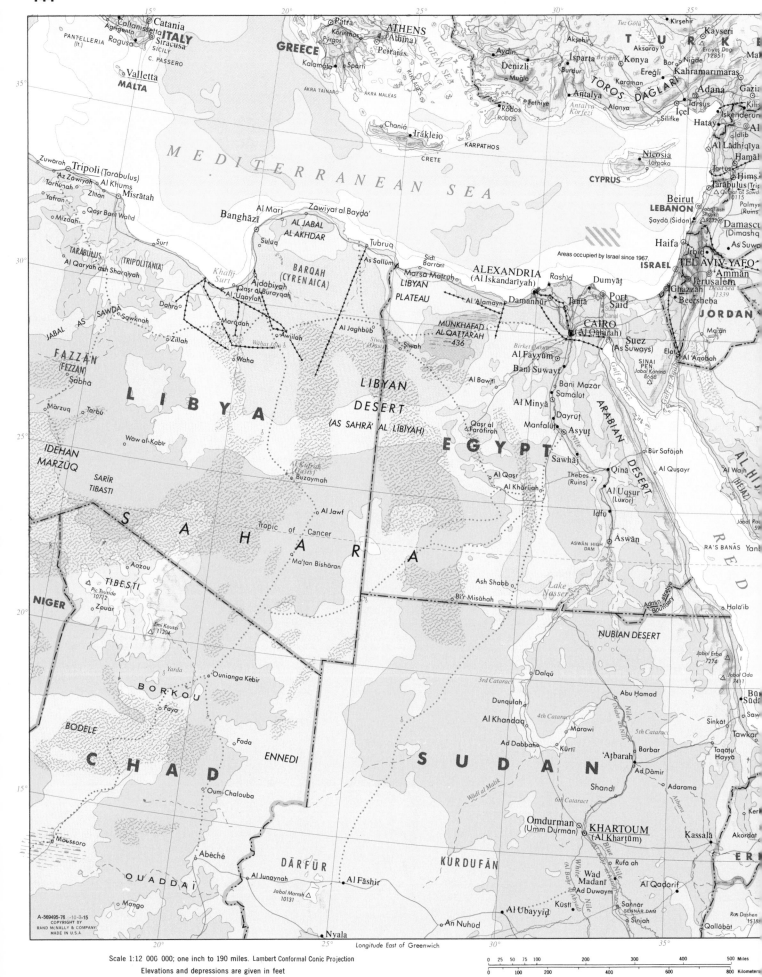

Scale 1:12 000 000; one inch to 190 miles. Lambert Conformal Conic Projection

Elevations and depressions are given in feet

Longitude East of Greenwich

A-569495-76 · -10-3-15
COPYRIGHT BY
RAND McNALLY & COMPANY
MADE IN U.S.A.

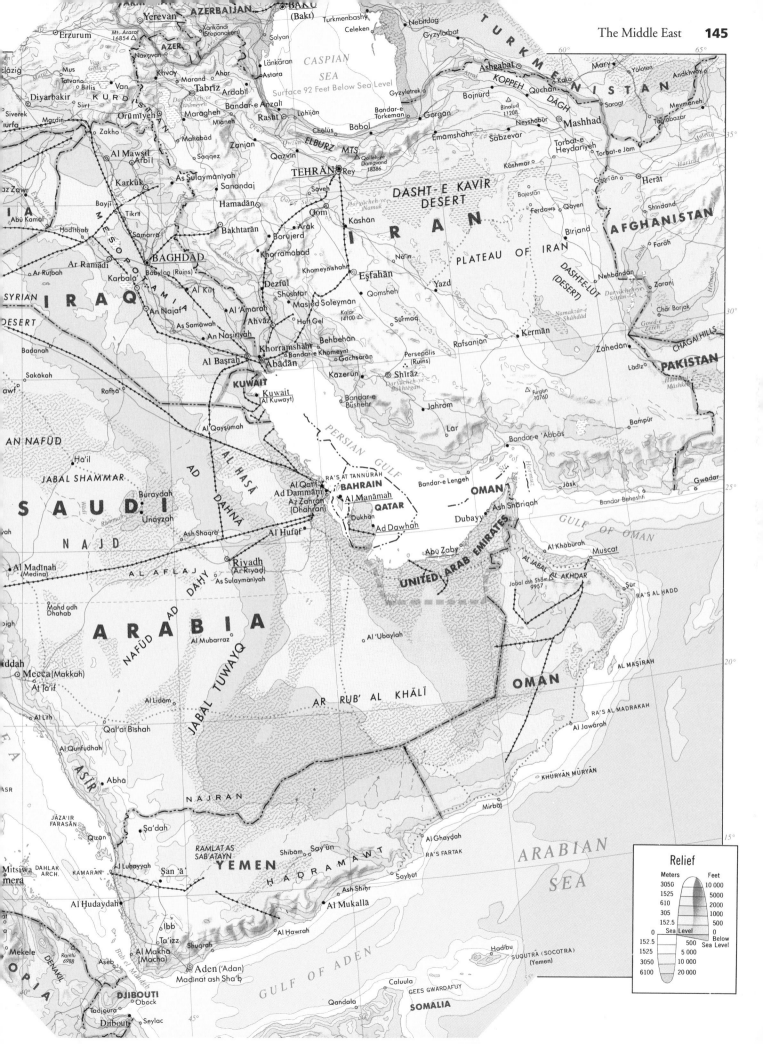

Yerevan
AZERBAIJAN
BAKU
(Bakı)
Turkmenbashy
Nebitdag
Celeken
Gyzylarbat
TURKMENISTAN
Mary
Yoloten
Andkhvoy

Erzurum
Mt. Ararat
16854
AZER.
Xankändi
(Stepanakert)
Salyan
CASPIAN
SEA
Surface 92 Feet Below Sea Level
Ashgabat
KOPPEH
Quchān
DAGH
Kaka
Sarogt
Meymaneh
Tagtabazar

Elâzığ
Muş
Tatvana
Bitlis
Van
Khvoy
Marand
Astara
Bandar-e Anzali
Rasht
Lāhijān
Bābol
Gorgan
Bandar-e
Torkeman
Bojnūrd
Binalud
11208
Neyshābūr
Mashhad

Diyarbakır
Siverek
Mardin
Orūmīyeh
KURDISTAN
Tabrīz
Ardabil
Chālūs
ELBURZ MTS.
Emāmshahr
Sābzevār
Torbat-e
Heydarīyeh
Torbat-e Jām
Harirūd

Zakho
Al Mawṣil
Arbīl
Maragheh
Miāneh
Qazvīn
Qalleh-ye
Damqvand
18386
Rey
Kāshmar
Ghariān
Herāt

Karkūk
As Sulaymānīyah
Sanandaj
Zanjān
TEHRĀN
DASHT-E KAVIR
DESERT
Bajestān
Shindand

Bayjī
Tikrīt
Samarrā
Hamadān
Arak
Qom
Kāshān
IRAN
Ferdows
Qāyen
Birjand
AFGHANISTAN
Farāh

Hadīthah
Bakhtarān
Borūjerd
Khorramābad
Khomeynīshahr
Eşfahān
Na'īn
Yazd
PLATEAU OF IRAN
Nehbandān
DASHT-E LŪT
(DESERT)
Zarani

BAGHDĀD
Babylon (Ruins)
Dezfūl
Shūshtar
Masjed Soleymān
Kalar
14100
Qomsheh
Persepolis
(Ruins)
Rafsanjān
Namakzār-e
Shāhdād
Darvācheh-ye
Sīstān
Char Borjak
Gowd-e
Zereh
CHAGAI HILLS

Ar Ramādī
Karbalā'
Al Kūt
An Najaf
Al 'Amārah
Ahvāz
Hoft Gel
Behbehān
Kermān
Zāhedān
Lādīz
PAKISTAN

Ar Ruṭbah
As Samāwah
An Nāṣirīyah
Khorramshahr
Bandar-e Khomeyni
Gachsārān
Shīrāz
Furglun
10760
Bāmpūr
Hāmūn-i
Māshkel

Badanah
Sakakah
Rafhā
Al Baṣrah
Abādān
KUWAIT
Kuwait
(Al Kuwayt)
Al Qayṣūmah
Kāzerūn
Darvācheh-ye
Bakhtegan
Jahrom
Lār
Bandar-e
Būshehr
Bandar-e 'Abbās
Jāsk
Bandar Beheshti
Gwādar

AN NAFŪD
JABAL SHAMMAR
Ha'il
Buraydah
Unayzah
Ash Shaqra
AD DAHNA
AL HASA
Al Qatif
Ad Dammām
Az Zahrān
(Dhahran)
PERSIAN GULF
RA'S AT TANNŪRAH
BAHRAIN
Al Manāmah
QATAR
Dukhān
Bandar-e Lengeh
OMAN
Ash Shāriqah
Al Khābūrah
Muscat
HORMUZ
Jabal ash Shām
9957

SAUDI
NAJD
Riyadh
(Ar Riyāḍ)
As Sulaymānīyah
Ash Shaqra
Al Hufūf
Ad Dawhah
Dubayy
UNITED ARAB EMIRATES
Abū Ẓaby
AL JABAL AL AKHDAR
Şūr
RA'S AL HADD

Al Madīnah
(Medina)
AL AFLAJ
AD DAHY
Mahd adh
Dhahab
ARABIA
NAFŪD
Al Mubarraz
Al 'Ubaylah
OMAN

Riyadh
JABAL TUWAYQ
Al Lidām
AR RUB' AL KHĀLĪ
RA'S AL MADRAKAH
Al Jawārah
AL MASIRAH

Al Qunfudhah
Al Lith
ASIR
Qal'at Bishah
NAJRAN
KHŪRYĀN MŪRYĀN

Abha
Al Lubayyah
DAHLAK
ARCH.
JĀZĀ'IR
FARASĀN
Qizan
Sa'dah
RAMLAT AS
SAB'ATAYN
Shibām
Say'ūn
Mirbāṭ
Al Ghaydah
RA'S FARTAK
ARABIAN
SEA

Mitsiwa
mera
KAMARAN
San'a
YEMEN
HADRAMAWT
Sayḥūt
Ash Shiḥr
RA'S FARTAK

Al Hudaydah
Al Mukallā
SUQUTRĀ (SOCOTRA)
(Yemen)
Hadibu

Ibb
Ta'izz
Shuqrah
Al Hawrah
Al Bayḍā

Mekele
Ramlu
6988
Al Makhā
(Mocha)
Aden ('Adan)
Madinat ash Sha'b
Caluula
GEES GWARDAFUY

DENAKIL
DJIBOUTI
Obock
GULF OF ADEN
SOMALIA

Tadjoura
Djibouti
Seylac
Qandala

Relief

Meters		Feet
3050		10 000
1525		5000
610		2000
305		1000
152.5		500
0	Sea Level	0
		Below
152.5		Sea Level
1525		5 000
3050		10 000
6100		20 000

Scale 1:16 000 000; one inch to 250 miles. Polyconic Projection
Elevations and depressions are given in feet

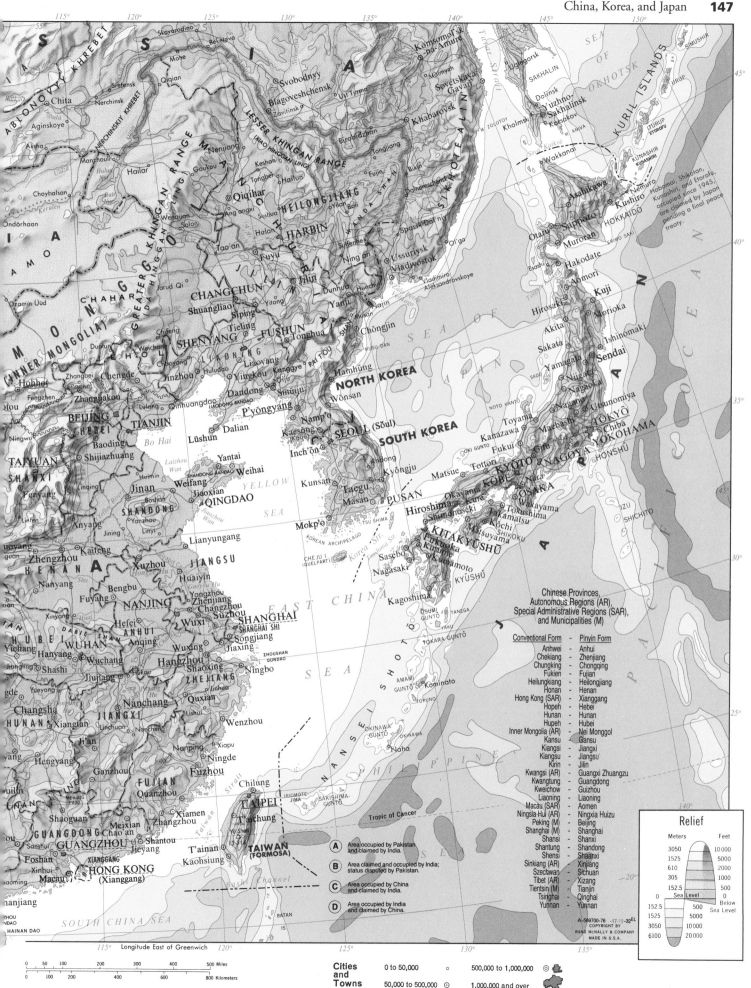

Chinese Provinces,
Autonomous Regions (AR),
Special Administrative Regions (SAR),
and Municipalities (M)

Conventional Form	Pinyin Form
Anhwei	Anhui
Chekiang	Zhenjiang
Chungking	Chongqing
Fukien	Fujian
Heilungkiang	Heilongjiang
Honan	Henan
Hong Kong (SAR)	Xianggang
Hopeh	Hebei
Hunan	Hunan
Hupeh	Hubei
Inner Mongolia (AR)	Nei Monggol
Kansu	Gansu
Kiangsi	Jiangxi
Kiangsu	Jiangsu
Kirin	Jilin
Kwangsi (AR)	Guangxi Zhuangzu
Kwangtung	Guangdong
Kweichow	Guizhou
Liaoning	Liaoning
Macau (SAR)	Aomen
Ningsia-Hui (AR)	Ningxia Huizu
Peking (M)	Beijing
Shanghai (M)	Shanghai
Shansi	Shanxi
Shantung	Shandong
Shensi	Shaanxi
Sinkiang (AR)	Xinjiang
Szechwan	Sichuan
Tibet (AR)	Xizang
Tientsin (M)	Tianjin
Tsinghai	Qinghai
Yunnan	Yunnan

A Area occupied by Pakistan and claimed by India.

B Area claimed and occupied by India; status disputed by Pakistan.

C Area occupied by China and claimed by India.

D Area occupied by India and claimed by China.

A-569700-76 -17-12-32EL
COPYRIGHT BY
RAND McNALLY & COMPANY
MADE IN U.S.A.

Relief

Meters		Feet
3050		10 000
1525		5000
610		2000
305		1000
152.5		500
0	Sea Level	0
		Below Sea Level
152.5		500
1525		5000
3050		10 000
6100		20 000

Longitude East of Greenwich

0 50 100 200 300 400 500 Miles
0 100 200 400 600 800 Kilometers

Cities and Towns

0 to 50,000	o	500,000 to 1,000,000	
50,000 to 500,000	⊙	1,000,000 and over	

125°　　　130°　　　135°　　　20°

PHILIPPINE

PHILIPPINES

15°

Catbalogan

Tacloban

LEYTE

Cebu

DINAGAT ISLAND

BOHOL

Butuan

Cagayan

MINDANAO

MT. APO

9692

Davao

10°

SEA

PHILIPPINE

TRENCH

PALAU

PULAU MIANGAS

SONSOROL
ISLANDS

5°

KEPULAUAN
TALAUD

PULAU SANGIHE

PULAU SIAU

nado

Tondano

Ternate

HALMAHERA

MOROTAI

KEPULAUAN
MAPIA

Laut Majuku
(Molucca Sea)

Laut
Halmahera
(Halmahera Sea)

PULAU
WAIGEO

Selat Dampier

PULAU BACAN

Labuha

Manokwari

SALAWATI

Sorong

BIAK

TG. PERKAM

Equator

0°

LAUAN
IGGAI

KEPULAUAN
OBI

PULAU
TALIBU

PULAU MANGOLE

PULAU MISOOL

PULAU
NUMFOOR

PULAU YAPEN

NINIGO GROUP

HERMIT IS.

ADMIRALTY ISLANDS

MUSSAU
ISLAND

EMIRA
ISLAND

KEPULAUAN
SULA

PULAU SANANA

JAZIRAH
DOBERAI

Teluk Berau

Teluk
Cenderawasih

Jayapura
(Sukarnapura)

Aitape

Wewak

MANUS
ISLAND

NEW HANOVER

Kavieng

BISMARCK

A S I A

Piru

CERAM
(SERAM)

Bula

Fakfak

Kaimana

PEGUNUNGAN VAN REES

Sepik

KARKAR ISLAND

LONG ISLAND

WITU
ISLANDS

NEW
IRELAND

Namatanai

Rabaul

ARCH

Kokopo

BURU

Ambon

PULAU AMBON

KEPULAUAN
BANDA

PULAU ADI

PEGUNUNGAN MAOKE

Puncak Jaya
16 503

Puncak Trikora
15 584

Madang

BISMARCK R.

Talasea

△Mt. Wilhelm 14 793

△The Father
7546

owoni

KEPULAUAN
TUKANGBESI

KEPULAUAN
LUCIPARA

KEPULAUAN KAI

KAI KECIL

Dobo

N E W G U I N E A

Mt. Giluwe 14 330

△Mt. Bangeta
13 520△

NEW BRITAIN

LAUT BANDA
(BANDA SEA)

PULAU
DAMAR

KEPULAUAN
ARU

PULAU
TRANGAN

YAMDENA

KEPULAUAN
TANIMBAR

PULAU
YOS
SUDARSA

Digul

PAPUA
NEW GUINEA

Lae

Huon Gulf

Morobe

NEW BRITAIN TRENCH

PULAU WETAR

DE-ATAURO

PULAU
MOA

PULAU BABAR

PULAU
SELARU

Merauke

Mt. Albert Edward
13 090

Buna

WOODLARK
ISLAND

PULAU
ALOR

Dili

EAST TIMOR

TIMOR

TANJUNG VALS

ARAFURA
SEA

Daru

Port Moresby

OWEN STANLEY RA.

△Mt. Victoria
13 238

TROBRIAND IS.

D'ENTRECASTEAUX IS.

125°　130°　135°

TIMOR

SEA

MELVILLE
ISLAND

COBOURG
PEN.

CROKER ISLAND

WESSEL IS.

BATHURST
ISLAND

Van
Diemen Gulf

Darwin

C. ARNHEM

AUSTRALIA

Gulf of Carpentaria

Torres
Strait

C. YORK

CAPE
YORK
PEN.

GREAT

BARRIER

REEF

CORAL SEA

Samarai

10°

140°　　　145°　　　150°

0   50   100   200   300   400   500 Miles

0   100   200   400   600   800 Kilometers

Inset map (Luzon, Philippines):

120°

Cabugao

Iguig

Tuguegarao

Vigan

Bangued

Narvacan

Lubuagan

Cabagan

Divilacan Bay

Candon

Bontoc

Ilagan

PALANAN PT.

Palanan Bay

Cervantes

CORDILLERA CENTRAL

Mt. Amuyao
8799

Cauayan

Luna

Santiago

Echague

Janes

DIJOHAN PT.

San Fernando S. Juan

Pulog
9626

Magabag

Solano

Bayombong

Dupax

PHILIPPINE

Bauang

Baguio

Bambang

Casiguran

SANTIAGO

Aringay

1388

CABARRUYAN

S. Fabian

S. Nicolas

Casiguran Sd.

CAPE SAN ILDEFONSO

16°

Bolinao

Bani

Alaminos

Lingayen
Gulf

Dagupan

S. Tayug

Agno

Burgos

CAIMAN PT.

Dasol Bay

San Carlos

Urdaneta

Rosales

S. Quintin

Baler Bay

Infanta

Mangatarem

Bayambang

San Jose

Baler

CAPE ENCANTO

Santa Cruz

Comsing

Muñoz

PHILIPPINES

SEA

Candelaria

High Pk.
6683

Gerona

Tarlac

Victoria

Cabanatuan

Dingalan Bay

LUZON

Gapan

Palauig

Concepcion

S. Miguel

POLILLO IS.

Iba

Pinatubo
5771

Angeles

Arayat

S. Fernando

POLILLO

PATNANUNGAN

S. Narciso

Guagua

Malolos

Infanta

Polillo

JOMALIG

S. Antonio

Subic

Sta.
Maria

BALESIN

CALAGUAS ISLAND

Olongapo

Orania

Malabon

Quezon
City

CABALETE

Capalonga

Paracale

SAMPALOC PT.

Orion

Balanga

Manila

MANILA

Pasig

ALABAT

Labo

Talisay

Mariveles

Cavite

Naic

Laguna

TALIM

Sta. Cruz

Daet

CORREGIDOR ISLAND

Bay

Silang

Calamba

Mauban

Lamon Bay

Mt. Labo
5066

San
Miguel
Bay

Nasugbu

Lipa

Nagcarlan

Atimonan

Macalelon

Ragay

Lagonoy

Balayan

Lubang

Lemery

S. Pablo

7177 Mt. Banahao

Gumaca

Catanauan

Mt. Isarog
6450

Naga

Pili

LUBANG

AMBIL
ISLAND

Balayan
Bay

Rosario

Lucena

Unisan

S. Narciso

Bato

Bula

IS.

GOLD
ISLAND

MARICABAN

Batangas

Loba

Tayabas Bay

Polangui

Moyong
Volcano
8077

Ligao

CABRA ISLAND

VERDE I. Passage

VERDE

Paluan

Mt. Halcon
8471

Calapan

Boac

S. Cruz

Torrijos

San Pascual

Legazpi

CAPE CALAVITE

Naujan

MARINDUQUE
ISLAND

BURIAS

Buti

Mamburao

Gasan

DUMALI PT.

Pinamalayan

Jones

SIBUYAN

TICAO
ISLAND

MINDORO

Sablayan

Mt. Baco
8163

BANTON

S. Jacinto

Aroroy

DONGON PT.

Odiongan

Romblon

TABLAS

SEA

Masbote

Scale 1:4 000 000

0   10   20   30   40 Miles

0 10 20 30 40 50 60 Kilometers

Knob Pk.
3031

ROMBLON ISLAND

Romblon

BUSUANGA

TARA

Mindoro Strait

S. Jose

ILIN ISLAND

Bulalacao

Tablas Strait

Looc

SIBUYAN

MASBATE

®RMCN.

®RMCN.

SOUTH CHINA SEA

Oceania (including Australia and New Zealand)

Oceania is comprised of Australia, New Zealand, eastern New Guinea, and approximately 25,000 other islands in the South Pacific, most of which are uninhabited. Many of the islands are coral atolls, formed by microscopic creatures over scores of centuries, while others are the result of volcanic action.

Bay of Islands, North Island, New Zealand

Oceania's largest landmass is Australia, which at three million square miles (7.7 million sq km) is the world's smallest continent. In fact, it is smaller than five countries—Russia, Canada, China, Brazil, and the United States. Australia is generally flat and dry. The interior is sparsely populated, with most people living in coastal cities such as Sydney.

The next-largest part of Oceania is Papua New Guinea, the country occupying the eastern half of the island of New Guinea, which has some of the most forbidding and remote terrain in the world. New Zealand, Oceania's third-largest country, is known for its natural beauty and its huge herds of sheep.

Oceania at a glance

Land area:
3,300,000 square miles (8,500,000 sq km)

Estimated population:
34,605,000

Population density:
10/square mile (4.1/sq km)

Mean elevation:
1,000 feet (305 m)

Highest point:
Mt. Wilhelm, Papua New Guinea, 14,793 feet (4,509 m)

Lowest point:
Lake Eyre, South Australia, 52 feet (16 m) below sea level

Longest river:
Murray-Darling, 2,330 mi (3,750 km)

Number of countries (incl. dependencies): 29

Largest independent country: Australia, 2,969,910 square miles (7,692,030 sq km)

Smallest independent country: Nauru, 8.1 square miles (21 sq km)

Most populous independent country: Australia, 21,135,000

Least populous independent country: Tuvalu, 12,000

Most populous metropolitan area: Sydney, Australia, population 4.3 million

The Outback, Australia

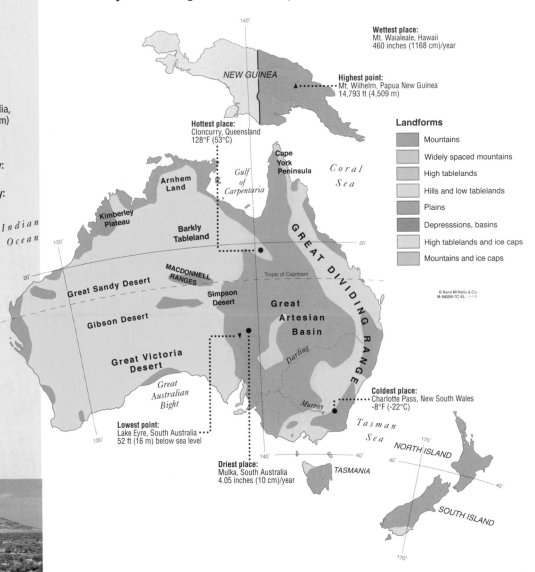

Wettest place:
Mt. Waialeale, Hawaii
460 inches (1168 cm)/year

Highest point:
Mt. Wilhelm, Papua New Guinea
14,793 ft (4,509 m)

Hottest place:
Cloncurry, Queensland
128°F (53°C)

Landforms

- Mountains
- Widely spaced mountains
- High tablelands
- Hills and low tablelands
- Plains
- Depresssions, basins
- High tablelands and ice caps
- Mountains and ice caps

© Rand McNally & Co.
M-590200-7C-EL -:-1-:-1

Lowest point:
Lake Eyre, South Australia
52 ft (16 m) below sea level

Driest place:
Mulka, South Australia
4.05 inches (10 cm)/year

Coldest place:
Charlotte Pass, New South Wales
-8°F (-22°C)

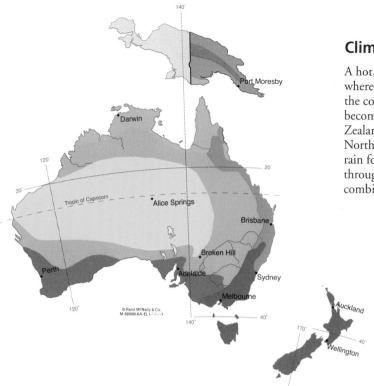

Climate

A hot, dry desert climate prevails in central and western Australia, where summer temperatures regularly rise above 100°F (40°C). Toward the continent's northern, southern, and eastern coasts, the climate becomes more temperate and less arid. Southeastern Australia and New Zealand enjoy a milder, rainier climate similar to that of the Pacific Northwest of the United States. New Guinea, which has a tropical rain forest climate, experiences heavy rainfall and high temperatures throughout the year. Equatorial warmth and moderating tradewinds combine to make tropical paradises of many of Oceania's islands.

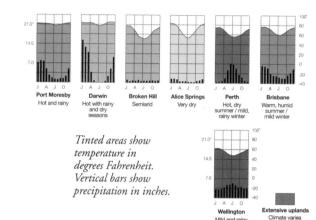

Port Moresby — Hot and rainy

Darwin — Hot with rainy and dry seasons

Broken Hill — Semiarid

Alice Springs — Very dry

Perth — Hot, dry summer / mild, rainy winter

Brisbane — Warm, humid summer / mild winter

Tinted areas show temperature in degrees Fahrenheit. Vertical bars show precipitation in inches.

Wellington — Mild and rainy

Extensive uplands — Climate varies with elevation and latitude

Population

Australia's population is concentrated in the coastal regions, especially along the stretch of southeastern coast that includes Adelaide, Melbourne, Sydney, and Brisbane. Almost all Australians speak English and are descendants of British settlers. In recent years, many immigrants have arrived from Asia, especially Hong Kong. Aboriginal people account for only about 1% of Australia's population. New Zealand has a similar ethnic make-up, but its indigenous people, the Maori, represent about 10% of the population. The North Island is home to approximately three out of four New Zealanders; the South Island, which is more mountainous and heavily forested, is sparsely populated.

Centuries of isolation have given rise to many distinctive cultures among the island groups of Oceania. There has been little immigration from other parts of the world.

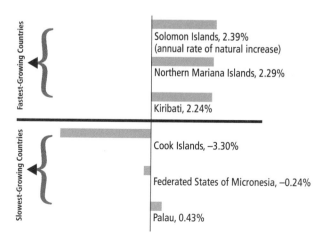

Fastest-Growing Countries

Solomon Islands, 2.39% (annual rate of natural increase)

Northern Mariana Islands, 2.29%

Kiribati, 2.24%

Slowest-Growing Countries

Cook Islands, –3.30%

Federated States of Micronesia, –0.24%

Palau, 0.43%

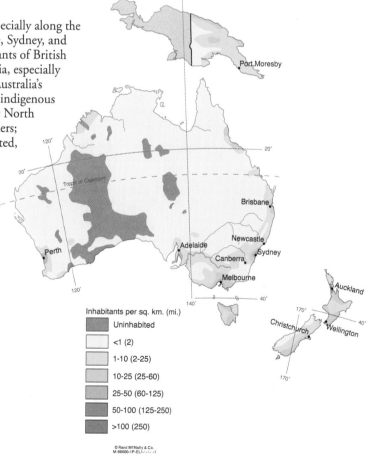

Inhabitants per sq. km. (mi.)

- Uninhabited
- <1 (2)
- 1-10 (2-25)
- 10-25 (25-60)
- 25-50 (60-125)
- 50-100 (125-250)
- >100 (250)

© Rand McNally & Co.
M-595000-1P-EL1-¹-¹- -1

Environments and Land Use

Much of central and western Australia is a dry, inhospitable land of sand, rocks, and scrub vegetation. Surrounding this desert region is a broad band of semiarid grassland that covers more than half of the continent and supports a huge livestock industry. Australia has more sheep—132 million—than any other country in the world, as well as sizable herds of cattle. The dry climate and sparse plant life, however, mean that each animal requires a dozen or more acres to survive. Six percent of the continent is suitable for crops; most of the arable land is found on fertile plains in the southeast. Major crops include wheat, sugar cane, oats, barley, sorghum, and rice.

Tourism plays an important role in Australia's economy. Among the continent's major attractions are its unusual wildlife, such as kangaroos, koalas, wombats, and platypuses; the Great Barrier Reef, which stretches for 1,250 miles (2,000 km) along the northeastern coast; and the ruggedly beautiful Outback, with its dramatic rock formations such as Ayers Rock (Uluru) and the Olga Rocks.

Thanks to its fertile land and temperate climate, New Zealand has a thriving livestock industry and is a leading world exporter of dairy products and lamb. Thinly populated and with little industry, it is one of the world's least polluted countries. Its pristine beauty encompasses a variety of scenery, including mountains, fjords, glaciers, rain forests, beaches, and geysers. Only the country's relative isolation restrains its growing tourism industry.

Dense tropical rain forests blanket much of Papua New Guinea. These forests have thus far escaped the large-scale deforestation that is taking place in other tropical forests around the world.

Tourism is central to the economies of many of the islands throughout Oceania. Abundant sunshine, pleasant temperatures, and beautiful beaches draw millions of visitors each year to islands such as Tahiti and Fiji. For islands with little or no tourism, the economic scene is less promising: many islanders rely on subsistence fishing and foreign aid from former colonial powers.

Farmland on North Island, New Zealand

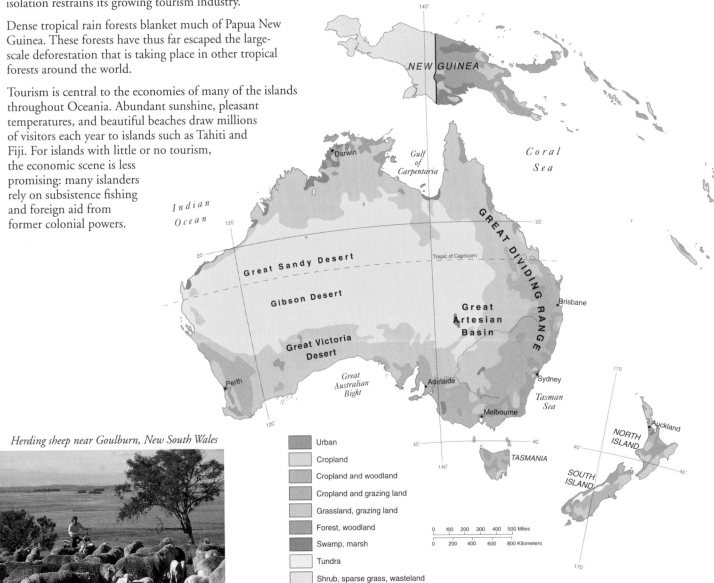

Herding sheep near Goulburn, New South Wales

Urban

Cropland

Cropland and woodland

Cropland and grazing land

Grassland, grazing land

Forest, woodland

Swamp, marsh

Tundra

Shrub, sparse grass, wasteland

Barren land

© Rand McNally & Co.
N-ANS95000-M1- --3-3-1

The Original Australians and New Zealanders

Many anthropologists believe that Australia's Aborigines are the oldest race of people on Earth. During the 40,000 years since they migrated to the island continent from Asia, they have developed a rich culture with an intricate spiritual and social life.

The original New Zealanders, the Maoris, arrived from other Polynesian islands in the 10th century. At the beginning of large-scale immigration from Britain in the 1800s, the British government signed a treaty with the Maoris which granted them full rights as citizens. With the exception of some disputes over land, this agreement has paved the way for the historically harmonious relations between the races in New Zealand.

Relations between the Aborigines and whites in Australia have been less harmonious. The arrival of the first European colonists in 1788 set in motion a chain of events that decimated the Aborigines and threatened their unique culture. Disease and skirmishes killed Aborigines along the coast, and thousands of others were forced from their lands by settlers. Some sought refuge with Aborigines already living in Australia's interior, the Outback. Alcoholism and other social problems became common among the Aborigines as they found themselves confronted by a society they did not understand.

Aboriginal boy with elders, Western Australia

Australia was slow to recognize the rights of its first inhabitants. In the early 1960s, official attitudes began to change as public embarrassment grew over the decades of discrimination. A significant step occurred in 1962 when full rights of citizenship were extended to the Aborigines.

Questions of land ownership, however, remain problematic for both sides. The government has set aside large reserves for the Aborigines, but much of the land is in the continent's hostile interior (see map at right). Only in the past two decades has an agreement been reached allowing Aborigines to share in the vast mineral wealth of their northern lands. Recent court decisions have awarded individual Aborigines rights to ancestral lands which were seized by settlers, but many local governments continue to fight these decisions.

In the face of indifference and hostility, there has recently been an upsurge of interest in cultural traditions among the approximately 240,000 Australians of aboriginal descent. Still, many of the traditions of the 500 different tribes that were present 200 years ago have been lost.

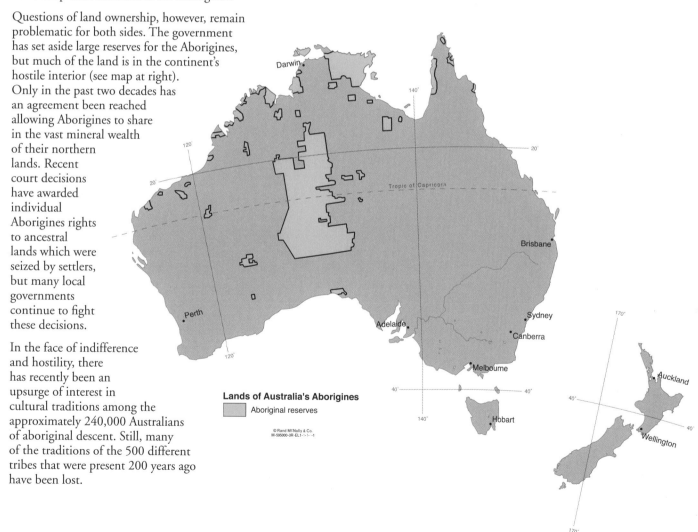

Lands of Australia's Aborigines

Aboriginal reserves

© Rand McNally & Co.
M-595000-3R-EL1-1-1--1

I N D O N E S I A

Pasuruan
G. Mahameru 12 060
G. Raung

Singaraja
Rinjani
LOMBOK Sumbawa-Besar
Lombok Selat

SUMBAWA
FLORES
Waingapu
SUMBA
SAWU
ROTI
Kupang

SAVU SEA

LOMBLEN PANTAR
ALOR
Dili
EAST TIMOR
TIMOR

SELARU

TANJUNG VALS

A R A F U R A   S E A

S U N D A   I S L A N D S

SUNDA TRENCH

TIMOR SEA

I N D I A N

O C E A N

C. VAN DIEMEN
MELVILLE
BATHURST
Van Diemen
COBOURG PEN.
CROKER
Darwin
Clarence Str.
Van Diemen Gulf
Dundas

WESSEL IS.
CAPE ARNHEM

CAPE LONDONDERRY
Joseph Bonaparte Gulf
Queen's Chan.
Anson Bay
Pine Creek
Katherine
Roper
ARNHEM LAND
Blue Mud Bay
GROOTE EYLANDT
Limmen Bight

GULF O
CARPENTAR
SIR EDWARD PELLEW GROUP
WELLESLE

BUCCANEER ARCH.
Sunday Str.
Collier Bay
CAPE LEVEQUE
King Str.
King
DAMPIER LAND
Broome
Derby
Roebuck Bay
LaGrange
EIGHTY MILE BEACH
LARREY POINT

Wyndham
Mt. Hann 2800
KING LEOPOLD RANGES
GEIKIE RANGE
Fitzroy Crossing
Halls Creek
Ord
Fitzroy

Victoria River Downs
Daly Waters
Newcastle Waters
Woods
Victoria
Birdum
Borroloola

N O R T H E R N
BARKLY TABLELAND
Burketown
Dobby
Camooweal
Mount Isa
Mal
Dajarro

Tanami
Tennant Creek

T E R R I T O R Y
Barrow Creek

DAMPIER ARCH.
Port Hedland
RIPON
DeGrey
Roebourne
MONTE BELLO IS.
BARROW
NORTH WEST CAPE
Millstream
Onslow
HAMERSLEY RANGE
Mt. Bruce 4052
Marble Bar
Nullagine
Jiggalong
Fortescue
Ashburton

GREAT SANDY DESERT
Disappointment
Mackay
Macdonald

Mt. Ziel 4955
MACDONNELL RANGES
Arltunga
Alice Springs
JAMES RANGE
Amadeus
Hay
Finke
SIMPSON DESERT

QU

POINT CLOATES
CAPE FARQUHAR
Tropic of Capricorn
Carnarvon
Geographe Chan.
BERNIER
DORRE
Shark Bay
DIRK HARTOG
STEEP POINT
Gascoyne
Murchison

W E S T E R N
GIBSON DESERT
Peak Hill
Nabberu
Carnegie
Wells
Gillen

Uluru (Ayers Rock)
MUSGRAVE RANGES
Mt. Woodroffe 4724
EVERARD RANGES
Charlotte Waters
Birdsville

S O U T H   A U S T R A L I A
Oodnadatta
STUART RANGE
William Creek
Marree
Farina
Woomera
Pimba
Parachil

HOUTMAN ROCKS
Geraldton
Dongara
Ajana
Northampton
Meekatharra
Nannine
Cue
Mount Magnet
Sandstone
Wiluna
Laverton
Yeo
Carey
Raeside
Austin
Barlee

A U S T R A L I A
GREAT VICTORIA DESERT
Ooldea Station
Hughes
Penong
Ceduna
POINT FOWLER
Eucla

FLIN
Port Augusto
Peterb
Whyalla
Port Pirie
Gladstone
Moonta
Port Wake
Gowle
FLINDERS RANGES
EYRE PENINSULA
Everard

Mingenew
Pithara
Milling
Moora
Lake Brown
Southern Cross
Coolgardie
Kalgoorlie-Boulder
Menzies
Dundas
Ballard
Ravensthorpe
Moore
Lefroy
Goddards Soak
Cowan
Rawlinna

NULLARBOR PLAIN
Eyre

DARLING RANGE
SWANLAND
Northam
York
Perth
Fremantle
Narrogin
Collie
Bunbury
Busselton
CAPE NATURALISTE
CAPE LEEUWIN
Normalup
Albany
PT. D'ENTRECASTEAUX
WEST CAPE HOWE
Norseman
Salmon Gums
Esperance
Hopetoun
Katanning
King George Sd.
Geographe Bay

GREAT AUSTRALIAN BIGHT

Port Lincoln
KANGAROO
Gulf St. Vincent
Spencer Gulf
Ade
Encounter
CAPE JAFFA
Kingst
Naro
Mt. Ga

I N D I A N   O C E A N

40,000 SQ MI
AREA

0   100   200
Miles

A-590200-26   5-18EL
COPYRIGHT BY
RAND McNALLY & COMPANY
MADE IN U.S.A.

Longitude   115°   East of Greenwich

Scale 1:16 000 000; one inch to 250 miles. Lambert's Azimuthal, Equal Area Projection
Elevations and depressions are given in feet

INDONESIA

Pasuruan

G. Mahameru 12 060
G. Raung
Singaraja Sunda Selat
Rinjani
Bali 9225
Lombken Pantar
Sumbawa Besar
Rapa
LOMBOK
SUMBAWA
FLORES
Waingapu
SAVU SEA
SUMBA
SAWU
ROTI
Kupang
Alor
Dili
EAST TIMOR
TIMOR

SUNDA
TRENCH

INDIAN OCEAN

SUNDA ISLANDS

TIMOR SEA

ARAFURA SEA

SELARU

TANJUNG VALS

CROKER
WESSEL IS.

CAPE ARNHEM

C. VAN DIEMEN
MELVILLE
Bathurst
Van Diemen Gulf
ARNHEM LAND
Blue Mud Bay
GROOTE EYLANDT

GULF O
CARPENTA

Darwin
Clarence Str.
Anson Bay
Pine Creek
Katherine
Limmen Bight
SIR EDWARD PELLEW GROUP
WELLESLE

CAPE LONDONDERRY
Joseph Bonaparte Gulf
Queen Chan.
Birdum
Borroloola
Victoria River Downs
Daly Waters
Newcastle Waters
Burketown
BARKLY TABLELAND

Wyndham
Mt. Hann 2600
KING LEOPOLD RANGES
GEIKIE RANGE
Derby
Fitzroy Crossing
Halls Creek
NORTHERN

Sturt Cr.

BUCCANEER ARCH.
CAPE LEVEQUE
King Sd.
DAMPIER
Broome LAND
Roebuck Bay
LaGrange
Woods
Alexandria
Dobby

Tanami
Tennant Creek
Camooweal
Mount Isa
Mall

LARREY POINT
EIGHTY MILE BEACH

TERRITORY

QU

Dajarra

DAMPIER ARCH.
RIPON
Port Hedland
De Grey
MONTE BELLO IS.
BARROW
Roebourne
Marble Bar
Nullagine
GREAT SANDY DESERT
Mackay
Barrow Creek
Mt. Ziel 4955
MACDONNELL RANGES
Arltunga
Alice Springs

Millstream
Onslow
HAMERSLEY RANGE
Mt. Bruce 4052
Jiggalong
Macdonald
JAMES RANGE
SIMPSON

NORTH WEST CAPE
Fortescue
Exmouth Gulf
Disappointment
Amadeus
Uluru (Ayers Rock)
Charlotte Waters
DESERT
Birdsville

POINT CLOATES

Tropic of Capricorn
CAPE FARQUHAR
Carnarvon
Geographe Ch.
Gascoyne
Peak Hill
WESTERN
GIBSON DESERT
Carnegie
Gillen
MUSGRAVE RANGES
Mt. Woodroffe 4724
EVERARD RANGES

BERNIER
DORRE
Shark Bay
Nabberu
Welb
The Alberga

DIRK HARTOG
STEEP POINT
Meekatharra
Nannine
Wiluna
Oodnadatta

Cue
Sandstone
STUART RANGE
William Creek
Marree
Grey
Coopers Cr.

Austin
Mount Magnet
Laverton
AUSTRALIA
Carey
SOUTH AUSTRALIA
Eyre
Farina
Patachin

HOUTMAN ROCKS
Ajana
Northampton
Ballard
Menzies
GREAT VICTORIA DESERT
Oodea Station
Woomera
Pimba

Geraldton
Mingenew
Moore
Kalgoorlie-Boulder
Rawlinna
Hughes
Penong
Whyalla
Port Augusta
FLIN

Dongara
Barlee
Lefroy
Goddards South
NULLARBOR PLAIN
Eucla
Ceduna
EYRE PENINSULA
Port Pirie
Gladstone

Pithara
Milling
Moora
Lake Brown
Southern Cross
Coolgardie
Cowan
Norseman
Dundas
Salmon Gums
POINT FOWLER
Moonta
Wallaroo
Port Wake

DARLING RANGE
SWANLAND
Perth
Fremantle
Northam
York
Ravensthorpe
Esperance
Eyre
GREAT AUSTRALIAN BIGHT
Port Lincoln
Gawle

Geographe Bay
Collie
Narrogin
Hopetoun
ARCHIPELAGO OF THE RECHERCHE
Spencer Gulf
KANGAROO

CAPE NATURALISTE
Bunbury
Busselton
Katanning
Nara

CAPE LEEUWIN
Nornalup
Albany
Kingsto
CAPE JAFFA

PT. D'ENTRECASTEAUX
WEST CAPE HOWE
King George Sd.

INDIAN OCEAN

Longitude   East of Greenwich

Relief

Meters		Feet
3050		10 000
1525		5000
610		2000
305		1000
152.5		500
0	Sea Level	0
152.5		Below Sea Level 500
1525		5000
3050		10 000
6100		20 000

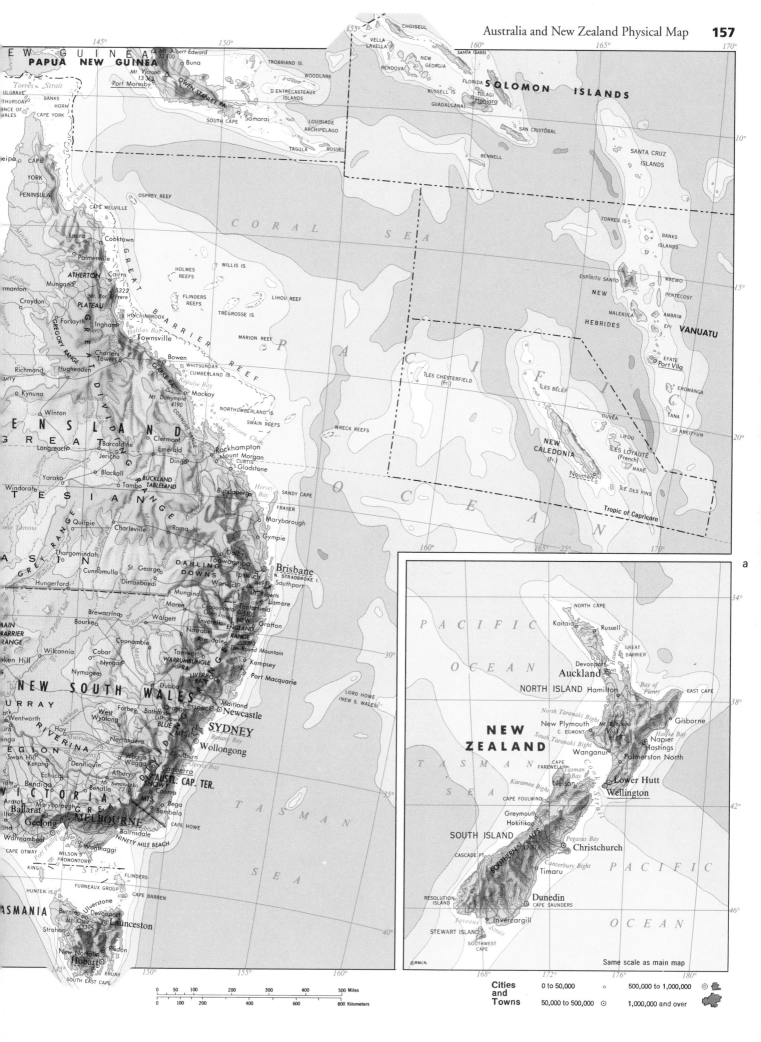

RUSSIA

KAZAKHSTAN

ZAPADNYYE SAYAN Irkutsk Baykal (Lake Baikal) STANOVOY KHREBET SEA OF OKHOTSK KOMANDORSKIYE OSTROVA BERING SEA Nome ST. LAWRENCE ALASKA (U.S.A.) Unalaska Attu ALEUTIAN IS. Petropavlovsk-Kamchatskiy P-OV KAMCHATKA

MONGOLIA Ulan Bator MANCHURIA HARBIN CHANGCHUN GOBI DESERT SHENYANG Vladivostok HOKKAIDO KURILS MYS LOPATKA

BEIJING TIANJIN Dalian KOREA SEA OF JAPAN HONSHŪ SEOUL (Sôul) TŌKYŌ YOKOHAMA KŌBE Nagasaki KITAKYŪSHŪ KYŪSHŪ JAPAN JAPAN CURRENT

CHINA KUNLUN SHAN Hwang NANJING WUHAN SHANGHAI Yangtze Fuzhou T'AIPEI NANSEI SHOTŌ BONIN IS. (Japan) MARCUS (Japan) MIDWAY IS. (U.S.A.) INTERNATIONAL DATE LINE

GUANGZHOU Hanoi HONG KONG TAIWAN (FORMOSA) Tropic of Cancer WAKE (U.S.A.)

THAILAND Hue HAINAN DAO CAPE ENGANO PHILIPPINE SEA NORTHERN MARIANA ISLANDS (U.S.A.) MICRONESIA NORTH MARIANA IS. GUAM (U.S.A.)

BANGKOK CAMBODIA Gulf of Thailand CHINA LUZON MANILA PHILIPPINES SAMAR SOUTH EQUATORIAL CURRENT MARSHALL IS. MARSHALL ISLANDS

HO CHI MINH CITY (Saigon) VIETNAM MINDANAO PALAU IS. CAROLINE IS. FEDERATED STATES OF MICRONESIA

MALAY PENINSULA Bandar Seri Begawan BRUNEI CELEBES SEA PALAU HOWLAND BAKER (U.S.A.) GILBERT IS.

MALAYSIA MALAYSIA BORNEO CELEBES HALMAHERA Manokwari Jayapura (Sukarnapura) Equator NAURU KIRIBATI KANTON PHOENIX IS.

SINGAPORE SINGAPORE MOLUCCAS TG. PERKAM NEW IRELAND MELANESIA TUVALU TOKELAU (N.Z.)

SUMATRA INDONESIA CERAM BISMARCK ARCH. NEW BRITAIN SOLOMON ISLANDS WALLIS AND FUTUNA (Fr.) SAMOA

JAKARTA Java Sea JAVA ARAFURA SEA PAPUA NEW GUINEA BOUGAINVILLE TRENCH TONGA

SUNDA TRENCH TIMOR EAST TIMOR TIMOR SEA THURSDAY I. CAPE YORK Port Moresby SOUTH CAPE CORAL SEA

CHRISTMAS (Austl.) Darwin Gulf of Carpentaria NEW HEBRIDES VANUATU NEW CALEDONIA (Fr.)

NORTH WEST CAPE GREAT SANDY DESERT Tropic of Capricorn MACDONNELL RANGES AUSTRALIA GREAT DIVIDING RANGE FIJI LOYALTY IS. EAST AUSTRALIAN CURRENT

Perth Fremantle Tarrens Brisbane NORFOLK (Austl.) TASMAN SEA

Albany Great Australian Bight Murray Adelaide Canberra SYDNEY KERMADEC IS. (N.Z.)

MELBOURNE CAPE HOWE Bass Strait NORTH CAPE NORTH ISLAND Auckland

TASMANIA Hobart SOUTH EAST CAPE SOUTH ISLAND NEW ZEALAND Wellington

INDIAN OCEAN STEWART I. SOUTHWEST CAPE Dunedin

Relief

Meters		Feet
3050		10 000
1525		5000
610		2000
305		1000
152.5		500
0	Sea Level	0
152.5		500
1525		5000
3050		10 000
6100		20 000

A-598500-76 012-30
COPYRIGHT BY
RAND McNALLY & COMPANY
MADE IN U.S.A.

Longitude East of Greenwich

→ Warm ocean currents
→ Cold ocean currents

Scale 1:50 000 000; one inch to 800 miles. Goode's Homolosine Equal Area Projection
Elevations and depressions are given in feet

a

Scale 1:4 000 000

0 10 20 30 40 Miles
0 10 20 30 40 50 60 Kilometers

PACIFIC OCEAN

HAWAI'I (U.S.A.)

Hanalei Bay
Kilauea
Kawaikini △ (5170)
Kaunakakai
Waimea
Lihue
KAUA'I
NI'IHAU
Kalalau Channel

KAHUKU PT.
O'AHU
Waialua
KA'ENA PT.
Wai'anae
Kāne'ohe Bay
Waipahu
Aiea
Waimanalo
'Ewa
Honolulu
Kaiwi Channel

MOLOKA'I
Halawa
Kaunakakai
Pailolo Channel
Wailuku
Pauwela
LĀNA'I
Kahului
MAUI
Lahaina
Keokea
HALEAKALĀ NAT'L PARK
Kalohi Channel
Haleakala Crater
Hāna
'Au'au Chan.
Kealaikahiki Channel
KAHO'OLAWE
Alenuihaha Channel

UPOLU PT.
Hawi
Pa'auilo
Kamuela
Laupāhoehoe
Mauna Kea △ (Vol.) 13,796
Honomu
Kailua Kona
Hilo
HAWAI'I
Mauna Loa (Vol.) △ 13,680
Hookena
Kalapana
Kapapala

Sitka
Prince Rupert
CANADA
ROCKY MOUNTAINS
Vancouver
Victoria
SEATTLE
Portland
CASCADE RA.
Salt Lake City
SAN FRANCISCO
COAST RANGES
SIERRA NEVADA
UNITED STATES
ST. LOUIS
Missouri
Mississippi
CALIFORNIA CURRENT
LOS ANGELES
SAN DIEGO
New Orleans
Galveston
GULF OF MEXICO
CABO SAN LUCAS
Mazatlan
M E X I C O
SIERRA MADRE OCCIDENTAL
Tampico
Rio Grande
ISLAS REVILLAGIGEDO (Mex.)
MEXICO CITY
Veracruz
Acapulco
BELIZE
GUAT.
Guatemala
HOND.
EL SAL.
NICARAGUA
Managua
CARIBBEAN SEA
COSTA RICA
Colón
Panamá
PANAMA
Panama Canal

HAWAI'IAN IS (U.S.A.)
Honolulu

NORTH EQUATORIAL CURRENT

PALMYRA (U.S.A.)
TABUAERAN
KIRITIMATI

EQUATORIAL COUNTER CURRENT

Buenaventura
ARCHIPELAGO DE COLÓN (GALÁPAGOS IS.) (Ecuador)
Quito
ECUADOR
Guayaquil

POLYNESIA
MALDEN

SOUTH EQUATORIAL CURRENT
MANIHIKI IS.
MARQUESAS IS.

COOK ISLANDS (N.Z.)
SOCIETY IS.
TAHITI
ÎLES TUAMOTU
AITUTAKI
RAROTONGA

FRENCH POLYNESIA

PITCAIRN (Br.)
DUCIE
PITCAIRN

ISLA DE PASCUA (EASTER) (Chile)
I. SALA Y GÓMEZ (Chile)

LIMA
Callao
PERU
Arequipa
Mollendo
PERU-CHILE TRENCH
Iquique
PERU CURRENT
Antofagasta

I. SAN FÉLIX (Chile)
I. SAN AMBROSIO (Chile)
Coquimbo
Valparaíso
ISLAS DE JUAN FERNANDEZ (Chile)
SANTIAGO
Concepción
ANDES MOUNTAINS
ARGENTINA
CHILE
Valdivia
Puerto Montt
CHILOE
Bahía Blanca

WEST WIND DRIFT

Punta Arenas
Estrecho De Magallanes
CABO DE HORNOS

Longitude West of Greenham

170° 160° 150° 140° 130° 120° 110° 100° 90° 80° 70° 60° 50°

0   500   1000   1500   2000 Miles
0   1000   2000   3000 Kilometers

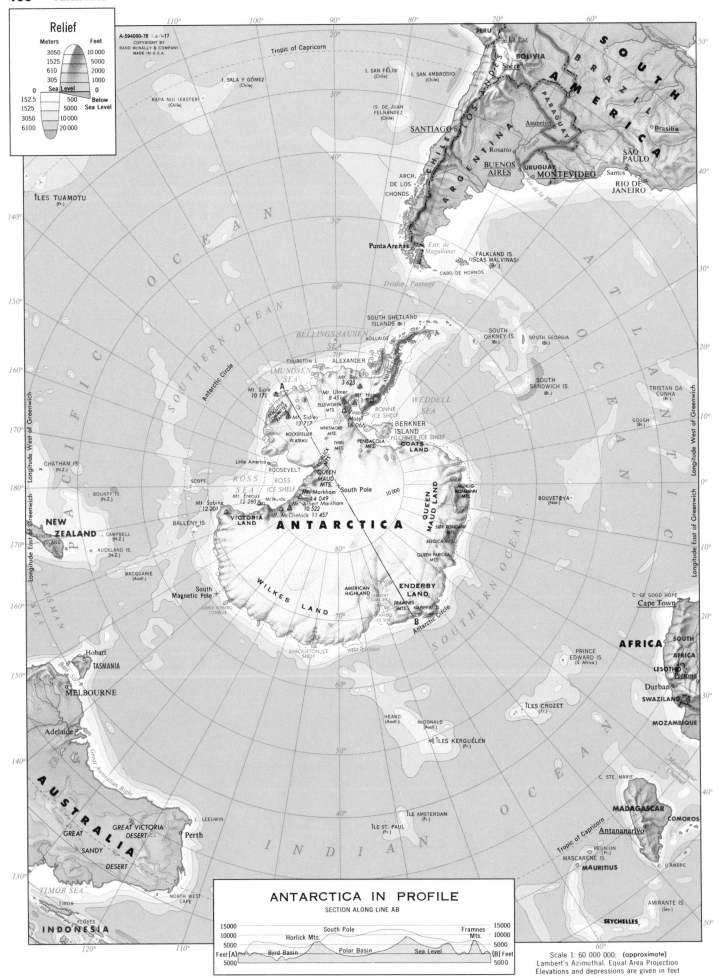

Glossary

Foreign Geographical Terms

Afk. ... Afrikaans
Ara. ... Arabic
Ber. ... Berber
Blg. ... Bulgarian
Bur. ... Burmese
Cbd. ... Cambodian
Ch. ... Chinese
Czech ... Czech
Dan. ... Danish
Du. ... Dutch
Est. ... Estonian
Finn. ... Finnish
Fr. ... French
Gae. ... Gaelic
Ger. ... German
Gr. ... Greek
Heb. ... Hebrew
Ice. ... Icelandic
Indon. ... Indonesian
It. ... Italian
Jpn. ... Japanese
Kor. ... Korean
Lao. ... Laotian
Lapp. ... Lappish
Mal. ... Malay
Mong. ... Mongolian
Nor. ... Norwegian
Pas. ... Pashto
Per. ... Persian
Pol. ... Polish
Port. ... Portuguese
Rom. ... Romanian
Rus. ... Russian
S./C. ... Serbo-Croatian
Slo. ... Slovak
Sp. ... Spanish
Swe. ... Swedish
Thai ... Thai
Tib. ... Tibetan
Tur. ... Turkish
Ukr. ... Ukranian
Viet. ... Vietnamese

-å, Dan., Nor., Swe. ... river
āb, Per. ... river
ada(lar), Tur. ... island(s)
adrar, Ber. ... mountains
ákra, akrotírion, Gr. ... cape
altos, Sp. ... mountains, hills
-älv, -älven, Swe. ... river
-ån, Swe. ... river
archipel, Fr. ... archipelago
archipiélago, Sp. ... archipelago
arquipélago, Port. ... archipelago
arroyo, Sp. ... brook
-ås, -åsen, Swe. ... hills
baai, Du. ... bay
bab, Ara. ... strait
Bach, Ger. ... brook, creek
-backen, Swe. ... hill
bælt, Dan. ... strait
bahía, Sp. ... bay
baie, Fr. ... bay
-bana, Jpn. ... cape
banco, Sp. ... bank
bandao, Ch. ... peninsula
bassin, Fr. ... basin
batang, Indon. ... river
bātlāq, Per. ... marsh
ben, Gae. ... mountain
Berg, Ger. ... mountain, hill
-berg, Afk. ... mountains
Berge, Ger. ... mountains
bi'r, Ara. ... well
birkat, Ara. ... lake
bocca, It. ... river mouth, pass
boğazı, Tur. ... strait
bogd, Mong. ... mountain
bolsón, Sp. ... enclosed basin
-breen, Nor. ... glacier
Brücke, Ger. ... bridge

Bucht, Ger. ... bay
bugt, Dan. ... bay
bukit, Indon., Mal. ... mountain, hill
-bukten, Swe. ... bay
bulu, Indon. ... mountain
Burg, Ger. ... castle
burn, Gae. ... brook
burnu, burun, Tur. ... cape
cabezas, Sp. ... peaks
cabo, Port., Sp. ... cape
campo, It. ... plain
cap, Fr. ... cape
capo, It. ... cape
catena, Sp. ... range
cayo(s), Sp. ... cay(s), islet(s)
cerro(s), Sp. ... mountain(s), hill(s)
chaine, Fr. ... range
château, Fr. ... castle
chiang, Ch. ... harbor, harbour
chott, Ara. ... intermittent lake, salt marsh
cima, It., Sp. ... peak
città, It. ... city
ciudad, Sp. ... city
co, Tib. ... lake
co., cerro, Sp. ... mountain, hill
col, Fr. ... pass
colina(s), Sp. ... hill(s)
colline, It. ... hills
collines, Fr. ... hills
con, Viet. ... islands
cord., cordillera, Sp. ... range
costa, It. ... coast
côte, Fr. ... coast, hills
cuchilla, Sp. ... hills, ridge
dağ, dağı, Tur. ... mountain
dāgh, Per. ... mountains
-dake, Jpn. ... mountain
-dal, -dalen, Nor., Swe. ... valley
danau, Indon. ... lake
dao, Ch., Viet. ... island
daryācheh, Per. ... lake
dasht, Per. ... desert
deniz, denizi, Tur. ... sea
desierto, Sp. ... desert
détroit, Fr. ... strait
dijk, Du. ... dike
distrito, Sp. ... district
djebel, Ara. ... mountain(s)
-do, Kor. ... island
-elv, -elva, Nor. ... river
embalse, Sp. ... reservoir
erg, Ara. ... sand desert
estrecho, Sp. ... strait
étang, Fr. ... pond
-ey, Ice. ... island
fjäll(en), Swe. ... mountain(s)
fjället, Swe. ... mountain
fjärden, Swe. ... fjord
-fjell, -fjellet, Nor. ... mountain
-fjord, Nor. ... fjord
-fjorden, Nor., Swe. ... fjord, lake
-fjörur, Ice. ... fjord, bay
-flói, Ice. ... bay
foce, It. ... river mouth, pass
forêt, Fr. ... forest
-forsen, Swe. ... waterfall
Forst, Ger. ... forest
-foss, Ice. ... waterfall
-fossen, Nor. ... waterfall
g., gora, Rus. ... mountain, hill
g., gunong, Mal. ... mountain
gang, Ch. ... bay
-gang, Kor. ... river
gave, Fr. ... mountain torrent
gebergte, Du. ... range
Gebirge, Ger. ... range
Gipfel, Ger. ... peak
göl, Tur. ... lake
golfe, Fr. ... gulf
golfete, Sp. ... bay
golfo, It., Sp. ... gulf
gölü, Tur. ... lake
gora, Rus. ... mountain, hill
gora, S. \ C. ... mountains
góra, Pol. ... mountain

gory, Rus. ... mountains, hills
góry, Pol. ... mountains
gr'ada, Rus. ... ridge
guba, Rus. ... bay
gunong, Mal. ... mountain
gunung, Indon. ... mountain
-guntō, Jpn. ... islands
Haff, Ger. ... lagoon
hai, Ch. ... sea, lake
-hama, Jpn. ... beach
hamada, Ara. ... desert
hāmūn, Per. ... lake, marsh
-hantō, Jpn. ... peninsula
hare, Heb. ... mountains, hills
-hav, Swe. ... sea, bay
havre, Fr. ... harbor, harbour
he, Ch. ... river
ho, Ch. ... river
-ho, Kor. ... reservoir
-holm, Dan. ... island
hora, Czech, Slo. ... mountain
Horn, Ger. ... point, peak
hu, Ch. ... lake, reservoir
Hügel, Ger. ... hill
-huk, Swe. ... cape
ig., igarapé, Port. ... river
île(s), Fr. ... island(s)
ilet(s), Fr. ... islet(s)
ilha(s), Port. ... island(s)
ilhéu(s), Port. ... islet(s)
Insel(n), Ger. ... island(s)
isla(s), Sp. ... island(s)
isola, It. ... island
isole, It. ... islands
istmo, Sp. ... isthmus
jabal, Ara. ... mountain(s)
järv, Est. ... lake
-järvi, Finn. ... lake
jazā'ir, Ara. ... islands
jazirah, Indon. ... peninsula
jiang, Ch. ... river
-jima, Jpn. ... island
-joki, Finn. ... river
-jökull, Ice. ... glacier
-kai, Jpn. ... sea
-kaikyō, Jpn. ... strait
-kaise, Lapp. ... mountain
kali, Indon. ... brook
kandao, Pas. ... pass
-kang, Kor. ... river
-kapp, Nor. ... cape
kepulauan, Indon. ... islands
khalij, Ara. ... gulf
khrebet, Russ., Ukr. ... range
-ko, Jpn. ... lake, lagoon
-kō, Jpn. ... harbor, harbour
kólpos, Gr. ... bay
Kopf, Ger. ... peak
körfezi, Tur. ... gulf, bay
kosa, Rus., Ukr. ... spit
kou, Ch. ... bay, pass
kuala, Mal. ... bay
küh(ha), Per. ... mountain(s)
la, Tib. ... pass
lac(s), Fr. ... lake(s)
lag., laguna, Sp. ... lagoon, lake
lago, It., Port., Sp. ... lake
lagoa, Port. ... lake, lagoon
laguna, Port. ... lagoon, lake
lagune, Fr. ... lagoon
laht, Est. ... bay
-lahti, Finn. ... gulf
län, Swe. ... county
laut, Indon. ... sea
liedao, Ch. ... islands
liman, Rus. ... estuary
ling, Ch. ... mountain(s), peak
llano(s), Sp. ... plain(s)
loch, Gae. ... lake, inlet
lomas, Sp. ... hills
lough, Gae. ... lake
lyman, Ukr. ... estuary
-maa, Est. ... island
-man, Kor. ... bay
mar, Sp., It. ... sea
marais, Fr. ... marsh

mare, It. ... sea
massif, Fr. ... massif
Meer, Ger. ... sea, lake
mer, Fr. ... sea
mesa, Sp. ... mesa
meseta, Sp. ... plateau
-misaki, Jpn. ... cape
mont, Fr. ... mount
montagna, It. ... mountain
montagne(s), Fr. ... mountain(s)
montaña(s), Sp. ... mountain(s)
monte, It., Port., Sp. ... mount
montes, Port., Sp. ... mountains
monti, It. ... mountains
monts, Fr. ... mountains
more, Rus., Ukr. ... sea
morne, Fr. ... mountain
morro, Port., Sp. ... hill, mountain
mui, Viet. ... point
munkhafad, Ara. ... depression
munţii, Rom. ... mountains
-nada, Jpn. ... sea, gulf
nafūd, Ara. ... desert
nagor'ye, Rus. ... plateau, mountains
-näs, Swe. ... peninsula
ness, Gae. ... promontory
nos, Blg. ... cape
nuruu, Mong. ... mountains
nuur, Mong. ... lake
-ø, Dan., Nor. ... island
-ö, Swe. ... island
o., ostrov, Rus. ... island
óros, Gr. ... mountain(s)
ostriv, Ukr. ... island
ostrov(a), Rus. ... island(s)
otok, S. \ C. ... island
ouadi, Ara. ... wadi
oued, Ara. ... wadi
-øy, -øya, Nor. ... island
oz., ozero, Rus., Ukr. ... lake
pampa, Sp. ... plain
pas, Fr. ... strait
paso, Sp. ... pass
Pass, Ger. ... pass
passe, Fr. ... passage
passo, It. ... pass
peg., pegunungan, Indon. ... mountains
pélagos, Gr. ... sea
peña, Sp. ... peak, rock
península, Sp. ... peninsula
pertuis, Fr. ... strait
peski, Rus. ... sand desert
phnum, Cbd. ... mountain
phou, Lao. ... mountain
pic, Fr. ... peak
pico(s), Port., Sp. ... peak(s)
-piggen, Nor. ... mountain
pik, Rus. ... peak
pique, Fr. ... peak
piton(s), Fr. ... peak(s)
pivostriv, Ukr. ... peninsula
planalto, Port. ... plateau
planina, S. \ C. ... mountain, range
plato, Afk., Blg., Rus. ... plateau
playa, Sp. ... beach
pointe, Fr. ... point
polje, S. \ C. ... plain, basin
poluostrov, Rus. ... peninsula
pont, Fr. ... bridge
ponta, pontal, Port. ... point
porto, It. ... port
presa, Sp. ... reservoir, dam
presqu'île, Fr. ... peninsula
proliv, Rus. ... strait
puerto, Sp. ... port
pulau, Indon., Mal. ... island
puncak, Indon. ... peak
punta, It., Sp. ... point, peak
qundao, Ch. ... islands
rão, ribeirão, Port. ... river
ras, ra's, Ara. ... cape
rās, Per. ... cape
récif, Fr. ... reef
represa, Port. ... dam, reservoir
-retto, Jpn. ... islands

ría, Sp. ... ria (inlet)
rib., ribeira, Port. ... brook
ribeirão, Port. ... river
rio, Port. ... river
río, Sp. ... river
riviera, It. ... coast
rivière, Fr. ... river
roca, Sp. ... rock
rocca, It. ... rock, mountain
rt, S. \ C. ... cape
sa., serra, Port. ... range
sahrā', Ara. ... desert
-saki, Jpn. ... cape
salar, Sp. ... salt flat
salina(s), Sp. ... salt marsh, salt flat
salto(s), Port., Sp. ... waterfall
-sammyaku, Jpn. ... range
-san, Jpn., Kor. ... mountain
-sanmaek, Kor. ... mountains
Schloss, Ger. ... castle
sebkha, Ara. ... salt flat
See(n), Ger. ... lake(s)
selat, Indon. ... strait
seno, Sp. ... sound
serra, Port. ... range, mountain
serranía(s), Sp. ... ridge(s)
shan, Ch. ... mountain(s), island
shanmo, Ch. ... mountains
-shima, Jpn. ... island
-shotō, Jpn. ... islands
sierra, Sp. ... range, ridge
-sjo, Nor. ... lake
-sjön, Swe. ... lake, bay
-sø, Dan. ... lake
Spitze, Ger. ... peak
sta., santa, Port., Sp. ... saint
ste., sainte, Fr. ... saint
step', Rus. ... steppe
štít, Slo. ... peak
sto., santo, Port., Sp. ... saint
stretto, It. ... strait
Strom, Ger. ... stream
-ström, -strömmen, Swe. ... stream
-su, Kor. ... lake
-suidō, Jpn. ... channel
Sund, Ger. ... sound
-sund, Swe. ... sound
-take, Jpn. ... mountain
Tal, Ger. ... valley
tanjong, Mal. ... cape
tanjung, Indon. ... cape
tao, Ch. ... island
teluk, Indon. ... bay
thale, Thai ... lagoon
-tō, Jpn. ... island
tônlé, Cbd. ... lake
-tunturi, Finn. ... hill, mountain
ujung, Indon. ... cape
-umi, Jpn. ... lagoon
-ura, Jpn. ... lake
valle, It., Sp. ... valley
vallée, Fr. ... valley
vårful, Rom. ... mountain
-vatn, Ice., Nor. ... lake
vdkhr., vodokhranilishche, Rus. ... reservoir
-vesi, Finn. ... lake
-viken, Swe. ... gulf
vodokhranilishche, Rus. ... reservoir
vodoskhovyshche, Ukr. ... reservoir
vol., volcán, Sp. ... volcano
wādī, Ara. ... wadi
wāhat, wāḥāt, Ara. ... oasis
wan, Ch., Jpn. ... bay
-yama, Jpn. ... mountain
yarımadası, Tur. ... peninsula
yoma, Bur. ... mountains
yumco, Tib. ... lake
yunhe, Ch. ... canal
-zaki, Jpn. ... cape
zaliv, Rus. ... gulf, bay
zatoka, Ukr. ... gulf, bay
zee, Du. ... sea, lake

Abbreviations of Geographical Names and Terms

Abbr.	Name	Abbr.	Name	Abbr.	Name
Ab., Can.	Alberta, Can.	Cro.	Croatia	Id., U.S.	Idaho, U.S.
Afg.	Afghanistan	Ct., U.S.	Connecticut, U.S.	Il., U.S.	Illinois, U.S.
Afr.	Africa	Ctry.	Country	In., U.S.	Indiana, U.S.
Ak., U.S.	Alaska, U.S.	C.V.	Cape Verde	Indon.	Indonesia
Al., U.S.	Alabama, U.S.	Cyp.	Cyprus	Ire.	Ireland
Alb.	Albania	Czech Rep.	Czech Republic	Is.	Islands
Alg.	Algeria	D.C., U.S.	District of Columbia, U.S.	Isr.	Israel
Ang.	Angola	De., U.S.	Delaware, U.S.	Jam.	Jamaica
Ant.	Antarctica	Den.	Denmark	Jord.	Jordan
Ar., U.S.	Arkansas, U.S.	Dep.	Dependency	Kaz.	Kazakhstan
Arg.	Argentina	Des.	Desert	Ks., U.S.	Kansas, U.S.
Arm.	Armenia	Dji.	Djibouti	Kuw.	Kuwait
Aus.	Austria	D.R.C.	Democratic Republic of the Congo	Ky., U.S.	Kentucky, U.S.
Austl.	Australia	Ec.	Ecuador	Kyrg.	Kyrgyzstan
Az., U.S.	Arizona, U.S.	El Sal.	El Salvador	L.	Lake
Azer.	Azerbaijan	Eng., U.K.	England, U.K.	La., U.S.	Louisiana, U.S.
B.	Bay	Eq. Gui.	Equatorial Guinea	Lat.	Latvia
Bah.	Bahamas	Erit.	Eritrea	Leb.	Lebanon
Bahr.	Bahrain	Est.	Estonia	Leso.	Lesotho
Barb.	Barbados	Eth.	Ethiopia	Lib.	Liberia
B.C., Can.	British Columbia, Can.	Eur.	Europe	Lith.	Lithuania
Bdi.	Burundi	Falk. Is.	Falkland Islands	Lux.	Luxembourg
Bel.	Belgium	Fin.	Finland	Ma., U.S.	Massachusetts, U.S.
Bela.	Belarus	Fl., U.S.	Florida, U.S.	Mac.	Macedonia
Bhu.	Bhutan	Fr.	France	Madag.	Madagascar
Bngl.	Bangladesh	Fr. Gu.	French Guiana	Malay.	Malaysia
Bol.	Bolivia	G.	Gulf	Mart.	Martinique
Bos.	Bosnia and Herzegovina	Ga., U.S.	Georgia, U.S.	Maur.	Mauritania
Bots.	Botswana	Gam.	The Gambia	Mb., Can.	Manitoba, Can.
Braz.	Brazil	Gaza Str.	Gaza Strip	Md., U.S.	Maryland, U.S.
Bul.	Bulgaria	Geor.	Georgia	Me., U.S.	Maine, U.S.
Burkina	Burkina Faso	Ger.	Germany	Mex.	Mexico
C.	Cape	Grc.	Greece	Mi., U.S.	Michigan, U.S.
Ca., U.S.	California, U.S.	Guad.	Guadeloupe	Mn., U.S.	Minnesota, U.S.
Camb.	Cambodia	Guat.	Guatemala	Mo., U.S.	Missouri, U.S.
Can.	Canada	Gui.	Guinea	Mol.	Moldova
C.A.R.	Central African Republic	Gui.-B.	Guinea-Bissau	Mong.	Mongolia
Cay. Is.	Cayman Islands	Guy.	Guyana	Mont.	Montenegro
C. Iv.	Cote d'Ivoire	Hi., U.S.	Hawaii, U.S.	Monts.	Montserrat
Co., U.S.	Colorado, U.S.	Hond.	Honduras	Mor.	Morocco
Col.	Colombia	Hung.	Hungary	Moz.	Mozambique
C.R.	Costa Rica	I.	Island	Ms., U.S.	Mississippi, U.S.
		Ia., U.S.	Iowa, U.S.	Mt.	Mountain
		Ice.	Iceland	Mt., U.S.	Montana, U.S.
				Mts.	Mountains

Abbr.	Name	Abbr.	Name	Abbr.	Name
Mwi.	Malawi	Para.	Paraguay	Swe.	Sweden
Myan.	Myanmar	P.E., Can.	Prince Edward Island, Can.	Switz.	Switzerland
N.A.	North America	Pen.	Peninsula	Tai.	Taiwan
N.B., Can.	New Brunswick, Can.	Phil.	Philippines	Taj.	Tajikistan
N.C., U.S.	North Carolina, U.S.	Pk.	Peak	Tan.	Tanzania
N. Cal.	New Caledonia	Plat.	Plateau	Ter.	Territory
N.D., U.S.	North Dakota, U.S.	Pol.	Poland	Thai.	Thailand
Ne., U.S.	Nebraska, U.S.	Polit. Reg.	Political Region	Tn., U.S.	Tennessee, U.S.
Neth.	Netherlands	Port.	Portugal	Trin.	Trinidad and Tobago
Neth. Ant.	Netherlands Antilles	P.R.	Puerto Rico	Tun.	Tunisia
N.H., U.S.	New Hampshire, U.S.	Prov.	Province	Tur.	Turkey
Nic.	Nicaragua	Qc., Can.	Quebec, Can.	Turk.	Turkmenistan
Nig.	Nigeria	R.	River	Tx., U.S.	Texas, U.S.
N. Ire., U.K.	Northern Ireland, U.K.	Ra.	Range	U.A.E.	United Arab Emirates
N.J., U.S.	New Jersey, U.S.	Reg.	Region	Ug.	Uganda
N. Kor.	North Korea	Res.	Reservoir	U.K.	United Kingdom
N.L., Can.	Newfoundland and Labrador, Can.	R.I., U.S.	Rhode Island, U.S.	Ukr.	Ukraine
N.M., U.S.	New Mexico, U.S.	Rom.	Romania	Ur.	Uruguay
Nmb.	Namibia	Rw.	Rwanda	U.S.	United States
Nor.	Norway	S.A.	South America	Ut., U.S.	Utah, U.S.
N.S., Can.	Nova Scotia, Can.	S. Afr.	South Africa	Uzb.	Uzbekistan
N.T., Can.	Northwest Territories, Can.	Sau. Ar.	Saudi Arabia	Va., U.S.	Virginia, U.S.
Nu., Can.	Nunavut, Can.	S.C., U.S.	South Carolina, U.S.	Ven.	Venezuela
Nv., U.S.	Nevada, U.S.	Scot., U.K.	Scotland, U.K.	Viet.	Vietnam
N.Y., U.S.	New York, U.S.	S.D., U.S.	South Dakota, U.S.	V.I. U.S.	Virgin Islands (U.S.)
N.Z.	New Zealand	Sen.	Senegal	Vol.	Volcano
Oc.	Oceania	Serb.	Serbia	Vt., U.S.	Vermont, U.S.
Oh., U.S.	Ohio, U.S.	Sk., Can.	Saskatchewan, Can.	Wa., U.S.	Washington, U.S.
Ok., U.S.	Oklahoma, U.S.	S. Kor.	South Korea	Wal./F.	Wallis and Futuna
On., Can.	Ontario, Can.	S.L.	Sierra Leone	W.B.	West Bank
Or., U.S.	Oregon, U.S.	Slvk.	Slovakia	Wi., U.S.	Wisconsin, U.S.
Pa., U.S.	Pennsylvania, U.S.	Slvn.	Slovenia	W. Sah.	Western Sahara
Pak.	Pakistan	Som.	Somalia	W.V., U.S.	West Virginia, U.S.
Pan.	Panama	Sp. N. Afr.	Spanish North Africa	Wy., U.S.	Wyoming, U.S.
Pap. N. Gui.	Papua New Guinea	Sri L.	Sri Lanka	Yk., Can.	Yukon, Can.
		Str.	Strait	Zam.	Zambia
		St. Vin.	St. Vincent and the Grenadines	Zimb.	Zimbabwe
		Sur.	Suriname		
		Swaz.	Swaziland		

Index

This universal index includes in a single alphabetical list approximately 4,100 names of features that appear on the reference maps. Each name is followed by geographical coordinates and a page reference.

Abbreviation and Capitalization

Abbreviations of names on the maps have been standardized as much as possible. Names that are abbreviated on the maps are generally spelled out in full in the index. Periods are used after all abbreviations regardless of local practice. The abbreviation "St." is used only for "Saint". "Sankt" and other forms of this term are spelled out."

Most initial letters of names are capitalized, except for a few Dutch names, such as "'s-Gravenhage." Capitalization of non-initial words in a name generally follows local practice.

Alphabetization

Names are alphabetized in the order of the letters of the English alphabet. Spanish *ll* and *ch*, for example, are not treated as distinct letters.

Furthermore, diacritical marks are disregarded in alphabetization. German or Scandinavian *ä* or *ö* are treated as *a* or *o*.

The names of physical features may appear inverted, since they are always alphabetized under the proper, not the generic, part of the name, thus: "Gibraltar, Strait of." Otherwise every entry, whether consisting of one word or more, is alphabetized as a single continuous entity. "Lakeland," for example, appears after "Lake Forest" and before "La Línea." Names beginning with articles (Le Havre, Al Manāmah, Ad Dawhah) are not inverted. Names beginning "St.," "Ste.'" and "Sainte" are alphabetized as though spelled "Saint."

In the case of identical names, towns are listed first, then political divisions, then physical features.

Generic Terms

Except for cities, the names of all features are followed by terms that represent broad classes of features, for example, *Mississippi, R.* or *Alabama, State.*

Country names and names of features that extend beyond the boundaries of one country are followed by the name of the continent in which each is located. Country designations follow the names of all other places in the index. The locations of places in the United States, Canada, and the United Kingdom are further defined by abbreviations that indicate the state, province, or political division in which each is located.

Page References and Geographical Coordinates

The geographical coordinates and page references are found in the last columns of each entry.

Latitude and longitude coordinates for point features, such as cities and mountain peaks, indicate the locations of the symbols. For extensive areal features, such as countries or mountain ranges, or linear features, such as canals and rivers, locations are given for the position of the type as it appears on the map.

Index